# The Magical Name—Awakening the Soul's Potentials

Uncovering the mysteries of our name and its effects within our lives is a high form of initiation. The ancient mystery schools taught their students the power of words. They taught the sacredness of names and the means to employ them for various purposes. They taught the use of one's name to touch the soul and awaken its potentials. Word and name magic were pre-eminent among the magical arts. This art of name enchantment has not been lost.

We have each been given a "magical word." It is a word that we can use to balance ourselves and to understand the forces operative within our lives. We can use this word to manifest energy, abundance and prosperity and to open us to unlimited possibilities. This magical word is our NAME!

More and more people are searching for some method to help lead them to greater enlightenment and to open the spiritual path. Most flounder in their quest, dabbling in the multitude of metaphysical sciences and teachings. Many do not know where to begin their spiritual studies.

The ancients emphasized one precept: "Know thyself and thou shalt know the universe." One of the easiest means of coming to "know one's self" is through the study of one's name. Our name is an energy signature that can reveal the soul's abilities and karma. By coming to a new understanding of the elements within one's name, the individual can learn to communicate more consciously and directly with the soul.

Our names are much more than a label by which people can identify and stereotype us. They contain great power and significance. As we open to that significance, we learn to activate and control those energies necessary to heal ourselves and all of our life manifestations.

It has been said that to hear the angels sing, you must first hear the song within your own heart. It is this song which is echoed within your name!

## About the Author

Ted Andrews is a full-time author, student and teacher in the metaphysical and spiritual fields. He conducts seminars, symposiums, workshops and lectures throughout the country on many facets of ancient mysticism. Ted works with past-life analysis, auric interpretation, numerology, the Tarot and the Qabala as methods of developing and enhancing inner potential. He is a clairvoyant and a certified spiritualist medium.

Ted is also active in the healing field. He is certified in basic hypnosis and acupressure and is involved in the study and use of herbs as an alternative path. He combines his musical training with more than twenty years of concentrated metaphysical study in the application of "Directed Esoteric Sound" in the healing process. He uses this with other holistic methods of healing, such as "etheric touch," aura and chakra balancing, and crystal stone and gem techniques, in creating individual healing therapies and higher states of consciousness.

He is a contributing author to various metaphysical magazines and is the author of a number of books, including *The Sacred Power in Your Name, How to See and Read the Aura, Simplified Magic,* and *Imagick.*

## To Write to the Author

We cannot guarantee that every letter written to the author can be answered, but all will be forwarded. Both the author and the publisher appreciate hearing from readers, learning of your enjoyment and benefit from this book. Llewellyn also publishes a bimonthly news magazine with news and reviews of practical esoteric studies and articles helpful to the student, and some readers' questions and comments to the author may be answered through this magazine's columns if permission to do so is included in the original letter. The author sometimes participates in seminars and workshops, and dates and places are announced in *The Llewellyn New Times.* To write to the author, or to ask a question, write to:

Ted Andrews
c/o THE LLEWELLYN NEW TIMES
P.O. Box 64383-014, St. Paul, MN 55164-0383, U.S.A.

Please enclose a self-addressed, stamped envelope for reply, or $1.00 to cover costs.

Llewellyn's Practical Guide to Personal Power Series

# The Magical Name

## *A Practical Technique for Inner Power*

Ted Andrews

1991
Llewellyn Publications
St. Paul, MN, U.S.A. 55164-0383

FIRST EDITION

**Cover painting by Robin Wood**

**Library of Congress Cataloging-in-Publication Data:**
  Andrews, Ted, 1952-
    The magical name : a practical technique for inner power / Ted Andrews.
        p.      cm. — (Llewellyn's practical guide to personal power series)
      Includes bibliographical references.
      ISBN 0-87542-014-1
      1. Magic.  2. Names, Personal—Miscellanea.  3. Alphabets—Miscel-
  lanea.  4. Spiritual life—Miscellanea.  I. Title.  II. Series: Llewellyn
  practical guides to personal power.
  BF1623.N3A52  1991                                              91-15677
  133.4'3—dc20                                                         CIP

Llewellyn Publications
A Division of Llewellyn Worldwide, Ltd.
P.O. Box 64383, St. Paul, MN 55164-0383

## About the Llewellyn Practical Guides to Personal Power

To some people, the idea that "magick" is *practical* comes as a surprise. It shouldn't!

The entire basis for magick is to exercise influence over one's personal world in order to satisfy our needs and goals. And, while this magick is also concerned with psychological transformation and spiritual growth, even the spiritual life must be built on firm material foundations.

Here are practical and usable techniques that will help you to a better life, will help you attain things you want, will help you in your personal growth and development. *Moreover, these books can change your life, dynamically, positively!*

The material world and the psychic are intertwined, and it is this that establishes the magickal link: that mind/soul/spirit can as easily influence the material and vice versa.

Psychic powers and magickal practices can, and should, be used in one's daily life. Each of us has many wonderful, but yet underdeveloped talents and powers—surely we have an evolutionary obligation to make full use of our human potentials! Mind and body work together, and magick is simply the extension of this interaction into dimensions beyond the limits normally conceived. *Why be limited?*

All things you will ever want or be must have their start in your mind. In these books you are given practical guidance to develop your inner powers and apply them to your everyday needs. These abilities will eventually belong to everybody through natural evolution, but you can learn and develop them now!

This series of books will help you achieve such things as success, happiness, miracles, powers of ESP, healing, out-of-body travel, clairvoyance, divination, extended powers of mind and body, communication with non-physical beings, and knowledge by non-material means!

We've always known of things like this . . . seemingly supernormal achievements, often by quite ordinary people. We are told that we normally use only ten percent of our human potential. We are taught that faith can move mountains, that love heals all hurt, that miracles do occur. We believe these things to be true, but most people lack practical knowledge of them.

The books in this series form a full library of magickal knowledge and practice.

## Other Books by Ted Andrews

*Simplified Magic*
*Imagick*
*The Sacred Power in Your Name*
*How to See and Read the Aura*

## Forthcoming

*Dream Alchemy: Shaping Our Dreams to Transform Our Lives*
*Sacred Sounds: Transformation Through Music & Words*
*The Feminine Mysteries of Christian Mysticism*
*How to Uncover Your Past Lives*
*How to Meet and Work with Spirit Guides*
*How to Heal with Color*
*Magical Dance*
*The Healer's Manual*

*TO MARGARET KATHRYN ANDREWS*
*WITH LOVE FOR SHARING MY NAME AND*
*ENCHANTING MY LIFE*

# Table of Contents

# Introduction

# Spellbinding

Abracadabra!

Hocus pocus!

In both high and low magic, the power of words has been a predominant element—in almost all societies. The world's literature is filled with myths and tales of how individuals have used magical words and names for everything from healing to shapeshifting to spiritual illumination. Most major societies still hold within their scriptures and myths references to the powers of sound, words and names.

In Ethiopian cosmology, God is said to have created the universe through the utterance of his own name. In Egypt, Thoth used words to create the universe, calling out over the waters of life "come unto me." In Babylonian cosmology, the gods mothered by Tiamat within the waters of life did not emerge as beings until they were named. Even the Christian scriptures tell us "In the beginning was the WORD..."

Word magic is worldwide, especially the belief that one gains power over a person or thing by having power and knowledge of its name (and all aspects of it). In the fairy tale *Rumpelstiltskin*, the miller's daughter is at the mercy of Rumpelstiltskin until she hears him sing his name in the woods:

"Today I bake, tomorrow I brew my beer;
The next day I will bring the queen's child here.
Ah! Lucky 'tis that not a soul doth know
That Rumpelstiltskin is my name, ho! ho!"

The ancient Egyptians taught that a word retained its power unless used lightly or inappropriately. "Unless the name of man was preserved, he would cease to exist." (Murry Hope, *Practical Egyptian Magic*).

A word or name that is understood and used correctly will lead to fulfillment of wishes, promises, illumination and connect one to his or her individual spark of life. In many traditions, failure to understand the names and words that we used would ultimately weaken the individual's innate ability to draw upon the creative power of the Word. This is why many societies held high the honor of fulfilling promises and "keeping one's word." It is tied to the creative power of the individual and if not kept, it could weaken that power.

Shamans, priest magicians and all masters were well aware of the power of sound and words and how they could truly be "spell binding." Many esoteric societies passed on their teachings through the proper use of techniques that enabled the students to assimilate the knowledge at whatever level they were at. In more recent times, these techniques have come down to us through the minstrels, the bards, the meistersinger, all schooled in the esoteric teachings of sound and music, one aspect of which is that of "name magic."

In Biblical times, Samuel founded the School of Prophets. He was the great initiate-singer of his day, and through his school, he passed on the teachings and techniques. The creative word—the feminine power within us all—is manifested through proper use of song, voice and dance and can liberate the soul from the body. This divine feminine power, called Shekinah by the Hebrew seers and Sophia by Christian Gnostics, would bless individuals with her presence when the soul awakened within itself joy and light—the joy and light that is reflected within one's true name.

One's true namesong can be spellbinding. It can open one to higher enlightenment and facilitate the breaking down of limitations. It can open the spiritual planes to conscious awareness and it can heal body, mind and soul.

The ancient Masters of Wisdom were careful about imparting knowledge of sound and words to their disciples. Students first had to prove their selflessness and love for humanity. They had to become educated in the mystical and metaphysical arts to the degree that they could bridge the higher and lower minds. They had to graduate from the "tests of silence." They had to learn how to speak, what to speak, and most importantly, when to speak—if they wished the higher knowledge of sounds, words and names.

Those who wished to learn the occult power of language and names had to first unlearn the previous use of language and names. They had to refrain from "ordinary" methods of talking. The concept of "strength through silence" must become a living reality. Students were taught three uses of sounds and names:

1. Intuitive—those aspects of our name which unveil our potentials and enable us to connect more fully with the divine while within the physical. This includes understanding the meanings, sounds, symbols and rhythmic significance within the name.
2. Scientific—those aspects of our name and its sounds and their effects upon our physical and subtle energies.
3. Astrological—the sounds, tones, elements and rhythms within our names which help connect us to the influence of the stars and how to use them to evoke greater or lesser influences within our lives.

What makes a word or name powerful? Is it its meaning? Its sounds? Its rhythms? The way it is conceived by the individual? In essence, all aspects add to the power of words and names. When a person can understand and employ all aspects simultaneously, then the name or word becomes "magical." It becomes "spellbinding."

Words and names vibrate to different parts of the body, different organs and systems within the body, different emotions and different mental and spiritual states. Some have power over the physical and some can quicken the emotions. The power of our names and words depends upon the depth from which the name or word arises—and upon how illumined the individual is about the name. This is why some individual's words will penetrate into the hearts of others as if spoken in "tongues of flame," while others may repeat the same words over and over again and they still won't penetrate.

Speech is a magical force. It works intimately with the ancient laws of manifestation—the crystallizing of energy into physical reality. The ancient magicians knew how to manifest through the proper use of silence and speech. They knew how to draw upon the inner resources, using their own names as a key to unlock those resources. They could open the doors between humanity and subtler beings.

The human voice is the most perfect of musical instruments. The light and darkness of the soul are revealed through the quality of one's voice. It has a tremendous ability to heal and nourish. Pythagoras recognized the considerable therapeutic power within human speech. He treated diseases through the reading of poetry. He recognized and taught his students how a skillful, well-modulated voice, beautiful words and their rhythm help to restore balance to the body and to the soul.

Jacob Grimm once wrote: "Each individuality, even in the world of languages, should be respected as sacred..." We must rediscover the sacredness of our own individuality. We must rediscover the sacredness of the creative power that lies hidden within us. This creative function is opened through an understanding of our name. As we grow in its discovery, our life changes. We become more empowered, and we learn to bridge the physical and spiritual kingdoms in full conscious awareness. Our names are no longer identification tags. They are spellbinding, words of power. They become prayers, that at once invoke and reverence the divine within each of our lives!

# PART I

# MAGICAL ALPHABETS
# & MYSTICAL NAMES

# 1

# Name Enchantment

Our names are tremendous symbols, concealing and revealing simultaneously truths about ourselves. The letters and their sounds reflect forces—archetypal and mundane—which can produce certain actions and effects when brought into conscious awareness and activation. Our name is a "spell," a formula, for releasing certain potentials and forces and for realizing certain lessons.

For any magical "formula" to work, it must be based on universal laws. It must be understood, especially from the points of symbology and analogy. There must be recognition of the law of cause and effect, operative within that formula. The individual must work with the formula from all levels—physical and spiritual—as we are all multi-dimensional beings. We must be careful of charging it or allowing it to be charged by others with the energies of false perceptions.

Our individual names fit all of these precepts. They reflect, like our astrological charts, an energy signature that we have come to work with and give greater expression within this incarnation. Names are susceptible to our own prejudices as well as those of others—due to personal likes and dislikes. (Overcoming name prejudice is a very powerful task.)

As we come to the realization of the inherent potentials and energies that we activate within our lives through the name(s) we use, we can then begin to take measures to use that knowledge to our benefit. In Chinese philosophy it is often said that to know something and then not *do* what you know is an indication that you really do not yet know, no matter how much you tell yourself otherwise. It is the task of this work to further strengthen and enlighten about the hidden significance of our names, and to demonstrate various ways in which we can take that knowledge and *do* something creative and constructive with it to enhance our lives.

Language is poorly understood. Misconceptions abound. It is presumptuous of humans to think that they know all they need to know simply because they use language to communicate. Philosophers have always shown great interest in language and its psychospiritual connections to humanity. Language and its expression are of central importance to understanding our individual thought processes. On other levels it is critical to understanding and realizing our spiritual aspects and how much they interplay within our physical life. Linguistics is the study of language in general, but there is also what can be termed *metaphysical linguistics*—how language affects humanity beyond the physical realms.

The study of language and its various sounds and uses has a long and ancient history. It is generally believed and accepted that most modern languages stem from various forms of Sanskrit, or what is now more often termed the Proto-Indo-European family of languages, and of the multitude of languages that do exist, only one in 20 has a written form.

Speech is the real language and writing is a secondary way of recording. Many of the mystery teachings were never to be recorded, but passed on by word of mouth. This protected the teachings from being profaned, but it was also understood by the masters that writing in any of its forms, pre-alphabetic (pictographs, hieroglyphics, etc.) and alphabetic (syllable scripts, single sound scripts, etc.), was a powerful means of invoking the play of energy into one's physical life circumstances. It draws the energies out of those more ethereal realms and grounds it in the physical. This will be explored in greater detail, when we demonstrate how to turn your name into a talisman of great force.

Our languages and their alphabets evolved and changed as humanity evolved and changed. Unfortunately, what was lost was the esoteric significance behind the scripts comprising the various alphabets throughout the world. Our modern English alphabet has a long and ancient history and is infused with the essence of almost every major society—each applying its own influence.

Pictographs were one of the first forms of written communication. They are pictures which communicate meaning. These eventually evolved into series of wedge-shaped lines called "cuneiform writing." Egyptian hieroglyphs were a combination of both. From the Egyptian hieroglyphs came the Phoenician (Canaanite) and Greek alphabets, followed by an Etruscan influence, Roman, Germanic, etc. As each society touched in with others, alphabets were adapted and changed.

Of the nearly 200 alphabets in existence, legends and stories abound, surrounding their spiritual formation and significance. The Chinese alphabet is attributed to Ts'ang Chien, the god with the dragon face and four eyes. Tradition tells how he looked up and saw the patterns of the stars and then looked down and saw marks on the back of the turtle and the footprints of birds in the garden. From these came the first Chinese characters. In essence, there is no true Chinese alphabet in the manner we normally think. Its script has over 40,000 characters and some can take as many as 32 strokes to form. In Egypt, Thoth is pictured with a reed brush and palette, as he is known as the inventor of the arts and sciences and the sacred writings we call hieroglyphics. Brahma in the Hindu tradition was waiting to write down his teachings and ultimately took Hindu characters from the seams in the human skull. The Runic alphabet was given to the Norse god Odin after hanging upon Yggdrasil, the World Tree, for nine days and nights. The twigs and branches that fell spelled out various words and formulas by which Odin could help raise the consciousness of humanity.

Many of the early alphabets were sacred writings, to be meditated upon and to help raise the spirituality of the individual. The Hebrew alphabet, comprised of twenty-two letters, is considered by the ancient Hebrew seers as the twenty-two steps to Wisdom. All one had to do was touch and absorb the significance of these mystical symbols. But as with many of the mystery religions, their teachings were not always obvious.

The ancients used symbology to communicate many of their teachings. They recognized the power of words and languages. Words were precisely selected by the teacher, so that each student would be able to absorb according to his or her own individual capabilities. The ancient teachers were well aware that certain words and names attracted blessings, bestowed power, brought release from difficulty, gave courage and strength, healed and comforted. Part of this is reflected in the Eastern teachings of mantric yoga.

Mantras are sounds or sentences containing ideas which display the characters and essences of various deities or archetypal energies. In Eastern philosophy there are considered ten karmas of mantras—ten ways in which these sounds and sentences can be used—from restoring peace to killing.

To use the name or the mantra of a deity is useless unless there is a proper understanding of it and it is approached with the right attitude. The individual must understand all correspondences or there will be an inability to connect with the archetype or to penetrate into the proper sphere of energy associated with the mantra. This is why symbology was of such great significance in all of the ancient mystery teachings.

Events and lessons were taught and recorded symbolically. Names were given and taken according to the individual's growth. In this way the student had the responsibility of translating it into his or her own symbolic interpretation and working with it. The symbology of the student was what would ultimately be tested by the masters to ensure that the student had achieved the proper depth to the meaning and significance of the lesson and especially of his or her name.

Understanding the true symbolic significance of one's name enables a transfer of consciousness, a new focus with all of its inherent physical and spiritual effects. The ability to form true names and significance from the letters is what name enchantment is all about. It leads us to reading the universal languages and the universal laws as they are being applied to us in this incarnation. We must learn to understand and use the elements of our names and *command* them! We must seek out their correspondences and analogies and thereby learn to re-create our lives according to their truest patterns. We must learn to use the esoteric language of our names to link us more fully to those archetypal energies playing within our lives and bridge them into a new harmony of body, mind and spirit! To simply "know" is not enough. We must also begin the process of *doing* what we *know*!

## THE SIGNIFICANCE OF OUR NAMES

Our names are energy signatures. They affect us on all levels—physical, emotional, mental and spiritual. Their meanings, sounds, letters and rhythms all indicate specific things about the lessons and potentials we have come to experience within this incarnation. The esotericism of letters needs to be understood in order to assist us all in our own life tests and initiations. The significance of the letters and their meanings—and their combinations within our names—is part of what was termed "knowledge of the Word."

The letters within our names are glyphs whose shapes, sounds and meanings can provide great insight into our own unique life circumstances. They provide clues to the innate abilities and potentials within us. They indicate lessons and learning experiences we have chosen during this incarnation. Every letter has power and qualities about it. The letters represent specific forces.

In order for those forces behind our names to manifest—be they archetypal or not—we must do more than intellectualize them. These forces must be invoked, felt and experienced. This alone makes them magical. This releases those hidden energies. A magical word or name is one which is created because the individual understands the complete analogy and significance of its elements (letters) and can reconnect with them at a primal level.

The Egyptians—as with many societies—attached great import to the power of the names of both those living and dead. Names were recognized as being as much a part of us as our own souls. Thus they knew we needed to know how to use our names properly. They knew that the gods and goddesses would only respond to the right name. They knew that to yield one's true name could place you within the power of the one to whom you yielded it.

There was a time in which all names were treated with great respect. The gods and goddesses of other countries and societies were always reverenced. Individuals knew that the divine could and would manifest under various guises to meet the needs of the society and its times. The Hebrew god Yahweh had many names. Prayers and invocations were used that would allow a specific manifestation of the one God to play more fully and specifically within their lives. This is why in the Hebrew Qabala, there are ten names for God—each an aspect of how the one divine force manifests in various avenues of human activity. These names range from Adonai to Jehovah, but they are specific "call signals" to specific manifestations of the Divine. Ra, the great Egyptian Sun god, was known as the god of many names. Many believed that the gods and goddesses of Egypt were little more than personifications of Ra under different names and thus different energy expressions and manifestations.

It is important to understand that "knowledge of the word" or name enchantment involves understanding basic universal principles. There is operating within all of our lives what is often termed the Hermetic principle of correspondence. Simply stated, it says: "As above, so below; as below, so above." Applying this to name magic is very simple. The name we use is an energy matrix or outline of what we have come to work with and work through in this life. It serves as a mirror reflecting certain archetypal energies into play within our lives. As has been stated, each letter and combination of letters are linked to specific universal forces. When we align ourselves to those universal forces in any way—through a name, a meditation, images, etc.—we activate and manifest those energies within our day to day life circumstances.

It is important to come to a greater understanding of what exactly is reflected within the symbols of our names—in the way of energies, potentials and lessons. This is not always easy, because our names and their elements have exoteric and esoteric significance. In Egyptian hieroglyphics, a picture can represent a thing, an idea or a sound. For example, the image of an eagle represents the eagle, the letter A or, when it has a human face, it represents the soul. The vowels and consonants within our names represent obvious sounds as well as many more subtle correspondences.

The vowels provide the great strength—the activating force within our names. The vowels provide and reflect the interior strengths and potentials that are not always apparent but are nonetheless influencing us. The consonants surrounding the vowels help to bring out those potentials so that they can become the keynote of the individual's life. The consonants are the skeletal framework which determines how we learn to express the potentials inherent within the vowels. Together they set a framework of energy in play within our lives, affecting us on physical, emotional, mental and spiritual levels.

## BIRTH, SOUL AND MAGICAL NAMES

We have many names within any incarnation. We have the birth name, which includes the given or first name, the surname or family name and, with most people, there is also a middle name. There are religious names, such as in the Catholic confirmation ceremony. There are the names of spouses, which in this society are generally taken by women. And there are initiatory names, new names that an individual may assume to reflect shifts in consciousness or awareness.

Our birth name is the most important name of all. It more than any other can reveal our potentials and lessons for this incarnation. We, of course, have free will and are not bound to those energies drawn to us by our name. We can change our names and thus the energy to which we are associated. In childhood, individuals often take on nicknames, but as one reaches maturity and steps out into the world away from the sheltered environment of childhood, the nicknames are often dropped and the true name is taken. We can evolve into our names, just as we can evolve into our higher potentials. Understanding the energies within the name will facilitate that evolution.

Of the birth names, the first name is the most important. It more than anything else reflects the individual creative energy one has come to learn to express. Its meaning, its elements, its letters and their correspondences will reveal much about that creative essence waiting to be expressed in a manner unique to the life circumstances of the individual.

The family name or surname reflects lessons and energies of the family—a kind of family "karma." It reflects the qualities most available to the person through the family heritage, which helps shape the expression of the individual's creative expression. One of the strongest karmic environs—one in which major lessons are experienced—is the family environment. The elements and significance of the family name can provide much information on those lessons.

The middle name is today more of an identification label, as it is more commonly used. But it has an influence within our lives also. Many individuals are called by their middle name, rather than by their first. Its significance can be great, in that it reflects forces and energies through its elements that can assist us in unfolding the potentials of our first name. It often reflects optional gifts and energies that can become accessible to us, if we learn how to invoke a more dynamic play of their energies. (This is one of the functions of this text.)

The name is a physical link to the spiritual essence of the individual. If understood and used correctly, it can summon up the characters, energies and essences that it represents. Our name is an intimate part of our lives, influencing us more greatly than we often imagine. Our name has a resonance with a particular universal energy that is operating within our lives—an archetypal energy to which we have access. The name is a direct link to the soul. The "creative word" or name, when employed with potent thought and focus, becomes a creative power which can fix the play of soul energy in any manner desired.

We have lost the ability to realize the true power in the names we use. We have lost the ability to use "name magic," a magic that lies at the essence of every soul and every name. It is a magic that "ties one to the spiritual path of the past" and can be used "to propel oneself to the future." Our name is a doorway to greater illumination, enlightenment and initiation.

Part of this process must involve discovering our real name— that which is called the SOUL NAME. It is the name of our most creative and individual essence. It is not the name we are using in this incarnation, but it is the name that resides behind all of our names throughout all incarnations.It is the signature that ties us directly to the Divine. Our other names, incarnation after incarnation, serve to manifest and bridge the Divine aspect, into our physical life situations.

Our names are special creations. They reflect energies from our true soul essence so that we can learn to manifest that essence in unique ways in this incarnation. Our names define the expressions of divine energies for this incarnation. We are not bound to them, but unless we become more aware of them and their very real effects, we can never unfold the soul potentials of which we are capable.

To bridge the process of connecting the birth name to a manifestation of the soul essence, individuals have utilized what are known as MAGICAL NAMES. Magical names are also called secret names, initiatory names, etc. They serve a variety of purposes ranging from linking the soul with the birth name, to assisting in changes of consciousness and energies within one's day to day life, to healing, to empowering one's life and essence, to activating higher forms of intuition, to facilitating out of body experiences and to giving greater access to the subtler dimensions and realms that interpenetrate and influence us.

Our name conveys who we are through a unique combination of meanings, sounds, rhythms, etc. It is a vehicle for personal self-expression. It is a tool of great self-discovery. By learning to utilize our names and their elements, we can open ourselves up to dimensions and realms that we have not even imagined.

We will learn to use the magical name to create a subtle body of energy—a magical body—that will enhance the persona and facilitate connecting with that soul realm. This magical body can be used to consciously explore the spiritual dimensions of the soul and crystallize its energies within our physical lives—creating greater fulfillment, abundance, prosperity, joy and love.

# 2

# The Mystical Power of the Vowels

While languages are comprised of vowels and consonants, they serve different and yet powerful functions. Vowels have the greatest power within languages and thus also within our names. Consonants find their true power only when placed with a vowel. This text will focus on how to use the name elements—vowels and consonants—to create an inner talisman of illumination and power.

Sound is a dynamic force within the universe. Every society and cosmology has spoken of the alchemical power of sound. This alchemical power is inherent within the sounds of our names. The vowels in many of the ancient alphabets were sacred. The Hebrew alphabet is comprised of consonants alone, as the vowels were too activating. The vowels had the life-giving power. They alone bring the energies and the potentials of the consonants to life. This is why the predominant vowel within one's first name is the strongest key to the soul's true potentials and forces. This force is adjusted according to the consonants—it may be enhanced or diminished.

The vowels, as with all letters of the alphabet, have certain characteristics associated with them, certain lessons, qualities, colors and even astrological correspondences—all of which can help us in the process of self-discovery. The vowels are links to archetypal energies and to archetypal elements within the universe. The predominant vowel within your first name provides a clue as to which of the elemental kingdoms you can most easily work with and which can assist you in expressing your own creative essence during this incarnation. These elemental kingdoms are not "the stuff of fiction" as we are so often told. The elemental kingdoms and the nature spirits that work within them are as real as any of us. They are simply comprised of a finer substance, and they work to assist humanity in its evolution and through the maintenance of the earth itself. The vowels within your name indicate which beings of the nature kingdom you have the greatest resonance with in this life.

| Vowel | Element | Archangel | Nature Beings | Direction |
|-------|---------|-----------|---------------|-----------|
| A | Ether | Christ | All four | All four |
| E | Air | Raphael | Sylphs | East |
| I | Fire | Michael | Salamanders | South |
| O | Water | Gabriel | Undines | West |
| U | Earth | Auriel | Gnomes | North |

(The associations and correspondences are not rigid. They simply provide a jumping off point for exploring some of the subtler associations with our names.)

The above information can be used in a variety of methods. It can be used in meditation to align your energies with those of the elementals and nature spirits. Those who are aligned with the ether element have been given opportunity to access all four of the elemental kingdoms. This gives greater opportunity, but it also indicates that there is a greater opportunity to be affected by all four of them more easily.

The primary element of your name is especially important for those wishing to align themselves and understand the astrological influences within their lives. When we incarnate, we choose a time and place of birth and a name whose energies will play upon us to help us learn what we need most. We choose these because when we enter the density of physical existence, there can be a tendency to forget our tasks and purposes once we are encased within physical flesh.

Each astrological sign is tied to one of the four elements as well. The birth sign reflects those energies we wish to evolve into. The element of that sign reflects what element of ourselves we wish to unfold and develop. The element of our first name indicates what we brought with us to assist us in accessing the astrological elemental influence.

| Vowel and Astrological Elements | | | |
|---|---|---|---|
| Element | Vowel | Signs of Zodiac | Qualities of Elements |
| Fire | I | Aries Leo Sagittarius | Courage, self-assertive, visionary, helpful, creative expression, strong, active life force, imposing, fanatic, self-indulgent, authoritarian. —Work with Salamanders |
| Earth | U | Taurus Virgo Capricorn | Providing necessities, grounded, good sense of timing, stable, self-aware, understands emotions, miserly, controlling, coarse, no empathy. —Work with Gnomes |
| Air | E | Gemini Libra Aquarius | Mental, inventive, intelligent, quick, alert, cooperative, humane, cold, aloof, imitative, nervous, superficial. —Work with Sylphs |
| Water | O | Cancer Scorpio Pisces | Understanding, emotions, psychic, sensitive, artistic, romantic, reserved, impressionable, self-indulgent, exaggerates feelings, sensual. —Work with Undines |
| Ether | A | Ether is substance from which all was created. | Ether is the spiritual aspect which overrides and influences all elements. It permeates all creation. |

Differences of opinion exist as to the vowel associations of the earth and ether elements. These are guidelines, what is most important is how you associate and what correspondences you build. The author has used the *U* for the earth element as it also is a vowel whose sound correlates to the functions of the base chakra. The *A* is assigned to the ether because ot its connection to the heart chakra which mediates all energies of the body, just as ether mediates the energies of all the elements.

| Elemental Combinations | |
|---|---|
| **Combined Elements** | **The Qualities and Relationships** |
| FIRE with FIRE | Tremendous impulse and stimulation; can burn self out; must find practical outlet; provides much energy toward life goal; must balance self-expression. |
| AIR with AIR | Excessively mental; not enough direction; whirlpool of ideas needing practical release; talkative and expressive. |
| WATER with WATER | Can give added depth; increased sensitivity; feelings easily hurt; intolerance; can lead to instability; requires a realistic focus. |
| EARTH with EARTH | Need stimulus to manifest latent fruit; can cause inertia; materialistic; must work self-expression and personal relationships; stabilizing; latent talents. |
| FIRE with EARTH | Learning boundaries of the activity of fire; practicalize high ideals; inspiring greater mobility; can ground the fire or stimulate expression. |
| FIRE with AIR | Very compatible; too much air and fire is out of control; fire can change properties of air for good or bad; strengthens and raises ideals. |
| FIRE with WATER | Fire turns water to steam; water puts out fires; when balanced they bring useful ideas/tremendous activity; alchemical processes are to be learned. |
| EARTH with AIR | Air stimulates earth qualities; fruit needs oxygen; earth stabilizes volatile air aspects. |
| EARTH with WATER | Very compatible as the two are necessary for anything to grow; earth stabilizes the restless water element and water prevents dryness and unfeeling nature. |
| AIR with WATER | Air keeps water fresh; water element can feel unfulfilled by air not understanding the emotions; intellect modifies oversensitivity; water broadens sympathies of air. |

The ether element accentuates the aspects of whichever element it is associated. It will enhance—or has the capability of enhancing—both the positive and negative aspects.

Knowing the elements associated with your name and your sign will assist you in utilizing the energies of the earth to grow and effect change. It helps us to grow more sensitive to the nuances of nature, so that we can come to see with the seer's eyes. We become aware of the play of the elemental beings in all aspects of our lives, and a cooperative effort occurs. Aligning with these beings of nature—be they angelic or elemental—is important as their consciousness is open and more concerned with life itself and its highest and truest expression, rather than the form in which that life resides. Humanity centers upon the emotional and the mental faculties, while the beings of nature center upon the higher intuitional. Aligning ourselves with them through processes of true "name awareness and enchantment," helps us to open our own higher faculties of intuition. We open ourselves to the wonders of other worlds and, more importantly, to the wonders of ourselves!

The letters or elements that comprise our names have a significance far beyond what we usually attribute to them. They have a glyphic significance, their shape and form provide clues to the inherent energies. They have a phonetic value, most apparent within the functions of the vowels. This phonetic value enables us to discern which chakra centers we have come to predominantly unfold within this incarnation. There are numerological correspondences which can provide clues to the significance of the letters within our names. The manner in which they interact with the letters around them can provide information as well. They are also tied to astrological correspondences and color and musical correspondences. All provide clues as to the essence of our personality and our soul potentials.

The Hebrew alphabet was created out of the Chaldean—specifically to convey certain mystical truths:

1. By the shape of the letters,
2. By that which they stand for,
3. By their sounds and
4. By their numerical value.

Our names and the elements within them activate the Law of Attraction: "Like attracts like." Our names attract energies which will play within our life and through us because we have aligned ourselves with them in a unique manner by way of our names. When we take our names, we begin to resonate with any energies that are of a like nature within the universe—physical and spiritual.

Understanding these energies more fully is one of the purposes of this book.

The predominant vowel—the vowel that is strongest and accented most within your first name at birth—is the KEYNOTE of your name. It determines much of the trends of personality and soul development for this incarnation. It is the key to interior strengths that you have come to understand and unfold. It is the key to those inner potentials that are not always so apparent. The vowels represent deeper states of consciousness that we have come to open—either for the first time or on a deeper level.

## THE VOWEL A

> KEYNOTE: Higher wisdom and illumination
> COLORS: White or light blue and gold
> ASTROLOGY: Element of ether/Sun and Uranus
> CHAKRA(S): Heart (long *A* sound as in "play")
> Throat (short *A* sound as in "bat")

The vowel *A* is the letter for activating the enlightened mind. It provides opportunities to balance the intuition with reason within one's life circumstances. It can give one the ability and potential for higher clairvoyance and command over all the elements of the earth. The *A* is the symbol of divine unity. It reflects the intellectual, one who strives for truth and ambition. It also shows great versatility, one with many talents and abilities. Unless these talents are focused, the energies will be very scattered. This can result in "always planning but never manifesting." This vowel represents the energies of the Sun.

The *A* is a symbol for the "Spirit of Aether." It is a symbol for the life breath of air and spirit, what is known as the Ruach in Hebrew mysticism. This vowel gives the ability for synthesis and for becoming a link between the mind of God and humanity. It involves developing the power to transform one's life through knowledge and the proper expression of that knowledge.

This vowel has a tendency to make one a receptor of power and inspiration for those who would open themselves appropriately. In actuality, the power of this vowel is manifested and expressed through inspiration (the magical word and breath).

*A* is the image-forming power that can be brought to life by the individual. This has ties to the ancient power of skaldcraft, the science of word magic or the craft of activating the magical force of poetry. This gives the ability to make magical connections between words and images through appropriate "sounding" or "toning" techniques. This is a craft that is tied to the god Odin of Teutonic and Scandinavian lore, and thus this is a vowel that also can be used to connect with this god-force.

The energies associated with this vowel can stimulate cynicism, scatteredness, hyper-sensitivity and an ability to be easily hurt if they are not focused and expressed properly. Once this is accomplished, ambition, versatility, concentration and inventiveness will unfold. This vowel is a creative force, for it is the element of ether from which all other elements came forth.

## THE VOWEL E

> KEYNOTE: Perception and universal consciousness
> COLORS: Blue or dark violet
> ASTROLOGY: Element of air/Mercury
> CHAKRA(S): Throat (short *E* as in "bet")
> Brow (long *E* as in "see")
> Crown (long *E* as in "see")

The *E* is a vowel which reflects the intellect and perception gained through chastity—proper direction of the sexual force. It holds the energies of the poet, the mystic and the lover of truth and intellect. Its energies are inventive and philosophical, and it gives wondrous strength on the higher planes, once unfolded.

The vowel *E* denotes action—physical and mental. It gives one the energy to illumine others if so desired. Developing the creative aspects inherent within it is the task of those who have the *E* as the keynote of their name.

This vowel opens one to divine ideas, ideas that link normal consciousness to the universal. It gives the potential for manifesting the highest form of intuition, although if undeveloped or uncontrolled, it may manifest in lower forms of psychism. This vowel can open the individual to realms beyond time and space, and the past of the soul can be unveiled.

The *E* can give the potential for creating harmony between any two working things. Its energy is that of a vehicle for self-transformation and will manifest conditions within life—unique to the individual—to assist with that process. It has an archetypal force behind it which can enable the individual to learn to move from one world to another in a fully conscious manner. It holds the lessons of trust, loyalty and lawful marriage and unity on all levels.

This is a vowel which can awaken true clairaudience within the individual, and communication with the angelic hierarchy. This is a vowel of communication on higher levels. It involves communication with those of the animal kingdom as well. As the perception of those with this vowel and its archetypal energies unfolds, so will the past, present and future for the individual.

The E brings with it lessons associated with hypocrisy, deceit, narrow-mindedness, lack of self-control and dogmatism. It may manifest the negative qualities of restlessness, self-righteousness and impurity which must be overcome to manifest the highest and truest energies. These include intuition, inventiveness, determination, persistence, electrical personality, mysticism and even genius. This is the letter for developing a greater ability to manifest universal consciousness within physical life circumstances. It is the letter for the development of strength and self-mastery.

## THE VOWEL I

> KEYNOTE: Divine love
> COLORS: Red-violet or opal
> ASTROLOGY: Element of fire/Mars
> CHAKRA(S): Medulla oblongata (long *I* as in "eye")
> Throat (short *I* as in "it")

The *I* is the vowel for divine love, with its color of red-violet. This is the color of transmutation through the power of love. It is the vowel for the linking of the heart and the mind into a powerful expression of compassion and healing.

This is a vowel which brings lessons in self-sufficiency in the unfoldment of its higher capabilities. Those with this vowel are very memory conscious, and have a capacity for seeing the law of cause and effect within their lives as well as the lives of others. This is the vowel which gives a capacity for spiritualizing the astral, the most activating principle for most life upon this planet. These individuals have an innate capacity to understand the metaphysical laws of life affecting them if they put their heart and minds to such endeavors.

The *I* is the activating vowel for the force of destiny within one's life. It attracts fire in all of its manifestations. It can endow the individual with a capacity for reading the hearts and minds of others. If not worked at, though, it may manifest an imbalance between heart and mind. Compassion without knowledge as to how best apply it is impotent.

This is a vowel of "contraction"—the condensing of the fires of illumination into the material world. Those with this vowel have come to walk the fire's edge of life, and they must keep in mind that what is not controlled will burn.

This vowel gives strength—spiritual, mental and physical. It endows the individual with natural healing capacities and a unique mentality. It contains the lesson of becoming without possessing. Its energies are aligned with Mars which gives great power for attracting love and great reservoirs for the outpouring of love and enlightenment for those within their lives.

These individuals must overcome emotionalism, selfishness, impulsive behavior and indifference in order to manifest the energies of healing, self-sufficiency, faithfulness and intuitive certainty. For it is these archetypal forces which are accessible to those of this predominant vowel.

## THE VOWEL O

KEYNOTE: Justice and balance
COLORS: Black and dark ultramarine
ASTROLOGY: Element of water/Saturn
CHAKRA(S): Spleen (long *O* as in "toe")
                Solar plexus (short *O* as in "pot")

The vowel *O* is tied to the archetypal energies of justice—particularly divine justice. It is the task of these individuals to attain harmony and to help others attain harmony, keeping in mind that what works for one may not work for all. This vowel gives an innate ability to attain a high sense of spiritual judgment and to comprehend legalities. It gives the power to evoke responses on any level.

Those with this vowel have a capacity to achieve satisfaction, security and success—as long as the dignity of the individual is held high at all times. Learning to see relationships—the cause and effects—facilitates their day to day life situations. Once they develop this capacity, they can teach this to others.

The *O* is the symbol of the sacred enclosure. It is thus the task of those with this as the predominant vowel to learn to work inside and out, and to selectively choose the time and circumstances of any barriers they may wish to employ in any avenue of life. Learning to order the forces of their emotions will be part of the task.

Those who truly open to the power of this vowel can discern the mysteries of the ebb and flow of life circumstances and learn to maintain the proper balance between both. For these individuals, control of emotions and anger is one of the tasks, but accomplishing it enables a true manifestation of the power of will-force.

The *O* is the vowel for the planet Saturn who is the teacher of this solar system. It is the influence of the laws of cause and effect, the ideal versus the real. This vowel—with its planetary influence— gives one the ability to connect and bind things together. It makes one sensitive to criticism, but it also makes him or her tenacious and faithful.

These individuals have an innate power for visualization and thus should only focus on that wished to be created. If encouraged to self-expression, there are no limits. If these individuals overcome lack of will, dogmatism, overly developed sense of criticalness and fear of failure, the gifts of power, imagination, initiative, generosity and teaching can manifest to untold heights.


## THE VOWEL U

> KEYNOTE: Birth giving
> COLORS: Earth tones and ivory black
> ASTROLOGY: Element of earth/Venus
> CHAKRA(S): Base (long *U* as in"cue")
>             Throat (short *U* as in "but")

At its highest level, this vowel can open the individual to a comprehension of the creative act and all of its ensuing karma. It activates the feminine energies of illumination and inspiration, and it is linked to one of the highest forms of intuition and clairvoyance. It gives one the strength for the task of mastering karma. If worked with, it can lead to conscious astral projection and out-of-body experiences.

The *U* has connections to Earth and to Venus—both of which are feminine planets. It is the feminine which holds the birth giving ability in any field of endeavor and in any form of manifestation. It has a fertilizing affect that can be unfolded to tremendous proportions in the life of any who has this as the predominant vowel.

The *U* provides protection through resistance. It gives one the ability to resist any invasion, and thus often needs love, patience and gentleness to open to the new. And it is important for those with this as the primary vowel to open to the new. Harshness can crush these individuals. They have strong intuitions, and they are often instinctively guided.

Conservative by nature, they make excellent judges of character. Those with this as a predominant vowel should pay close attention to their dreams, for their dreams will be of great significance. (Dreaming is part of the feminine expression of energies within us all.) These individuals can also range from being very quiet to very boastful in their outward expressions.

It is important for those of this vowel not to resist new opportunities, for this can attract losses. Theirs is the inherent force of formation and the "will to form." Fire when blended with water upon the earth plane can remove weaknesses or become a force of destruction. It is this force that those of this vowel have a capability of manifesting within their lives. When controlled and directed, it can open them to other dimensions.

## THE VOWEL Y

KEYNOTE: Transmutation
COLORS: Light golden brown and pink
ASTROLOGY: Elements of fire and water/Venus and Mars
CHAKRA(S): Varies from any of the chakras of the head
(throat, brow, crown and medulla oblongata),
depending upon the  sound the *Y* takes
within the name. It has no sound of  its own.

On its highest level, this vowel gives one the capacity for understanding the origins and rhythms of life and how to use the creative process. It can awaken profound intuition and aspiration. It is linked to the gift of true prophecy—as in the tradition of the secret wisdom school of ages past. When activated fully, it can open sight to the archetypal energies behind all life and all life circumstances.

This vowel links the male and female. Whenever there is a uniting of these two forces, there is a new birth—a transmutation. The male and female in a united and balanced expression gives birth to the "holy child within." Even the glyph of this letter reflects this uniting of the male and female. The stem of the letter is the male, activating force, and the upper V is the feminine, the yoni of creation. They are united within this vowel, and thus those with this as the primary vowel can unfold a tremendous creativity within his or her life.

The color is light golden brown, like ripened wheat. Wheat grows from the earth (feminine) when activated and fertilized through the flames of the sun (the masculine). Wheat is the food of new life.

This vowel holds the lesson of freedom from bondage, and these individuals must be handled gently, as they are ruled by love. They have come to build strong mental powers and link the heart and mind in a new union. They have great potential for manifesting power—positive or negative.

The vowel *Y* can manifest opportunities within the individual's life for healing, wisdom and aspiration. Theirs can be the way of loving guidance and self-sufficiency, especially if they overcome any imposed bondage (by self or others) and do not allow themselves to be so easily hurt. Theirs is the Quest for the Holy Grail, the quest of the transmutation of energies, the quest for the alchemical process of life and life circumstances.

These individuals have a capacity for being visionary, nurturing and gentle souls. Theirs is the innate ability to sense the thoughts, feelings and motives of others, but they must learn to trust in those feelings and not resist the expression of the new.

# 3

# The Vowels as
# Inner Talismans

Ultimately, we need to awaken the life force of the vowels within us. One way of initiating this process is to turn the vowel into an "inner talisman." Meditating upon its significance and on all of its correspondences is an excellent means of doing so. Visualizing the energy of the vowel surrounding you and flowing forth from you into your life is part of that process. The second part involves the use of sounds and toning.

Assuming the posture and visualization on page 27 during the practice of the following exercise will facilitate the activation of the archetypal energies of your predominant vowel.

1. Determine the primary vowel of your first name. (Use your first as it appears on your official birth certificate.) This will be the vowel which is most strongly stressed within your name. If two vowels are together, it is the vowel which is sounded.

2. Familiarize yourself with the correspondences and symbology of the vowel. Although methods to bring the vowels to life will be discussed, it is most important to keep in mind and concentrate upon the important aspects of the vowel.

3. Allow yourself to relax, making sure you will be undisturbed.

4. Visualize the vowel forming around you, its energies awakening all of the abilities and potentials that are associated with it. See yourself filled with the color of your vowel. See yourself as the vowel symbol itself, a spiritual glyph with all of its inherent en-

ergies.

5. Begin slow rhythmic breathing. With each in-breath, pull the letter and its color energy within you, let it fill you completely. With each out-breath, imagine that energy pouring forth from you to be given expression somewhere in your own life circumstances. Remember that we are manifesting and bringing to life the energies you have come to unfold and express within this incarnation.

6. Repeat for approximately 5 to 10 minutes, until you begin to feel a definite energy change. This will most likely be noticed first within the area of the body associated with the element of the vowel:

    Fire (head and the heart)      Air (chest and head)
    Water (abdomen and groin)    Earth (feet and legs)
    Ether (throughout the body)

7. Ten minutes a day of this exercise will bring to life the energies that are working through your vowel within a relatively short time. It will vary according to the individual, but a noticeable change could occur after only a month's time.

8. In the imaging process, try to visualize the physical, emotional, mental and spiritual energies being affected. This facilitates linking the physical with the spiritual. The change will be felt first upon the physical, but this will carry over into the spiritual aspects. Remember that we are working on evolution, which moves from the physical to the spiritual.

9. Practice of this exercise will ultimately enable you to evoke the energies to which your vowel is connected any time they are needed. Before long you will be able to picture and perceive the corresponding virtues and energies in a conscious manner in all of your day-to-day life circumstances.

A: Ether
Keynote: Illumination
Colors: White or light blue

I: Fire
Keynote: Divine love
Colors: Red-violet or opal

E: Air
Keynote: Strength/self-mastery
Colors: Blue or dark violet

O: Water
Keynote: Justice/balance
Colors: Black or dark ultramarine

U: Earth
Keynote: Birth giving
Colors: Earth tones and ivory black

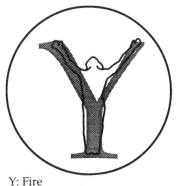

Y: Fire
Keynote: Transmutation
Colors: Light golden brown and pink

### *Postural Glyphs of the Vowels*

## Positive and Negative Traits of Vowels

| A | | E | |
|---|---|---|---|
| ambition | cynicism | intellectual | hypocrisy |
| intellectuality | sarcasm | intuitive | deceitful |
| versatility | scattered | inventive | restless |
| inventiveness | lack of concen- | philosophical | argumentative |
| concentration | tration | determined | narrow-minded |
| aspiration | immersion in | electrical | impurity |
| truth | sensuality | genius | dogmatic |
| idealistic | overly critical | mystical | easily irritated |
| sensitivity | disharmony | strength of will | self-righteous |
| broad-minded | hypersensitive | strong | nervous |
| creative | possessive | | afflictions |
| organized | lack of will | | |
| | easily hurt | | |
| | planning, not | | |
| | manifesting | | |

| I | | O | |
|---|---|---|---|
| healing | stifled creativity | stable | melancholy |
| self-sufficiency | emotional | power | lack of will |
| selfless | indifference | psychic | dogmatic |
| greater love | selfish | love of music | nagging |
| stimulating | jealous/ | orderly | critical |
| faithful/loyal | possessive | sympathetic | fear of failure |
| demonstrative | oblivious | generous | suppressed |
| intuitive | stubborn | strong willed | feelings |
| certainty | impulsive | sociable | arbitrary |
| active/energetic | apathetic | sense of justice | sensitive to |
| outspoken | distrust | | criticism |
| | | | domineering |

| U | | Y | |
|---|---|---|---|
| strong intuition | harshness | loving | lustful |
| conservative | easily hurt | insight/ | overly emotional |
| visionary | selfish | intuition | impatience |
| lucid dreaming | haughty | can manifest | egotism |
| patient | bragging | great power | negative |
| gentle | secretive | healing | indecisive |
| nurturing to | misuse of power | wisdom | imposed |
| children | miserly | self-sufficiency | bondage |
| tenacious | overly protective | positive | inability to |
| quiet | deceitful | aspiration | manifest |
| progressive | resists change | loving guidance | easily hurt |
| reliable | clannish | patience | lack of |
| protective of | | | common sense |
| others | | | |

## Table of Correspondences for Quick Reference

| Vowel Glyph | Vowel Sounds | Chakras | Effects of Energy When Activated |
|---|---|---|---|
| A | ay (hay) | Heart | Chest, lungs, circulation, heart, blood (love, healing, balance, Akashic Memory) |
| | ah (cat) | Throat | Throat, respiration, mouth, trachea, etc. (creative expression, clairaudience) |
| | aw (saw) | Solar plexus | Stomach, digestion, left-brain, intestines (inspiration, clairsentience, psychism) |
| I | I (eye) | Medulla oblongata | Balanced brain function, mental clarity (mind over emotions, "intelligence of heart") |
| | ih (bit) | Throat | Throat, respiration, mouth, trachea, etc. (creative expression, clairaudience) |
| E | ee (see) | Brow | Head cavity, sinuses, brain, pituitary, glands (clairvoyance, third eye, spiritual vision) |
| | | Crown | Skeletal system, pineal (Christ Consciousness) |
| | eh | Throat | Throat, respiration, mouth, trachea, etc. (creative expression, clairaudience) |
| O | oh (note) | Spleen | Muscular system, reproduction, navel area (creativity, reserve energy, higher emotions) |
| | aw (cot) | Solar plexus | Stomach, digestion, left-brain, intestines (inspiration, power, psychic sensitivity) |
| U | oo (boot) | Base | Genitals, pelvis, lower body, circulation (vitality, life force, Kundalini) |
| | uh (but) | Throat | Throat, respiration, mouth, trachea, etc. (creative expression, clairaudience) |

## TECHNIQUE #1 - ACTIVATING THE INNER SOUNDS

1. Breath refers to that quick life intake of energy. Esoterically, it is that which carries an image or thought to the subconscious. It is life itself, and breath with the sounds of our name activate our most intimate life forces.

2. The function of directed esoteric toning with the primary sounds within one's name serves to restore the primal vibration pattern of the bodies (physical and subtle).

3. Taking the primary vowel within your name, review its significance. Visualize its activation as you have learned to do through the previous exercise—include color and posture.

4. Relax and close your eyes. As you inhale slowly through the nose, sound or tone the vowel silently within your mind. Use the vowel sound as it is pronounced within your name. Imagine it echoing within the head and mind and across the infinite realms of inner space. As you do so, feel the color grow brighter and more intense around you.

5. Exhale slowly through the mouth, vibrating or toning the sound audibly. Allow it to find its own volume and length. Do not try to hold it to a particular pitch. As you work with it, it will find its own.

6. Repeat the process. Inhale, sound it silently. Exhale, sound it audibly. In, out. Silent, audible. In, out. Spiritual, physical. This process activates the archetypal energies associated with the sound and begins the process of bringing them out into the physical. It links and bridges the two worlds.

7. Repeat the toning and keep in mind that the effects are amplified by visualizing the colors becoming more brilliant and vibrant.

8. After ten minutes, the sound will begin to assume the same pitch with each toning. The inner, silent sound will begin to connect and become inseparable from the outer, audible sound.

9. This becomes even more effective if you focus upon the chakra center that is affected by your vowel sound. This chakra center is one you have come to work upon more intensely during this incarnation. As you inhale, feel the chakra accumulate a reservoir of energy. As you exhale, see and feel this energy surround you,

filling your entire being with its color and radiance. Then imagine your entire aura filled with its brilliant intensity.

10. At the core of the chakra, visualize the glyph of the vowel, the letter itself, forming within you to radiate energy out to you. With practice, all you will need to do is close your eyes and visualize this spiritual glyph that we call a letter shining within you. This will activate a release of its energy into your life. THIS IS THE INNER TALISMAN!

Take time at the end of the exercise to meditate upon all you will now be able to do because of this spiritual activation.


## TECHNIQUE #2 - BALANCING THE POLARITIES

We are all a combination of masculine and feminine energies. The masculine aspect within us all is the electrical, assertive energy. The feminine is the magnetic, intuitive aspect. The vowel sounds can be classified as feminine or masculine, thus they provide clues as to which aspect we have come to more fully unfold within this incarnation. The vowels that take on a short sound within your name are the feminine sounds. Those that have a long vowel sound are masculine. We can use the short and long sounds of our primary name vowel to balance out the male and female energies within us. We can use both of the sounds of our primary vowel to re-align the electro-magnetism of body, mind and soul.

1. Take a comfortable position, making sure you will not be disturbed, and relax.

2. Review the significance of your primary vowel.

3. Determine the masculine and feminine sounds associated with your vowel—the short and long sounds.

4. Begin with the short or the feminine sound. The feminine is the receptive and the masculine is the assertive. We will use the vowel *E* as our example:
   a. As you inhale, sound the short *E* sound (as in "bet") silently within your mind, as you learned to do in the previous technique.
   b. Exhale, toning the long *E* sound (as in "see") audibly.
   c. Inhale the short *E* sound silently; exhale the long *E* sound

audibly. Continue for five to ten minutes.

d. Visualize the appropriate color with each breath cycle. See and feel it coming to life, first within you, and then outside of you. See the energy pouring forth and surrounding you and your world with each audible exhalation. This assists in learning to control all aspects of your energy and direct it where you wish. You are learning to accumulate, assimilate and express your energy in conscious awareness.

5. As a conclusion to this exercise, do a cycle of three breaths, using only the primary sound of your primary vowel. If in your name, your vowel has a "short" sound, do three breaths in which you inhale silently the sound, and then exhale the same sound audibly. If your name has a "long" vowel sound, then do likewise. This serves to activate the expression of your innate energies in a balanced manner.

6. This balancing exercise brings the masculine and feminine into alignment. It balances the hemispheres of the brain which facilitates the learning and creative processes within one's life. Esoterically, whenever the male and female are aligned and united, they give birth to a new expression of energy—that which is often referred to as the Holy Child within.

### SPECIAL HINTS

You are learning with the previous exercises to attune to and tone the primary creative sounds you have come to work with in this incarnation. As you practice, it is important to see the vowels take shape around you as you tone them, as well as within you. Keep in mind that the sound, the glyph and the colors associated with them are all tied to archetypal energies that are playing within your life. Try to imagine and feel the energy filling your body, your environment and your universe. Ultimately, you want to be able to visualize these energies into activity—like turning on a light switch. You must also learn to dissolve it, or turn the switch off. In this manner, you learn to activate and de-activate according to your individual needs. We don't need to leave lights on. All we need to do is learn to turn them on and off at will. To absorb the activated energy back into the body, simply visualize its form in the area of the body associated with its element or the chakra center associated with the vowel itself. See it radiating out as generator of force and light.

In learning to fill the room and the universe with the essence and energy of the letter, you must first bring it to life within you. This is the import of the silent toning with the in-breath. Then as you breathe out, see and feel the energy radiating out from your body to begin the process of filling your environment or universe. You are learning to draw upon unlimited reservoirs to which you have access, but which for most people, go untouched. With each in-breath, the letter and its corresponding energies will become increasingly intense and vibrant, so there is more energy to breathe out into your life.

Assuming the postures as previously depicted, while performing these exercises, will enhance the effects. Physical movements and postures create electrical responses within the body and the mind, facilitating an accessing of energy. It enables you to build a thoughtform around your name symbols, empowering them, just as one might with a talisman. In this manner, the vowel becomes an "inner talisman" that is always carried within you, simply waiting to be evoked by you for your own individual purposes.

# 4

# The Consonant Charms

Just as the vowels reflect inherent potentials we have come to try and manifest, the consonants also activate a certain play of archetypal energies within our lives. To a great degree, the vowels relate to the inner drives of the soul during this incarnation. They are the urgings of the inner self to move itself forward in a particular manner. They reflect the often hidden forces behind our actions and attitudes. They reflect the heart's desires, the ideals and the individuality that can be uniquely expressed. They are representative of the often unseen spiritual force within us that can become a permanent soul force in our lives if developed.

The consonants on the other hand play a rather different role. Just as with the vowels, they too are tied to specific archetypal energies which play themselves out within our lives. The energies linked to the consonants are often more easily detected and brought to life, as they are often the soul forces we have worked to develop in past lives.

All of the experiences mastered, controlled and overcome register upon the soul as growth. These experiences are often reflected within the consonants of our names. They reflect lessons experienced in the past, skills and qualities developed as a result of those experiences. At the same time they reflect those forces we can most easily re-awaken in order to more fully tap the hidden resources reflected within the vowels of our name.

This does not mean that those abilities are automatically accessible from the moment of birth. We still have to go through a process

*35*

of re-awakening those soul energies into expression within our day-to-day life circumstances. This means that we access those soul energies and bring them out. This may involve going through certain life experiences, using a ritualistic method of re-activating them or even something as simple as the techniques that are described throughout the rest of the text. Because they do indicate that we have developed and expressed their corresponding energies in some manner in the past, they will be more easily awakened within this incarnation.

The consonants help us to form a skeletal framework by which we can begin to manifest the hidden forces of the soul (that which is reflected by the vowels). They set a pattern that allows us to remanifest the forces and abilities of the past , so that we can build upon them with the soul forces of our future.

The consonants represent the foundation we have come to build upon in this lifetime, adding to it the hidden forces reflected within the vowels. They represent the solid part of us and our outer personality. They reflect the self-knowledge that we have come into this life with to add to on even greater levels. This adding process has lessons and gifts associated with it, both of which are reflected in the consonants of your name.

The consonants also reflect the outer mask we wear so as to hide the inner urges and impulses from others. They reflect what people can most easily discern about you, and it is often who they think you really are. The consonants provide personality clues, as they often reflect what we most know and feel about ourselves.

As we grow older, the influence of the consonants and the vowels tend to blend together more. The inner blends with the outer, and we begin to unfold into our true potential, building upon the foundations of the past (consonants) with new materials (vowels) for the future. Our name can be considered a sign of destiny, as it is our destiny to grow. The new ever builds upon the old. We must conserve the elements of our past that have enduring worth. Just such elements are reflected within the consonants of our names. We must also leave behind those elements that are a hindrance to life and growth. The energies invoked by the elements of our names stimulate circumstances, unique to our individual environments, that will enable us to discern what is a hindrance and what should be built upon.

Part of the responsibility of growth is to make our own rules and then follow them. We must learn that we are each a creator in our own right and as such we are expected to give free expression to our own genius—in strict adherence to the laws of our own being and circumstances. In order to do this fully, we must first come to understand the energies we are trying to give expression to within this life. It is our name which holds that key!

The consonants, in the evolution of the soul, indicate lessons learned and energies more accessible. It does not mean that you have mastered *all* that is indicated by the letter, but that you have learned some of the lessons within it and can activate it more easily within this incarnation. They indicate abilities learned through past labors, abilities that the individual can grow even more into in this lifetime and unfold to an even greater degree. They are the energies that will assist in unfolding the hidden potential.

The energies of the vowels and the consonants are neutral and impersonal. They are neither positive nor negative in and of themselves. Archetypal energies are energies that we can activate and direct in our own life in accordance with our own free will. It is how we choose to express the energies that determine their "goodness" or "badness." We can choose to unfold them and use them in the most beneficial manner or to ignore them and simply let life play upon us. We can choose to activate them and express them in a negative manner as well.

The name reflects energies to which we have greater access, and that plays in our life because of our association with that name or its elements. Those energies can take positive, negative or even alternative forms of expression within our life circumstances. The more we become aware of the forces and energies that lie behind our names, the more we can control how they express themselves within our life. We can take a negative expression and find an alternative or positive form according to our individual situation. We are not bound to them and to a particular form of expression. The energies that are tied to the elements of our name are the ones most easily directed and controlled. This is why it is always good to come to a complete understanding of the significance of one's true name before instituting a process of change.

Our names reconnect us with the moment and with the archetypal energies playing behind the moment of our lives. Understanding the elements of our name is the key to living within the moment. The vowels are in essence a state of consciousness we hope to achieve within this lifetime—endowed with all the energies available to such a state. The consonants serve as pathways to help open those states of consciousness. The energies of the consonants serve to stimulate a drawing upon our inner resources. By working through even more of the lessons of the consonants and expressing their energies even more fully in this life, we open ourselves to the opportunity to more fully express the touch and be touched by the creative and soul activating energies of the vowels.

When we change our names, we change the archetypal energies to which we have greater access. The new consonants within our name re-open doorways of the soul. These new doorways are tied to lessons and abilities that we have also developed to varying degrees. There is often a tendency among those working to unfold to believe that each learning experience is entirely new. The truth is that we work on many aspects of energy and have done so for a long time. Each incarnation simply provides an opportunity to develop the skills and energies a little more fully, until that time in which we have fully integrated the archetypal into the full expression of our day-to-day lives.

We can look upon our soul as a resource of infinite experience. We choose a name and an environment that enables us to draw upon and develop those soul resources even further within any incarnation. When we change our name, we access a different resource file to assist us with our life circumstances.

The problem arises when we try to change the name too frequently or too indiscriminantly. People need to understand their birth name first and learn to rejoice in its effects and forces. The magic of an individual is first manifested through the birth name. It is attuned in most cases to the energies of the environment in accordance with whatever peculiar lessons and experiences that soul has chosen to undergo in this incarnation.

Our name at birth gives a true indication of what we have come to do within this incarnation. It indicates the goals, the tools and the handicaps to be overcome. It lets us know just why we have signed on this planet at this particular time. It lets us know what lessons we have chosen to teach ourselves through the life circumstances that will be set in motion around us, and it lets us know what gifts and abilities we have come to unfold and develop more fully through these life circumstances. When we understand this, and then when we learn to direct the communications with the soul much more consciously, we discover the divine magic that lies within the heart of all of us.

Changing the name too frequently or changing without full awareness of the intricacies of the process can create very trying periods within one's life. The name we came into physical life with is our primary energy signature. It is most closely aligned with the energy of the environment and enables us to grow from that environment. There is resonance of varying degrees. When we change our name, resonance must be re-established. This can take as long as seven to nine years in some cases. In others, it may take seven to nine days. It depends upon the individual, the new energies being activated and the alignment with other factors which will be discussed in the section on creating a magical name.

It is important to understand that for a name change to be beneficial there must be efforts to create entrainment. Entrainment is the mixing and blending of energies. In the case of name changes, it is done to create a transfer of consciousness. The name and its elements are direct links to the soul and its infinite files of experience, abilities and energies. A change of any kind should be given due consideration, or energies will be evoked that are discordant and disruptive until a degree of entrainment and resonance can be established.

The names we use or choose reveal only what we wish them to reveal. They reflect energies from our true essence, so that we can learn to manifest such energies, qualities, etc. in all circumstances. They define the expressions of energies for this incarnation. We are not bound to them. We can change those energies, but unless we become more aware of their very real effects, we can never unfold the potentials of which we are capable. Our names are special creations; inherent within them is the creative principle that operates throughout nature and the universe. It is what grounds our essence into a unique life of learning and expression. We can learn to control and direct this creative aspect and thereby control and direct our lives and our evolutions.

## DETERMINING THE PREDOMINANT CONSONANTS

The consonants reflect abilities and potentials that we have worked on and developed to some degree in the past. They contain energies and qualities that can assist us with the unfolding of the inner potentials reflected by the vowels, and they provide a tie to archetypal energies that can assist us in handling in a creative and productive manner the circumstances and environments of our lives. The key is understanding their significance and learning to manifest and direct those energies more consciously. There are two predominant consonant influences within a name:

1. CORNERSTONE—This is the initial consonant of the name, even if not the initial letter of the name. Many names do not have initial consonants (*e.g.* Irene).

2. CAPSTONE—This is the final consonant of the individual's first name, even if not the final letter in the first name. Many names do not end in consonants (*e.g.* Nancy).

The CORNERSTONE is the initial consonant within the individual's first name. It reflects the starting point of construction of new soul energies in this lifetime. It is the essential and primary influence of past abilities that have been brought forward into this incarnation to assist the unfolding of the inner potentials of the vowels. It is the chief foundation upon which the new growth of this lifetime is to be constructed. When the cornerstone is the initial letter of the name as well, it has an even greater impact. This can indicate that the individual must first awaken its qualities to unfold the inner potentials reflected by the vowels. It provides a reserve force to be drawn upon during those more trying times that one may encounter.

The cornerstone is the consonant reflecting the strongest abilities and qualities that can assist one within this incarnation. These qualities are those abilities the individual may have a greater facility in unfolding, but they still must be unfolded and re-awakened. The cornerstone often reflects the formative lessons of youth that enable us to come into our own expression of individuality. It is what leads each of us uniquely to the inner soul potential and growth.

When the cornerstone precedes the predominant vowel, the consonant helps to bring out that hidden force of creative expression so that it can become the keynote of the person's life. When the cornerstone consonant follows the predominant vowel of the name, it can indicate several possibilities about the soul growth:

1. The individual has come in with that hidden potential already revealing itself.

2. The strongest learning lessons will occur in youth, but they

won't be synthesized until later in life as the energies of the cornerstone consonant will be more easily accessed in the post youth period.

3. The individual has come to tie up past life lessons before the new cornerstone of soul growth is laid.

For example, in the name IRENE, the predominant vowel is the *I*. The initial consonant of the name or its cornerstone is the *R*. This may mean that the individual known as Irene may have past life lessons dealing with and reflected by the energies of the *I* before the new cornerstone of growth can be laid. This indicates that the individual has come not only to tie up a lot of loose ends, but also to lay new foundations. This is why names that begin with vowels have abundant activity and a wide-range of situations experienced by the individuals. Thus the more one becomes aware of the subtle influences and correspondences of the name, the more easily one will be able to deal with the circumstances of one's life.

The CAPSTONE is the final consonant within the name. It is the finishing stone of the monument called life. It is the indicator of that which will highlight and high point your life when the cornerstone energies have been applied to awaken the inner potentials of the vowels. When this occurs, the energies of the capstone letter are triggered into greater activity. The force of the awakened inner potentials of the vowel produce a period of great opportunity and productivity, reflected by the capstone.

The cornerstone assists us in touching the inner potentials of the vowels, which when activated enable us to place a capstone of great achievement upon our lives. Although we treat them all initially as separate and distinctive elements, there is an intimate and intricate interrelationship.

It is the interplay of these three elements that provides the clue to our growth. The two predominant consonants and the primary vowel are the key elements of our name. These three provide the clues to the new birth you have come to give to yourself within this incarnation. All of the other letters are elements that influence this birth and growth. All vowels and consonants, found within the name between the cornerstone consonant and the capstone consonant, reflect energies and lessons that influence the creative and developmental process of the individual in varying degrees.

Three is the creative number. It is the number of new birth. It is the linking of the male and female into a new expression. When the male force (cornerstone consonant) is united with the feminine force (vowel), it gives birth to a new expression of energy and creativity which is the capstone.

Names which end in a consonant (capstone) often indicate the culmination of life energies and expressions in a manner that corresponds to the significance of that consonant. For example, with the name PAT, the energies of the *T* indicate what can be the potential highlights of this person's life, if the cornerstone of *P* and the vowel *A* and their inherent forces are activated. It the cornerstone and vowel forces are not accessed fully and balanced properly within one's life, then the negative expressions of their energies will be felt. This occurs through experiencing certain life lessons and situations. Thus the more we are aware of all the inherent reflections of the vowels and the consonants, the more we can prepare for the capstone of our lives and use the energies to facilitate our daily circumstances.

Some names do not have a capstone. This does not mean that there will be no highpoint or culmination of life experiences for the individual. Names such as JO, which have no capstone, can simply indicate that the individual has chosen to focus more upon the in-depth development of the cornerstone and vowel. This has its own "highpoints," and does not lead one to a particular field of expression for its culmination, but can lead to a variety of highpoints and expressions. These individuals often have the opportunity to develop the creative energies of their name elements and apply them to a variety of endeavors, rather than just building toward one "capstone." Of course, caution must be taken so as not to become too scattered in that deeper expression of energies.

Some names with no capstone do have third elements. The name SUE is a prime example. Its cornerstone is the *S* and its predominant vowel is the *U*. It is the male and female, but in this case it gives birth to a silent expression of energy, *i.e.* the silent *E*. It creates an inner development and awareness, rather than an outward expression or culmination of energy. One name is neither better nor worse than another, simply different in the manner in which energies can be manifested or expressed within one's own environs.

By now, one should be able to discern that there is an intricacy of interplay among the elements of one's name. Generalizations are difficult to follow, and thus it is important to begin with understanding the elements themselves as energies, and then work, through analysis, meditation, etc., to synthesize them as they are playing out within your own life.

## REMINDERS:

1. Keep in mind that the cornerstone is that element which will facilitate the unfolding of the inner potential. It indicates past life abilities that you can awaken and re-manifest with greater ease. It is the first consonant of your name!

2. As you awaken the cornerstone abilities, you can begin to more fully access the inner potential, reflected by the vowel.

3. As the vowel unfolds, your life is imbued with power and a greater ability for manifestation and productivity (the manner of that productivity often reflected by the capstone).

4. The predominant vowel usually follows the cornerstone. It is the vowel most strongly accented. Some names have several vowels which are accented, and some names have vowels which both precede and follow the cornerstone consonant. In a name such as IRENE, the predominant vowel is *I* and the cornerstone is the *R*. The *E* following the *R* though is also accented. It can be considered the predominant vowel as well. In cases such as this, it indicates that the influence of the *I* is a carry over from a past life, and it can indicate that certain lessons and potentials have been chosen to be experienced and developed before the cornerstone of new growth for this incarnation is set in motion. It can indicate that certain forces are wanting to be settled and manifested before the individual concentrates upon those peculiar to this incarnation. In this case, the lessons would involve the cornerstone *R*, the vowel *E* and the capstone *N*.

5. The cornerstone is considered strongest when it initiates the name, but only because the soul comes in working from day one upon its soul task of new growth and development. When it is not the initial letter, it indicates that there may be some delay (the length of which will vary from individual to individual) while the individual takes care of tying up the loose ends of a previous life, as in the previous example. In such cases the cornerstone germinates and simply then comes out stronger when it does emerge.

6. The capstone is the final consonant of a name. It is strongest

when it ends the name, but only in the sense that it tends to tie up the individual's growth neatly. It indicates that the soul has come with a particular task or endeavor or ultimate goal which can serve as a culmination of life experiences. It does *not* mean that the individual will only meet success at the end of the life, but it more often means that a specific pattern of success is established for this incarnation—a pattern by which the energy can best be applied for individual success.

7. When the capstone does not come at the end of a name, such as in the name NANCY in which the C is the capstone, it simply indicates that the individual has chosen not to be limited to a particular expression of success, but may use the capstone energy to open even greater expressions and even gain a jump on the next incarnation. This is most often the case in names that not only end in vowels, but in silent vowels especially, *i.e.* Jane. When the vowel is silent at the end, the individual is building toward future soul growth that he or she is not necessarily concerned with expressing in this incarnation. When the name ends in a vowel that is sounded, *i.e.* Nancy, the vowel indicates that the individual wishes to keep expressing his or her energies even after developing and placing a capstone upon the learning of this incarnation. They are open to even newer expressions.

8. Begin by determining your predominant vowel(s) and your cornerstone consonant and your capstone consonant (if applicable). Review the significance of them. Study the energies associated with them, and take time to meditate upon them to understand how the archetypal energies associated with them have been and are playing within your own life circumstances.

9. Examine the other elements of your name—the other minor consonants and vowels. Although they are not as dynamic within the influence of your name, they do reflect other energies and abilities to which you have access. They just do not influence as strongly as the predominant vowel(s) and the cornerstone consonant and the capstone consonant.

10. Pay close attention to any double letters within your name. Any letters that repeat themselves will intensify the play of those energies and their corresponding lessons and potentials. Double letters, especially when next to each other (ee, ll, oo, mm, etc.), will amplify the play of energies on both the physical and the

metaphysical levels of your life. They are as powerful and significant as any of the predominant letters—vowel or consonant. They give twice the potential, but they also may manifest twice the tests in order to manifest that higher energy. Keep in mind that the letters are symbols linked to archetypal energies of the universe. By aligning ourselves with them through our names, we set their energies in motion within our lives and our unique life environs. It is important to understand them and learn to employ them in manners other than for identification. It is important to use them to open the windows of our souls and manifest that soul light within our physical existence.

11. Consider also any consonant combinations (th, ch, etc.). Consonant combinations, especially if they form a cornerstone or capstone, create a unique combination of energies in your life. They are two distinct consonants forming one unique sound. This indicates that the individual has come to blend and harmonize specific energies and abilities. For these individuals, it would be most beneficial to study carefully the information on both and examine the possibilities and ways in which those energies can combine. Harmony, creating or maintaining, will be a task for those of the consonant combinations on some level. This harmony must either be developed or re-established for the true inner potential, as reflected in the vowel, to manifest. As the individual develops inner harmony, the inner potential can manifest most fully, and the past talents and abilities are more easily activated to assist in this process.

12. Whether we are dealing with the vowels or the consonants, keep in mind that the alphabet was considered sacred. Keep in mind that everything associated with the elements in your name provide clues to the elements of our soul. The glyphic significance (shape and form of the letters), the phonetic value, astrological and numerological correspondences, position within your name, color correspondences and all esoteric associations are linked to the archetypal divine energy working with you through your own SOUL! Remember that above the portals of the ancient mystery schools was but one rule: "KNOW THY-SELF!"

# 5

# The Hidden Essences
# of the Consonants

Although the vowels most strongly represent the inner potentials to which we have access, the consonants are also strongly symbolic of energies playing within our lives. The vowels are those we have come to unfold, and the consonants are the means by which we can most effectively do so. The consonants are reflections of those archetypal energies that we have accessed in the past and developed to some degree. They do not reflect mastership of their energies, but working with them to unfold our inner potentials helps to lead to that—be it in this life or some future life.

The correspondences are guidelines. They are not LAW. They are to facilitate a starting point by which we can begin the process of unfolding them more fully. The energies they reflect are neutral and impersonal. They operate whether we are aware of them or not. The more we become aware of them, the more we can control them and then the less we are at the mercy of our life circumstances. We are no longer passive.

The manner in which they are allowed to play within our life can be positive or negative and everything in between. The correspondences listed are designed to give you a starting point to discerning just how they are playing in your personal life, so that you can then adjust them accordingly.

Some of the correspondences are arbitrary. The colors are not set. The first color listed is the easiest vibration associated with the letter; the second is the color of the letter at a more intense activation. As you begin to work with the letters and other elements of your name, you may find differences in the colors. This is normal, and to be expected from time to time. These elemental energies of your name adjust themselves to you and your own vibrational frequency so that you can access them and experience them in the manner best for you.

One of the best ways of discovering some of the hidden aspects of the letters is by exploring some of the earlier alphabets that preceded our own English alphabet. Eight different alphabets are listed in chapter 20. There are any number of books that define the hidden significance of the letters. For example, the Ogham alphabet of the early Celts is an alphabet in which the letters are associated with specific trees. Discerning the tree and its qualities can provide clues to the hidden aspects of the letter itself. Some of these correspondences will be touched upon in the descriptions of the consonants.

The consonants, just like the vowels, can have positive and negative aspects unless we learn to tap and use their energies appropriately. That, of course, is the purpose of this text. These different manifestations of energy are also described for each consonant. There is an exercise at the end of this chapter to help you to alter the expression of the consonant's energy, if you discern it to be operating in a negative manner. Because we have worked with them in past lives, they are much easier to turn around to our benefit. We can change the condition of the archetypal energy as it manifests simply by activating the inherent creative force.

There are many ways of working with the combinations of vowels and consonants, too many to work with within the boundaries of this text. It is important to know that the influence of a vowel before the consonant and the vowel that follows a consonant is different in how they manifest within your own life. There are three steps to truly understanding one's name elements:

1. Understanding the vowels and the inner potentials they are attempting to activate within your own life.

2. Understanding the consonants and the abilities through which you have the greatest access, and through which you may fully unleash the inner potentials of the vowels.

3. Understanding the elements as they work together in all of their various combinations—the significance of each vowel with each consonant and how they modify and create unique expressions of energy.

It is also important to understand that the effects of the vowels and the consonants are going to be experienced, regardless of the individual's awareness. It will just be to a much lesser degree and with seemingly little control. Even without conscious awareness, the primary vowel and its energies will unfold to some degree through the course of life, simply because it activates the play of archetypal energies by its glyph, sounds and other correspondences.

This is also true for the consonants. Their energies will also be felt, and the individual will find that he or she, more or less, will reflect the energies and experiences that are triggered by association and connection to those consonants and all of their glyphic and symbolic ties to universal energies. The trick is to control and direct the intensity and manner in which those energies manifest within one's life.

This is what name enchantment is truly about. It is about developing a greater wisdom of one's true potentials and learning to use that wisdom to take greater responsibility for one's life circumstances. It is about the task of re-creating our life. It is about softening the difficult aspects, healing the hurts and accelerating the growth. It is about recognizing that growth and development require effort, but do not require that we traumatize ourselves in the process. Name awareness is a gentle and consciously active process of enlightenment. It touches the heart of each of us, for it is from the heart that our name sings forth its song to our soul!

## THE CONSONANT B

KEYNOTE: The constructive and creative power of wisdom
COLOR(S): Yellow and violet-indigo
ASTROLOGY: Mercury

The consonant *B* is connected to that archetypal energy capable of making one a true magus of power and wisdom. Its colors are those of higher intellect (yellow) and cosmic consciousness (violet-indigo). It is a letter that is tied to those universal energies which enable one to concentrate energy expression into very definite forms. It gives one the innate ability to combine elements of one's life and energies in novel ways.

Its glyph is the straight line, attached to two half circles. This is the body and mind connected to the spiritual. It is also similar in appearance to the number 13. Although this has always been considered an unlucky number, in ancient times it was a powerful symbol of the one great sun around which circled twelve other stars. This is more recently reflected in the life of the Master Jesus and the 12 Apostles. On a lesser level it is also the one and the three brought together. This is reflected in many ancient teachings concerning the Trinity, three persons in one god and in the divine father-god, mother-god and son-god which comprises the manifestations of the One Divine source of Life in the Universe.

This consonant enables the individual to draw upon an innate understanding and perception of life. Those with this as a predominant letter within the name soon discover that nothing is in vain— even the negative and the positive experienced within one's life.

It enables you to draw upon the qualities of loyalty and sympathy that have been developed by the soul in the past. Those with this consonant can often be "late bloomers," experiencing their greatest success later in life—in the post 40 period. It can make the individual very electrical in the expression of energy. As the individual learns to manifest this electrical aspect, he or she can become a strong influence in the lives of others—with an apparent ability to be catalytic in the fate of others. It is important that precautions be taken by the individual so as not to interfere with the free will and karma of those within their lives.

These individuals have a capability of tapping into soul recesses to draw upon knowledge and/or experiences that facilitate working with all aspects of polarity and sexual magic. If this is accessed and expressed appropriately, it can be a remedy for any disharmony within the body. They can learn to work with and control the polarities of life and death when the energies associated with this letter are accessed at the highest level. The power to construct is inherent in those who have this letter predominant within his or her name. It provides the energies of balance and new expression from that balance. It is a letter that brings the opportunity to build the new upon the old, the opportunity to learn the constructs of new magic.

This is a letter of great fertility, and indicates a lifetime opportunity of blossoming when one is brought within its rhythms. For this blossoming to occur in the most beneficial manner, resistance toward the cyclic flow of life must be overcome. It requires an activation of modesty, patience and fairness. This is inherent within the character development of those of this letter, but overcoming self-criticism is the key to its full manifestation.

These individuals have a unique ability to grow in spite of outside forces and influences. It is that ability they have brought forth to give even greater expression to this incarnation and thus inspire others toward their own development. These individuals have the ability to break open the seeds of their lives and create dynamic growth. Theirs is the energy of fertility, transformation and the innate power of mystical eroticism. It is the alchemy of the WORD that they have experienced somewhere within their pasts and have come to build upon it even more so.

As with all letters, there may be weaknesses to overcome and strengths to obtain and build upon. Individuals that have this as a predominant consonant may have blocked vision from time to time. There may be an innate sense of restlessness and an inability to balance the rational and the intuitive. It may even manifest an unwillingness to take advantage of growth opportunities. On the other hand, it is a letter that stimulates a release of energy that provides a sense of self-nourishment and inner dexterity. It can open one to true seership, and even activate an awareness of those lifetimes in which that seership was utilized. It gives great artistic energy and expanded intelligence. It endows the individual with the innate realization that he or she can construct this life in the manner that he or she desires. This is truly the constructive power of inner wisdom!

## THE CONSONANT C

KEYNOTE: Creative cyclic expression
COLOR(S): Red-orange and violet
ASTROLOGY: Moon

The consonant *C* is tied to the archetypal energies of creative expression, manifesting through cycles. Recognition of the cyclic flow of these energies and accessing them is something that those with this as a predominant letter can do more easily than others. It is the symbol of the in-flow and out-flow of expression. It is the rhythm of the tides and the cyclic fluctuation of energies and life patterns. One who is capable of recognizing the true rhythms and omens of nature can move beyond mere divination into the realms of prophecy, unbounded by superstition.

The glyph is the open circle. Energy and life can flow in and flow out, but discernment and discrimination must be developed so only that which is healthy will flow forth. This is the glyph for the open mouth, the power of expression. It is the creative aspect of expression. These individuals need to heed the adage "It is not what goes into the mouth that will create imbalance as much as that which comes out." The words of these individuals are felt more deeply by others, and words spoken to them touch more deeply as well. The things said more lovingly will be felt more lovingly. The things said more cuttingly will cut more deeply.

This is the symbol for the spoken "WORD," the creative force. Creativity is strong in those that have this as a predominant letter within the name. It indicates that creativity was developed in the past and can be drawn upon and taken to new heights. This is a symbol of new birth, the bringing forth out of the womb. It is the energy and drive to give new expression to themselves and their abilities.

The drive in these individuals is usually strong, but they can be impatient if others do not respond as strongly or as quickly. They can be irritated by others that are slow. Within them is a desire to give up the old and move into a new expression.

Those of this consonant are working with a process of self-spiritualization. At its highest level is the "Mystery of the Eucharist," the alchemical process of change. It is the blending of the male and female into a new form. These individuals have often accomplished to some degree the balancing and uniting of the male and female forces, and now there is an inherent drive to give that unity expression in some dynamic way (reflected within the open mouth of the circle). Determining the area of that expression is the difficult part and often gives these individuals the greatest difficulty.

As the individual learns to more fully activate the energies of this letter, it stimulates control of the astral body and the entire auric field. This facilitates the process of shapeshifting in its truest sense. The individual can learn to shift and mold and transmute his or her energy. The individual has developed strong ideals in the past and is often searching for a new form of expression for them. They have the ability to modify the change process through the use of the "WORD" in any of its forms.

This is a cyclic letter. It implies transition, the death and rebirth cycle, on some level. It stimulates an opening up of the self to newer forms of creativity and expression. It provides the energies so that in the course of the individual's life, he or she may chase back the shadows and develop greater clarity and concentration. It is a letter of new growth and new effort. It indicates tasks of giving more light and searching out more light.

The kind of cyclic energy activated by this letter brings lessons of giving up the old expressions so as to have new opportunities to develop greater and deeper inner stability. These individuals work with the lessons of patience. They must learn to put forth their energies, allow them to find their own unique rhythms and then allow time for the new to unfold, yet the individual must remain stable while doing so. This is the giving out and absorbing cycles of creative expression and manifestation!

This is the letter for Moon-fire. This is the fire of change and illumination, the fires that bring new light with each phase of the Moon. It burns away the dross so that the gold beneath is given greater expression and grows stronger with each passing Moon.

## THE CONSONANT D

KEYNOTE: Fertility
COLOR(S): Emerald green and rose pink
ASTROLOGY: Venus

This is the letter of fertility. It is pregnant with life, as is reflected in its shape, the swollen womb that is ready to burst forth with new life. This letter is tied to those archetypal energies that can reveal the mysteries of creation—as they are playing within our own unique life circumstances.

Astrologically, it is associated with the planet Venus, a planet of beauty, attraction and the sharing of love which produces new life.Those with this as a predominant letter have an innate ability to attract material things. It activates the magnetic aspect of them, the magnetic which draws other people and things into the individual's life.

This is the letter of magnetism—physical and spiritual. It can make one pregnant with life, and individuals with this letter predominantly placed within their name have an instinctual facility at social grace. They know how to act and when. This can also stimulate sexual magnetism as well. They instinctively touch the sexual core of others in ways not often understood. Sexual energy is a powerful life force, the secrets of which are still shrouded in mysticism. It is so much more than just a physical drive, but a force that touches and opens the doors to the soul.

For these individuals, there are lessons of blending and joining the male and female into ever higher forms of expression and manifestation. It is a letter that requires a balancing of wisdom and folly (knowledge and ignorance) on all levels, reflected within the glyph itself. The half circle (pregnant with life ) touches the bottom of the vertical line and the top as well. This fertility needs to be expressed in a balanced manner on both the physical and spiritual realms.

At some point in the past, evolvement of the individual has become a knowledge of the birth process and a belief in the impossible. As long as the individual does not give in to the susceptibility of disbelief and feeling unattractive, great joy and creativity can manifest in his or her life and in the lives of those he or she touches.

Those with this letter's influence will have to learn to master the ego and the mental body. When this is accomplished, the significance of all erotic energies can be revealed, and love and sex in all of its spiritual forms can become available. The individual has the opportunity to become a "Master of Love." All procreative acts within your individual life circumstances can fall under your charge.

This is a letter of final transformation. The pregnant letter is you, about to give birth to a new you. When we balance the male and female within us, we give birth to the Holy Child. This is what has come to be termed the Rite of the Mystic Marriage.

This letter indicates that you have made major breakthroughs in your own growth and development in the past, and it will stimulate the energies that provide opportunity to continue that process. This letter can bring radical changes into one's life. A new child changes much within the lives of the parents. Things are never the same. And although the outcome may not be predictable, it is assured. It will bring new birth and life!

Inherent with this letter, are energies that teach trust. Its Runic counterpart tells us that "the Warrior nature reveals itself." This is, of course, the spiritual warrior aspect. This letter allows us to draw upon past achievements and methods of prosperity so as to institute changes within one's present life circumstances.

Individuals with this as a predominant letter seem to lead "charmed" lives—lives that are often a paradox to themselves and to others. It may bounce from extremes, but even the negative passes quickly to be replaced by the positive and fertile. The more we can attune to the archetypal energies behind this letter, the more it can work for us.

This is the paradox of fertility. It is linking the male and the female, the electrical and the magnetic, the Sun and the Moon, the dawn and the twilight. It teaches how to use the edges of extremes, the intersections that create powerful vortices of energy by which new growth can be brought forth into manifestation.

This is a letter that allows the individual to draw upon the ability to work hard so as to produce great joy and abundance. This capability of working hard was brought into this incarnation to assist the individual and enable the individual to bring to fertility the hidden power and potential of the predominant vowel within the name.

## THE CONSONANT F

KEYNOTE: Dynamic fulfillment through harmony
COLOR(S): Light red-orange and black with gold flecks
ASTROLOGY: Taurus

This is the consonant of harmony and the distilling of light through harmony. It activates an innate cheerfulness that the individual can easily draw upon to assist in manifesting harmony within the outer life. It gives a tendency toward idealism.

Its glyphic form reflects much. It is made of two lines pulling away from a third. It is the process of pulling away from the physical into a new perspective which is often necessary for harmony to ensue. These individuals must look at things differently. The bottom of the vertical pole has no horizontal line attached to it, indicating that those with this consonant have begun the process of pulling away from lower level perceptions, and to activating higher levels of idealism.

It is important for these individuals to work to remain positive and receptive to higher influences. These higher influences are those of mysticism, intuition and imagination which have been awakened in the past. It is important though that these individuals learn to harmonize these elements and synthesize them into constructive expressions within their physical lives or discord may result. Learning to do so is what is reflected in the higher color vibration associated with this letter. The gold is the light of the spiritual manifesting in the physical (the black).

This letter gives one the ability to harmonize will and intellect, feeling and physical life. This ability was initiated in previous times and can be built upon within this life. Those with this letter predominantly placed can learn to control these in the self and in others, for they lead to true mastery of one's own spirit.

Harmony is the true key to mastering one's spirit and the four elements that comprise it. At its highest level, it brings understanding of universal laws and abstract ideas, with the ability to link the physical with the metaphysical. Part of what the individual will learn to do is to work within the four-fold quadrants of the world and all of their corresponding energies.

This is a letter of dynamic power. It brings the promise of fulfillment and nourishment, but the individual must work through and understand the true process of profit and loss and how it manifests on levels other than just the physical and material.

Self-rule is the lesson of this letter, and constant vigilance is required. Learning not to succumb to frustration, and learning that there are lessons in all things (even when one falls short) is the true key to successfully unfolding the highest potential. The individual must become ever mindful of each experience, and many times, he or she must learn the shadow side of things to understand and harmonize with the power of light.

This is a letter tied to the "force" which lies hidden in all things. Uncovering that force, harmonizing it within one's own life circumstances and utilizing it in a productive manner is the true lesson and the ability of those with this letter. It is the task and the potential of those with this letter to draw light and life up out of death, to raise one's self above the physical, to draw upon often unseen forces to lift the consciousness through will and self-mastery. As this develops, so too will the intuitive and the spiritual imagination.

This letter is linked to those archetypal energies which make one steadfast and loyal. It is a letter of affection—giving and receiving—for others instinctively feel the harmonizing capability that lies within. It is important for that harmony not to be forced, but to be recognized as a power that will adapt itself to each person and each situation. Being careful not to become too stubborn and over-emotional is the key, along with not allowing oneself to be drawn too strongly into material and physical appetites. If these are controlled, this dynamic harmonizing power will bring fertility, intense sensitivity and understanding.

## THE CONSONANT G

KEYNOTE: Gifts of faith and discernment
COLOR(S): Deep blue and silvery blue
ASTROLOGY: Moon

This is the letter that brings gifts of the spirit into one's life. It enables the individual to draw upon those spiritual gifts, developed within the past, to facilitate the present and the move to the future. It is the letter of memory, patience and perseverance. It is the letter of spiritual energy and essence.

Its glyph is the open circle with the intersecting line. It is the symbol for the act of intercourse, the creative act itself that will give birth to new expressions of energy, but which in itself is one of the most powerful forces to which humanity has accessibility. In alchemy, one learns all of the elements necessary to prepare for a transmutation of energy, but even if all preparations are performed properly, the transmutation itself will not occur. Enacting the transmutation process, placing oneself fully and completely in it, is required. The actual act itself creates a stimulation of energy whose effects then are determined by one's faith. In Biblical scripture, one reads of the alchemical process of changing the water into wine. The change occurs during the mixing, not after they are mixed. As the water is poured forth, in faith as wine, the alchemical process occurs.

This is the lesson and the ability of those of this letter. Learning to do in faith what one believes and knows is right for him or herself is the key. Recognizing that it is the path and not where the path leads that provides the rewards is the true test and ability of the individual. It is learning to do something for the joy of it, rather than for what may be "gained" from it.

The act of intercourse raises tremendous forces on both physical and spiritual levels. Those with this consonant must learn to control and direct the flow of those energies for the most beneficial expression. This energy can ultimately be channeled to create an alchemical change on the cellular structure of the body and allow it to open to spiritual ecstasy and a higher mind that in turn creates the true body of light—"The Golden Wedding Garment." These energies enable individuals of this letter to discover their own "Ark of the Covenant," their own "Holy Grail," their own "Holy of Holies," and manifest it within the sacred energies of their own auric fields.

Learning to balance peace and strife is part of the task. Anger and sarcasm cut more deeply, and they must practice constant awareness of their own words, for our words are a dynamic expression of that same spiritual-sexual energy. These individuals are often aware of this force, and may shrink from the responsibility they feel from it. It is important that they learn to trust the subconscious urgings, as the intuitive and inventive aspects of it are dynamic. Developing faith is the key.

There is an innate sensitivity to these individuals, a subconscious empathy with others. Discernment is necessary for the balance in their lives. Discernment of mercy in all situations is strong. Understanding mercy as it plays in the lives of humanity and in animals is inherent with those of this letter.

This letter gives one the ability to generate happiness, success and wealth—along with their proper perspectives. Most obstacles encountered will be self-made obstacles, again an indication why the innate discernment needs to be awakened and drawn upon. For some there may be an inability to see the purpose in all things in life, and faith must be drawn upon, a faith that knows there is a purpose, even if it is not recognized. Learning to remove the barriers between the inner and the outer worlds is part of the lesson, as is reflected by the open circle within the shape of the letter itself.

This letter awakens the past ability to unite with higher levels of consciousness. This is the letter of the alchemical marriage. It holds the force of the exchange of power—the giving and receiving and the bringing of opposites together. It is the linking of the inner and the outer, and there is always within some field of endeavor a communion with the higher self which is drawn upon—a force of inspiration that can be applied within one's work, home, etc.

This letter holds the gift of consciousness and the energy of life-breath. It is the letter that indicates the individual knows there is freedom through unity. These individuals know that through unity, one does not lose individuality but gains greater expression of it. This is the letter of exchanged force, a force that requires quiet balance and applied concentration if it is to bring the light out of the dark and turn faith into a true force that is not a test.

## THE CONSONANT H

KEYNOTE: The power of the word, imagination and intuition
COLOR(S): Brilliant reds
ASTROLOGY: Aries

This is the letter tied to the power of speech and its manifestations. In the physical, speech is our primary means of communication. It is through this faculty that we can communicate what we experience through the other senses. It is tied to the ability to express what is seen.

With our speech we can make others feel as if they are standing in God's shadow or as if they are existing in Hell. It is the power of the word which is the creative force, but that force must first be controlled before it will become an innate power. Fire by itself is a force, but it must be controlled and directed if it is to be applied practically. Otherwise it becomes destructive, burning free.

Those with this as a predominant vowel have a great ability to make their words felt and heard, but they can take on a pure "elemental" force. This force can become a sacred manifestation of the creative feminine energy—the wisdom aspect of the universe. This is referred to as the Shekinah by ancient Hebrew seers or Sophia by Christian Gnostics. It is pure intuition, guided and directed through the imagination and manifested through the proper use of words (in the form of prayers, invocations, chants, songs, poems, etc.). "The letter *H* in the sacred alphabet represents the exalted feminine, the intuitive or wisdom principle, which when awakened through processes of initiation, gives the ability to 'see no more through a glass darkly,' but face to face" (Corinne Heline).

Its glyph is the beginning of a ladder. It is the first rung to new birth and higher manifestations of wisdom and intuition. It indicates, when it is a predominant letter within one's name, that the individual has come to begin to climb a new ladder to new heights. It indicates that preparatory processes have been worked through so that this new climb could be undertaken in this incarnation. This ties it also to its astrological correspondence of Aries. Aries is the first sign of the zodiac. It is the beginning. It is said that God fashioned the world while the Sun was in Aries and that Moses led the Hebrews from the bondage of Egypt during this time of the year. It is the sign of spring—of new birth and new expressions of life.

Its glyph is also tied to the union of opposites, that they may be transformed and new birth occur. The horizontal pole stabilizes the opposite forces, the male and female within us, so that they can be brought together in a new expression. It is a symbol of linking the physical and the spiritual, both requiring equal attention. It is the union of fire and water to generate new expressions of energy.

This is a letter that stimulates the intuitive and imaginative faculties of the mind, thereby opening new insight. This has been activated in the past by those with this letter prominent within their names. This enables them to further develop their faculty of sight and to see greater ways of manifesting the hidden potentials reflected through the vowels in the name. Thus the imagination is strong, for it is what enables us to move from the known to the unknown. It will be the task of those with this letter though to use the will in conjunction with their strong imaginations. There can be a tendency towards always beginning and never completing. This is often due to their strong imaginations by which they can see so much, but the will-force to follow through with that which is imagined is not directed strongly enough.

This is a letter which gives new life and new opportunities for life. It is a letter of transformation of great measures. It is a letter of transformation through initiation. In the ancient scriptures, Jesus was known as Yeshua. At the time of his baptism and the descent of the Holy Spirit, he then became known as Yeheshua.

In the Hebrew Qabala, there was a name for God that was too sacred to be spoken aloud, known as the Tetragrammaton. It is comprised of four letters: JHVH. The *H*, the feminine intuition and image-making ability, is key. It is the power of the word, it dynamizes the creative capacity of the individual.

At its highest, this letter can awaken an innate understanding of languages and their power within human lives. It is the true "gift of tongues." Individuals with this letter always have a fascination with languages and speech. This letter indicates they have come to breathe new life into their soul growth. It brings with it strong clairvoyance and a symbolic and intellectual sensing of the divine. These individuals have a capacity for influencing the fates of others.

This letter stimulates the energies of change, freedom and inventiveness. Individuals with this as a predominant letter have an inner need to break free from that which hinders and constricts their lives. In the early years, many events may seem beyond their control, but it will ultimately have a reverse effect. The negative will lead to the positive. These individuals seem to walk through the "new doors" backwards. It is important for them though to follow their own instincts.

This is a letter that demands growth and change. It is a powerful energy and holds the pattern for anchoring oneself upon a new path and soul direction. These individuals must keep in mind that the more radical the change within their lives, the more significant it is to the overall growth of the soul. Those who have this letter within their name, chose it so growth would be demanded from them. In this way they can boost themselves up on the ladder, so that they can breathe new air and see new light, the light they have always imagined! It is the light of the "Sun of the Morning"! It bestows great vision and imagination to one's life. It strengthens and inspires so that one will move toward that morning sun!

## THE CONSONANT J

KEYNOTE: Harvesting of cosmic love
COLOR(S): Yellow-green and dark opal
ASTROLOGY: Virgo

This is a letter of enthusiasm and mysticism. It stimulates new ideas and an intensity within the individual. Those with this as a predominant letter are much better at leading than following. They bring into this life an energy of pioneering and a desire for new methods and expressions. This is a consonant that will stimulate and bring great light to the hidden potentials reflected by the vowel which follows it within the name.

Its glyph is the symbol of a fishhook. The fishhook is that which drops out of the spiritual to lift one out of the waters. It is true love that enables us to be lifted. Fishing though does require individual effort. The fish do not just jump up out of the water. For those with this as a predominant consonant, there must be manual effort to accomplish anything on a physical or metaphysical level. It is the lesson of growth through application of one's own efforts. This alone will bring a harvesting, but the harvest will only be as great as the love of the task.

Those with this letter need to involve themselves in tasks they truly love and enjoy. They should focus on balancing the physical, and working on physiological changes so as to be a better temple of the spirit. In any area that the individual truly commits him or herself there will be a beneficial activity and outcome, although that commitment is often what is most strongly tested in the lives of individuals with this name. How strongly are you committed to your ideals, activities, lifestyle, etc.? It is not unusual to find the commitment of these individuals tested for a minimum of a year in most endeavors. Afterall, crops are harvested once a year.

These individuals must learn to keep their spirits high and to cultivate that which they plant. Patience is often a test, for the individual must learn that growth cannot be forced. Learning to recognize cycles within one's life is key to enjoying the harvesting process in all areas of life. With a little introspection, it should not be difficult for these individuals to discern the various cycles, and the endless return of that which is not truly cultivated and harvested properly. These individuals have learned in the past that the rewards of one's work and effort is balanced with the quality of that work and effort.

When the Sun enters the sign of Virgo, autumn begins. Autumn is the time of spiritual recapitulation—the time of harvest. Virgo also has ties to the Holy Grail Mystery, and thus so do those of this letter. There have been quests for such in the past. It is the time of the year in which individuals desiring to can begin to prepare themselves for a new cycle within their lives, draw themselves up and out of the physical mire into new expressions of the spiritual. It is a time in which individuals can begin the process of re-opening themselves to the flow of cosmic love and manifest it within the circumstances of their own lives.

At its highest level, this letter awakens within one's life high love with great feeling and giving. This letter is also tied to the water element, with its glyph of the fishhook and its colors of yellow-green and dark opal. It holds the mystery of ecstasy of water upon the earth. These are the qualities often seen as sympathy and empathy. It is the expression of will, love and intellect within the physical life circumstances.

These individuals have a unique power of attraction. There are usually certain things, circumstances, kinds of people, that the individual seems to attract more than others. Introspection will provide insight into exactly what it is. This is particularly important in the first 20-30 years. Examining the events and situations that you have attracted in that time frame will reveal much about how your power of attraction was used or misused in previous incarnations.

Learning to master that and direct it according to your highest good is part of the process of harvesting the cosmic love within this incarnation. Learning to master evoking and diminishing love and sympathy at will serve to benefit you. True "love magic" can be achieved by those of this letter. This gives one the ability to evoke sexual desire and increase it in others. There is strong karmic repercussions in its misuse, which is why those of this letter need to express a harvest of cosmic love rather than a harvest of physical sex. Worked with appropriately, these individuals have a capacity to predetermine and influence the sex of a child and bestow the child with specific qualities at the moment of the sexual act. It all depends upon the individual's focus and expression of cosmic love, and their ability to first connect with the archetypal energies operating through that particular letter.

When this is accomplished, the ability to completely empathize with others grows. The individual discovers that he or she alone determines the harvest within life, and there awakens an intelligence of will for the proper expression of love in all circumstances. The individual learns to recognize cycles and rhythms and can work within them, making his or her life one of self- fulfillment.

## THE CONSONANT K

> KEYNOTE: New journeys through creativity
> COLOR(S): Blue and violet
> ASTROLOGY: Jupiter

This is a letter which contains the creative vibrations of life. It indicates that the individual has developed to some degree the ability to draw inspiration out of the spiritual ethers and manifest them within the physical life circumstances. This is most evidenced by the glyph of the letter itself.

The glyph of the *K* is comprised of one vertical line and two diagonals which touch. The diagonal line is always a symbol of the dynamic aspect of energy. It reflects movement. In this letter it reflects movement out of the spiritual. The upper "v" of this letter is a drawing forth of creative energies out of the spiritual. This creative energy can then be poured forth into one's physical life circumstances. This is part of the significance of the inverted "v" comprising the bottom half of the letter. Because it is also formed from a diagonal line, it indicates great creative activity or the potential for it in many areas of physical life. These individuals thus have very active minds and lives.

When the *K* is a predominant letter within one's name it indicates a love for loving, manifesting sometimes as a strong sense of romanticism. There is always a strong desire for enlightening humanity in some area—or at least that part of humanity closest to the individual.

It is important for these individuals to balance the physical and the spiritual, to learn to work with the flow and flux of energies of both or it can manifest an energy of extremes within life. It is important for those of this letter to find an avenue of work or endeavor in which they can meet.

This letter bestows upon the individual either great sympathy or a lack of tolerance, and part of the test that it brings with it is that of learning to find and hold a middle ground. It brings a great capacity for enlargement, these individuals once balanced—and once finding their creative outlet—have a unique ability for manifesting that which they treasure in life. When applying the creative to life circumstances, they then discover an ease at getting what they want.

This letter gives great power, a power at its highest level that can be utilized for what the ancients referred to as a working of miracles. There is a unique ability to manifest ideas into reality—no matter the idea—if followed through. Thus one of the lessons inherent in the lives of those with this letter predominant within the name is that of courage and learning to overcome fears and doubts, as well as assisting others with it.

This letter brings with it various weaknesses, yet to be overcome in varying degrees, and strengths to be developed. There can be an inability to see choices at times. Sometimes the creativity blinds one to the realities. There can also be an underlying sense of discontent because these individuals are instinctively visionary and know that events are not as yet ideal. There can also manifest a sense of self-pity and universal unfairness.

On the other hand, it endows the individual with qualities and strengths that have been developed in varying degrees in other lifetimes. There is usually a strong sense of maturity and responsibility. They have great perseverance and a unique ability for self-preservation. They have a capacity for seeing the divine laws operating within physical events and can usually detect the cause and effects of life. These individuals have also come to continue their own "Quest for the Holy Grail"—a quest that may take them through many adventures, both mundane and extraordinary. It is important for them to recognize that in their own unique manner they will be discovering their true soul essence and how best to express it within the present life circumstances.

This is a letter of "new openings"—openings whose pattern has been set in the past and will take even greater dimensions in the present. These individuals have a knack for pushing away the dark that clouds others' lives—and thus are able to shed more light upon their own. This is a letter of great creativity and enchantment. And even though the individual must learn to face change and give up the old for new expressions of creativity, they have the capacity to shape their lives any way they desire.

This is the letter of artistic inspiration and controlled fire. It can give great charisma, and the energies of these individuals can usually be felt as they come into their own sense of individuality and creativeness. They often are endowed with the ability to assimilate great technical knowledge and skills and can develop great craftsmanship. This is a letter which connects sexual energy with creative manifestations. They have learned in the past how to channel the creative forces of sexuality into other avenues, and they will build upon it within this lifetime as well. Thus by working from both realms—physical and the spiritual—they can reshape their world according to whatever ideas they wish to focus upon. This opens many journeys and paths for them within life—for these individuals are becoming the "Masters of the Forces of Life."

## THE CONSONANT L

> KEYNOTE: Magnetism, the power of attraction
> COLOR(S): Emerald green and sea green
> ASTROLOGY: Libra

This letter is one which can manifest true powers of attraction on all levels. The power of magnetism and attraction is part of the feminine energies, and these energies are to be expressed in a balanced manner by those with this letter predominantly placed within the name.

The feminine is the intuitive, the receptive aspect. It awakens greater receptivity of insight, psychism and spirituality—that in turn are to be expressed within the physical life. This is evidenced by the glyph of the letter itself. It is comprised of two lines, perpendicular to each other. They do not cross each other, but they do touch. The horizontal line extends outward at the base, indicating that as one makes him or herself receptive to the higher energies (reflected by the vertical line) the physical life will extend itself. This horizontal line is anchored at the base also as a signal to maintain balance and focus. It is through the physical that we grow and unfold, and the spiritual path is not a path that leads upward into a blinding light into which all of our troubles are dissolved. It is the path for spiritualizing the physical. It is the task of the individual to manifest the spirit while in the physical. This implies that one must become receptive to higher influences, but also apply such influences to the daily life circumstances.

For those of this letter, it is important not to become lost in the feminine energies. As one opens up the intuitive and psychic there can be a tendency to use it as a form of escapism. It is the balancing horizontal pole that is a key to reminding oneself.

Astrologically, this letter is also tied to the sign of Libra. Libra is the sign of the scales, the balance. It can be easy for those of this letter to become lost in the imaginative worlds, as their imaginations are very active. Finding a way of applying that strong imagination constructively within the physical life circumstances will be part of the individual's task. The glyph is a bringing down of the spiritual into the outer expression of the physical.

This letter endows the individual with intellect and artistic energies which have been developed in some area in the past. At its highest vibration it can open one to the spirit of prophecy. The individual may run with extremes unless balance is maintained. It can awaken and manifest opportunities for great virtue or great baseness.

This letter is the letter of equilibrium. It involves balancing the serpent or sex-force within the individual's unique life circumstances. As this equilibrium of the serpent force is maintained, the individual will become "receptive" to comprehending the greatness of the divine.

These individuals, by touching the archetypal force behind this letter, can come to understand true morality as it manifests in all worlds. It can open one to the importance of purity and to understanding how virtue operates within our lives on all levels.

The magnetic quality of this letter not only opens the individual to great sensitivity—a hypersensitivity that can manifest on any number of levels within the individual's life—and enlightenment, but it can lead to states of true saintliness. This magnetic quality is the key to the true mysteries of magic. It connects the individual to the fluid and moldable forces of the astral and can help the individual learn to master astral light. It is this astral light and energy which operates through the physical sex force and strongly influences health, beauty and vitality. It can endow the individual with the ability to learn to shapeshift—to mold one's energy to resonate with the occasion.

This magnetic quality when balanced and directed can enable those of this letter to condense and transfer the astral vitality for healing or to create harmony where there was disharmony. It is because of this quality that those with a predominantly placed *L* in the name attract individuals of all types into their lives. They can relate to almost all people on some level.

This letter also may reflect weaknesses that must be overcome within the individual's life as well as strengths that can be built upon. There is often a duality in the personality of the individual. They may have a quiet side and a very raucous side as well. The individual may be very wild and also very calm and rational. Also because of the magnetism, the ability to attune to others, there may develop an inability to make decisions. On the other hand this magnetic aspect endows them with artistic energies, along with an ability to inspire others. They can blend the physical and the spiritual in practical ways and are very sociable and impartial.

A predominant *L* influence indicates that the individual has been preparing through the past to heed an inner call for self-transformation. These individuals are learning to connect with the intuitive on levels never experienced. They are cleansing and re-aligning, and although they are never quite sure just where events are headed, they seem to know that they are leading somewhere very important to them.

These individuals have established in the past a reconnection with the feminine waters of the universe. Now they will begin the process of drawing them out of the ethers, out of themselves and into new expression. It is important for them to honor the feminine, the intuitive and creative. They must learn not to overextend themselves, for if they draw off too much water, the river will run dry. (This is also reflected within the glyph, as the horizontal bar at the base of the letter is shorter than the vertical.)

This is a letter that contains all life potential—the potential to draw and attract a multitude of energies into one's life. These energies may cause the individual to become scattered or to be overwhelmed with opportunities until it is balanced. The *L* is like a waterfall. Life, power and vitality pour down into a pool or river which can carry that vitality onward.

Within these individuals is the ability to work with the ebb and flow of life. There is an innate capacity to manifest "the unknown"—in ways that often catch them by surprise. They often do not recognize the magnetic aspect of their focus, but it reflects the life energy that is strong within them—even when not recognized by them. It is a life force which stimulates organic growth in all they touch. They rest in a point between evolution and involution and assist others to achieve such a point. It is for this reason that those of this letter never lead dull or boring lives. They are lives of constant change and growth, for where there is outward flow there is never stagnancy.

## THE CONSONANT M

> KEYNOTE: Regrowth and rebirth, the waters of life
> COLOR(S): Deep blue and mother-of-pearl
> ASTROLOGY: Neptune and the Moon

The letter *M* is a powerful letter, touching the individual on primal levels. It is tied to the process of initiation, new birth and new growth. It is tied to the primal element of water—the primal feminine wisdom, that which was called Shekinah by the ancient Hebrew seers and Sophia by Christian Gnostics. In Hebrew Qabalistic teachings, its esoteric title was "Spirit of the Mighty Waters," and it is this spirit that individuals with this as a predominant consonant have come to awaken and manifest.

Its glyph is that of the waves of the sea, rising and falling. Many societies hold within their mythologies of how all life came forth out of the great waters of the universe. Water is the feminine energy of creation. The waves of the sea are disturbed in the birth process, and it is the sea which has a great depth of power and hidden activity that is not usually apparent until the waves are noticed. Those waves can be soothing or of tidal proportions, indicating the depth of power available to be tapped by those of this letter. It is as though their task is to control the activity of waters within their lives, which is reflected in the parallel points of the letter itself. They are of equal height and depth—indicating control.

There is usually great depth to those of this letter and there is often a great deal of activity—even if only mental. There is a great capacity to giving birth in any endeavor to which they are drawn. They are also endowed with a great sense of empathy and often they may put up a calm front while underneath, the waters are churning.

These individuals are pregnant with the life force, which can be applied to almost any avenue of existence. They are often looking for something new to be born within their lives, and they must come to understand that it is they themselves who will give birth to themselves. Learning to work with this birth-giving force often manifests in trials and temptations. It can be very easy for them to draw upon the depths of power to manipulate others. Thus service is the key, as this is a letter that demands honesty and faith. They must keep the waters clean and calm and they usually have an innate sense of poise that has been developed.

These individuals have in the past begun the process of controlling and directing the astral waters. They have a capacity to develop conscious out-of-body experiences often more easily than others. These individuals have strong sensitivities. Although often accused of being overly emotional, they are just hypersensitive. They have a capacity to feel the full impact of whatever energy is being expressed around them.

This letter endows the individual with the opportunity to begin the process of becoming a master of feeling. This includes control of life and sensations—and the birth process. This is a letter of change and growth. It is the letter of initiation. The astrological correspondence to this letter is Neptune, the planet of the unconscious mind and initiation. It gives great intuition and understanding. It is also tied to the energies of the great Archangel that we in the Western world know of as the Christ. In esoteric Christianity, part of the purpose of the Christ Mysteries was to restore the balance between the male and the female—to give new birth and new expression to the feminine.

This is a letter which indicates that the individual has been working on overcoming various weaknesses and working on developing certain strengths in the past. It is important for these individuals to guard against depression—getting caught in a mire of waters.

It can stimulate unproductive daydreaming, self- indulgence, a lack of compassion and render the individual overly impressionable. On the other hand, it does indicate that there is developing an ability to see new perspectives, a new sense of compassion and trust in one's own instincts. It awakens great psychic energies and a powerful ability to affect others.

This is a letter of change. There must be a flow to the waters. These individuals have a capacity to live the ordinary in a very non-ordinary manner. This is a letter which manifests opportunities for great growth and a great rectifying of the past. The waters of the individual's life must be allowed to flow free. Only in the free flow of one's life can the individual clear him or herself of that which would block and hinder growth.

These individuals have a strong, almost genetic tie to divine consciousness. The study of myths would benefit them greatly, as there is a strong link—an almost innate belief in their descendence from the gods.

There are also ties to the Moon with those of this letter. The Moon, like the great seas, is always changing and yet it is ever the same. The individual must keep alive a willingness to change and grow while simultaneously remaining stable and true to one's inner nature. In this manner the individual can keep alive the "Spirit of the Feminine Waters" in him or herself and in all they touch. They can nurture and discipline, love and teach, heal and inspire. They give birth to others and thereby are reborn themselves!

## THE CONSONANT N

KEYNOTE: Willed transmutation and fertility
COLOR(S): Blue-green
ASTROLOGY: Scorpio

This is the letter of willed transmutation and transformation so that greater fertility in all areas of life may manifest. Those with this letter predominant within their names have an innate and extraordinary fertility, deriving from a nearly inexhaustible life-force which has been awakened in the past.

Its glyph reflects much about this. It is comprised of three lines. Three, of course, is a creative number, reflecting fertility on some level. The outer lines are equal and parallel. This is the balance of the male and the female, the physical and the spiritual. They are connected by a diagonal line, extending from the top of the first vertical line to the bottom of the second. All diagonal lines are activating, and in this case, since it touches both extremes, top and bottom, it indicates the individual has the ability to work from all levels—the physical and the spiritual, the male and the female, the base and the noble.

This aspect is also reflected in its astrological counterpart. Scorpio is a sign of great force and transmutation. Scorpio has several symbols associated with it. The scorpion reflects the baser expressions of its energies, but the eagle is also a symbol for Scorpio. The Scorpio individual has a capacity to fly to great heights. Learning to transmute the lower instincts into higher expression is thus the task, and those with the N as a predominant consonant have begun that process.

This is a letter that involves willed transmutation. This requires that the life force (sexual energy), which is strong within these individuals, must be controlled through its cycles so that it may become the instrument for the alchemical process within one's life.

This letter endows these individuals with a quiet sense of understanding and nourishment. They seem to know what to say and when to say it. In the early years, they often learn to deal with constraints and limitations—whether self-imposed or imposed from without. Throughout their life, they hold a strong love of home and they recognize the importance of the sexual act in the weaving of lives together on levels beyond the physical. There is also often a push in the early years toward marriage, resulting in offspring while young. This often serves as a catalyst for initiating a process of controlled change and life direction that will last throughout the entire incarnation. They begin to come more into their own.

Those individuals with a prominently placed N within the name often have a fine sense of smell. This physical sense is related to other senses operating on more subtle levels. It usually indicates that there is developing a sense of spiritual discernment. On the astral level, it is connected to a strong sense of emotional idealism and upon the spiritual plane it is tied to pure idealism—the kind that leads to the fulfillment of one's personal vision. This idealism is an ability to stand focused amidst a world of ideas that may be swirling about.

When one touches the archetypal force behind this letter, it opens a transference to high states of happiness. This is enhanced by the ability to set up a mental energy matrix that will result in physical manifestations. It stimulates the ability to see and work with auras and thoughts of others, and they often need to be aware that they have come into incarnation with the intuitional "lights" already on and thus they should not be discouraged if they do not have the "development" experiences so often described by others when their "lights click on."

These individuals have developed in the past an ability to enlighten others and to help others solve problems, as they have an innate ability for coherence and cohesion. They have an ability to assist others in asserting their will forces more appropriately.

In the early years of these individuals there is often a cleansing required on at least some level, if not more than one. This is often because they have chosen to come in and take care of the most difficult first. It is important for them not to resist changes and cleansing, and it is most important for them not to take things personally. Learning that all setbacks are teachers and that they pass with time is part of the lesson for those of this letter.

Resistance to change, fear of change, failure to leave the past, seductiveness and an inability to understand other's conflicts may be issues to be dealt with by the individual. On the other hand, this letter endows one with all the strength (and more) necessary for transformation of any condition in life. It gives a great capacity for understanding when touched and activated fully within one's life. It enables the individual to begin or to intensify the ability to merge the physical and the spiritual, to use the sexual life force as a tool to assist all transformations and changes. A friendship established with someone with this as a predominant letter will become a true friendship that can last beyond time.

There is a strong sense of protectiveness about these individuals, with an ability to draw upon energies that powerfully guard all that is treasured. And even though there may be painful lessons, there is always recognition of learning as a result.

These individuals have ties to the ancient myths of the Fates or the Norns, those beings that measured the time, the quality of time and the length of time upon the planet. Their fate is in their own hands. They have asked for the opportunity to use the transmutational force and to learn to direct it within this incarnation. Thus they set their own cycles, their own rhythms. As they learn to move within those rhythms gently and willfully, great movement occurs and extraordinary fertility manifests in all endeavors. The individual becomes a "Child of the Great Transformers."

## THE CONSONANT P

KEYNOTE: The power of hidden expression
COLOR(S): Scarlet
ASTROLOGY: Mars

Inherent within the power of this letter is the force of expression—the Power of the Word. The mouth is known as the Gateway to the Soul as life breath enters in through us and is then reflected by what comes out. Our speech reveals who and what we are. It can reveal great beauty and great ugliness; it can create harmony or discord.

Many of the ancient mysteries were taught through the use of song and story—the myths and tales of various peoples filled with mystical truths in all its various guises. The initiates would learn scores of songs and tales, replete with symbolism that would touch each individual in accordance with his or her own growth. In Ireland they were known as the Ollahms and Shanachies. In France they were the troubadours, in Africa they were the Griots, in Germany they were the Meistersingers. They were English bards, Anglo-Saxon Gleemen and Norse Skalds. They knew and worked with the power of expression—the power of sound, music and voice. They used this power through myths, tales and songs so that the Truth could be revealed but not profaned.

This is the power of those with this as a predominant letter. It is reflected within the glyph itself. The letter is comprised of a circle, out of which drops a vertical line. The circle is the spiritual force and knowledge to which the individual has access. The vertical line is a drawing down of that force into one's physical life. The spiritual force is drawn down in a controlled and direct manner.

This is a letter which ties one to those ancient traditions of the bard initiates and skaldcraft. It gives an innate sense of the power of poetry and words. Individuals with this as the predominant letter move into such a power as they mature. The words they speak and write begin to take on greater power and force. That which is said more lovingly is felt more deeply. That which is said more cuttingly cuts more deeply.

Those of this letter seem to instinctively know that they have great power, even if they don't know how to manifest it. This force may remain hidden within one's life until a certain degree of maturity is reached or until the individual begins to consciously take up the task of asserting one's own direction in life. This does not mean though that there is nothing going on prior to that, it just indicates that the transformations are more internal—particularly in the early years. Nothing is insignificant in the lives of these individuals, as their whole life process is one initiation and forms of psychic death and rebirth.

Things come to these individuals in "unordinary" ways, and they should not expect too much at once. They are destined to be like the phoenix that will rise from whatever ashes may ensue. Theirs is a life of deep inner transformations, and the more they develop a faith in the heavens and the spirit, the smoother their life circumstances become.

These individuals must investigate, understand and overcome the cause and effect elements of their lives. In Teutonic lore, it is the process of learning the "way of wyrd"—learning to synthesize realities, recognizing that the past is intertwined with the present so as to shape one's individual forces for the all-becoming future. It ties one to the Well of Urdhr of this lore where live the three Norns or fates. Urdhr is the eldest and oversees "that which has become." Verdhandi, the second Norn, oversees "that which is becoming." And the third, Skuld, oversees "that which should become." Thus those of this letter must learn to work with the evolutionary force and its laws of cause and effect and synchronicity.

Mars is the astrological correspondence for this letter. In its highest aspect, Mars is the force which creates matter by drawing it down out of the spiritual realms (also reflected within the glyph of the letter itself). It is an active male force, although it comes from the primal feminine—the vertical line (male) out of the circle (female) as reflected within the glyph. The Greeks were not too fond of the god Ares, but the Roman counterpart had many positive characteristics: giver of fertility, protector and inspirirer of new ideas.

Those who have this letter predominantly placed within their names will find its influence powerful. It can lead one towards impatience, and there are often emotional and mental conflicts. Insecurity may reflect itself with an ensuing feeling of being lost. On the other hand, when activated and balanced fully, it endows one with great endurance, courage and faith. It stimulates great self-awareness and an energy to change one's fortune.

There is always a longing for spiritual progress within those of this letter. When the archetypal force operating behind the letter is touched by the individual, there occurs an alignment with the laws of evolution and great devotion and even religious experiences may result. There will occur lessons in humility to balance the power to which these individuals have access—especially if it has not been developed in the past.

These individuals are excellent to call upon when assistance is needed for they have come to give much to humanity, and they have brought their ability to do so from the past into the present. They have a unique ability to uplift spirits. There is a strong maternal instinct and a great love of children or the child within other people. Any lessons in purification and transformation of the individual's character serve to develop a high perception of the beauty that resides within all, regardless of outer appearances, and there unfolds a grace that touches the heart of all.

## THE CONSONANT Q

KEYNOTE: Intelligence of the heart
COLOR(S): Violet and crimson
ASTROLOGY: Pisces

The *Q* is a letter that does not always have counterparts in other languages. It has no sound of its own, but it has ties to awakening psychic centers within humanity that are often neglected. It is a consonant of great balance, joy and harmony, and it has ties to a unique expression of archetypal energies within one's life.

The *Q*, like the vowel *I*, has ties to a minor chakra center located at the stem of the brain in the area of the medulla oblongata. This is a center focused upon in the Egyptian Mysteries as well as in some of the more shamanic societies. It is a center important to linking the mind with the heart—the emotional with the higher mental forces. It is a center whose importance to healing and being healed has yet to truly be revealed. It is a center for creating what the Egyptians called "Intelligence of the Heart"—hence the keynote for this letter.

This linking is reflected within the glyph of the letter itself. The letter is comprised of the circle that is pierced by a diagonal line. The diagonal line is an activating force, linking the inner with the outer, the male with the female, the mind and the heart, the spiritual and the physical. It indicates that the individual has come to work for a new dynamic expression of the spiritual within the physical. This is reflected by the line slanting downward out of the circle. Those whose name have this letter predominant within it have come to make a dynamic expression in linking opposites—be they the male and female, physical and spiritual or the heart and mind.

This is a glyph of intercourse—be it intercourse of a physical nature, an intercourse with the spiritual or an intercourse of heart and mind. This indicates an activation of tremendous energy and power on whatever level the individual approaches such intercourse. It is this act which is key to releasing energy to assist the body in transforming itself so as to manifest even greater occult powers.

The astrological correspondence is that of Pisces, often considered the most misunderstood of the astrological signs. This fits well with humanity's concept of intercourse and the sexual act. It also is misunderstood, not only in the energies associated with it, but with its influence in all aspects of our lives. It is the life force which frees us and which can tie us to other individuals in ways most people cannot understand. It is not just a tool for procreation or recreation, but is a physical reflection of the primal life force of the individual. The symbol for Pisces has similarities to the letter Q. The Piscean glyph is comprised of two semi-circles united by a single line, representing the finite consciousness of humanity linked with the cosmic consciousness of the universe. It reflects the dualistic aspect of life and the need to unite the two in a balanced expression. This is also hinted at within the glyph of the letter Q. It is the task of the individual to bring the spiritual into expression within the physical. The individual is learning to link the two realms—reflected by the downward slanting line of the letter.

This is a letter tied to the archetypal energies of unity and aspiration. It indicates intellectual focus and development. In the English language, it is most often followed by the vowel U which indicates the need of the individual to find a pragmatic and practical application for that intellectualism and the spiritual energies that are manifested. It indicates a desire to find a practical approach to mystical concepts—a search for a means to make such concepts accessible to humanity. It can reflect intense efforts that will be made toward uplifting humanity, to bring the inner worlds and realms to life in the outer for others to more readily experience.

This letter indicates the development of judgment and the balancing of it with the emotions. These individuals have a strong capacity for empathy and must develop the correct mental perspective of such feelings so as to apply the empathic energies appropriately for the individual. This empathic sensitivity is a strong psychic sensitivity, with the ability to read the character of others quite accurately. It is important for those of this letter though to learn to read others without overly influencing or interfering with their free will. They must learn to practice the Law of Privacy, realizing that even if they are aware of various aspects of another's life, one does not always have the right to reveal to them that they are aware. This is part of the process of spiritual discernment that is being developed by those of this letter.

The archetypal force behind this letter is one which can manifest in the gifts of healing, and at its highest level a "working of miracles." This is the power of manifestation and directing of energies in a conscious manner. Control of the imaginative forces is the key, as these individuals have strong imaginations. Until the individual comes into his or her own, this imagination may be ungoverned and can help manifest unpleasant circumstances. There may be lessons of vulnerability to be dealt with, excessive empathy and even times of withdrawal.

As the individual comes into his or her own power, this letter awakens within the soul of the individual a greater expression of unselfishness, faith and optimism. The intuition becomes highly accurate on all levels, and there comes the ability to fully understand and work with animals and all the forces and elements of nature. It awakens control of sleep consciousness and dreams.

This is another of the letters of initiation. It indicates a life of new beginning, a beginning that is like the first fires of the morning. It awakens the creative imagination and unfolds the ability to apply it with serious and undistracted concentration. It brings one out into the light and awakens one to that which must change, endowing the individual with the power to effect the change. This letter has connections to the esoteric title: "The Child of the Sons of the Mighty."

## THE CONSONANT R

KEYNOTE: Spiritual fires of love, wisdom and freedom
COLOR(S): Orange and amber
ASTROLOGY: Sun

The consonant *R* has ties to the power of love and wisdom and all the potentials inherent within them. It gives great force and inspiration, and an ability to inspire such a force in others. It is the force of fire, manifesting within the physical life of the individual. It is a fire that is unique in intensity to the individual, as no two will ever express the fire in identical manners.

Its glyph is the symbol of activating one's own creative fires and applying them to one's life. It is the symbol of drawing from many sources, testing independently and then synthesizing in a manner that provides perpetual growth that is best for oneself. The glyph is comprised of three aspects. It has an upper circle, the universal and spiritual realm from which we are fed knowledge, wisdom and love. It has a vertical line, the channel of energy from that universal source into all physical lives. This reflects the fact that there is a lifeline to the spiritual that is always operative for all of us, whether we realize it or not.

The third aspect of the glyph is a diagonal line also emanating from the upper circle. It is the activating force and indicates that the individual has come to more consciously access and utilize the spiritual and psychic forces to which we all have access. It indicates that the individual has entered into physical incarnation, drawing more greatly from the source of light and life and will be drawn into circumstances that will force a greater activation of its qualities.

This is the letter of love, wisdom and freedom and the greater application of them within one's life. This means that most life experiences will center around the further development of them. They will be of great importance to the individual. Any hindrance of any of these within the individual's life will cause great tension and strife. Those with this letter predominantly placed within the name have come to manifest the energy and light of these qualities on a physical and material level.

This kind of fire quality always stimulates a powerful sense of attraction and desires, which if not expressed, may bubble to the surface at inopportune times. This is a letter which provides a powerful reservoir of energy to be drawn upon. Its astrological correspondent reflects this. Just as the Sun radiates energy outward toward the Earth, those of this letter have a capacity to radiate energy out that can affect those within their lives. This is also reflected in the glyph of the letter itself. The diagonal line is the radiation of the soul energy into one's physical life.

Those of this letter are usually generous in some area of their life. They innately know that they have much to offer—even if it is not recognized by others. As the individual learns to draw more actively upon those great soul forces, he or she will become like a second sun in the lives they touch.

The *R* is one of the most powerful modifiers of vowels. It adds great strength to them, and it accelerates the opportunities to manifest the hidden energies reflected by them. It facilitates the understanding of one's inner potentials and also makes it easier to understand how best to express them within this incarnation. It is often easier for those of this consonant's influence to discern the path of endeavor most beneficial.

This is a letter which lends a great intellectuality in some area of one's life. It is a letter which activates the inner sun centers (chakras) of the head. These centers, particularly those of the brow and crown chakras, are linked to our ability to assimilate knowledge, understand it and then express that understanding in life. This expression is the wisdom aspect of consciousness. It is this letter which helps one to discern which area of life will bring the greatest sunshine.

With understanding and wisdom comes freedom, another of the qualities associated with this letter. There are always lessons associated with freedom for anyone with this letter in their first name, and most often these lessons about personal freedom arise most strongly in the early years, and if not handled appropriately, they will re-manifest until the individual does express personal freedom with wisdom. It is the proper use of one's personal freedom which will activate the sun of one's life for those with this consonant.

There can arise a strong sense of independence and a sense of guardianship of personal freedom. These individuals have come to keep alive the fires of their own freedom and thus influence others to do so as well.

Security is important to these individuals, and at its highest level, this letter can connect one to that archetypal force which facilitates manifesting security on any level. It leads to freedom of will and of mind, and it can open to the knowledge of how spiritual and natural laws are violated and upheld. It endows one with ingenuity that can be applied to a variety of areas. It creates a widening of intellect and knowledge that can be understood and expressed within the physical life.

The *R* is a consonant which does require a development of humility, gratitude and devotion for its full force to become effective within one's life. Once these are developed, the individual has the ability to see both sides of an issue and to inspire others to their inner worth and higher perceptions. These individuals can determine "the right course"—for themselves and others, if given the freedom to do so. Theirs is a journey toward self-healing, by learning to manifest and work towards their inner aspirations.

There may be weaknesses to overcome on this journey. Selfishness, idleness and lack of diligence can hinder it. The individual may also have to learn not to allow fears and half- formed ideas imprison them and hinder their pathwork. As the individual begins to follow the inner fires, there comes a true recognition of purpose, replete with joy and optimism which have repercussions upon all touched. Tremendous artistic inspiration may occur, greater productivity and a development of self-mastery.

This is the letter of healing and the alchemy of light. It is the power of chasing back shadows through love and wisdom. It can manifest a test of one's humor, but the individual must remember that detours are only disguised opportunities. This can endow one with knowledge of right order and rhythms which is tied to the mystical powers of dance, music and poetry. This is the letter of "becoming"—a coming into one's own sunlight. It is the power of ritual cognition and a spiraling concentration that makes a vehicle and tool of the cosmic power that infuses the earth plane. It is a letter tied to the archetypal force which enables one to become a master of the fires of the world!

## THE CONSONANT S

KEYNOTE: The serpent wisdom
COLOR(S): Blue
ASTROLOGY: Sagittarius

The consonant *S* has ties to many of the ancient serpent mysteries. The serpent is one of the most misunderstood and yet most powerfully symbolic totems. It has been linked with the destructive elements within humanity and also the most constructive forces as well. It is tied to the forces of fire and of healing, of shedding the old for the new.

Its glyph is like a coiled snake. The snakes upon the caduceus are symbols of the wisdom expressed through healing. It is a symbol of the sex force, raised up through wisdom into new expression of healing and wisdom.

This is the symbol of eternity, and it reflects that the individual has found his or her path, whether aware of it or not, and has set the pattern for unfoldment for ages to come. It has been said that with certain initiatory rites one will set the course of one's evolution for thousands of lifetimes. It is this which is reflected within the symbol of this letter.

This symbol also has ties to the energies of Sagittarius. Sagittarius is a sign that indicates personal evolution will enable the individual to activate the vital life force to maximum mobility. The arrow is a symbol for Sagittarius, shooting straight toward its target. Such is the bite of the snake. It raises itself up and strikes quick and hard and true to its mark. Thus it is best not to anger those of this letter. Although slow to lose their tempers, once lost, their bite is quick, sharp and direct. They almost always hit their mark.

This is the letter of clairvoyance and prophecy. It is a letter whose archetype can awaken within them a mastery of the electrical fire element, which can enable them to control their own consciousness and those of others as well. It indicates also that there have been past lives in which there has been development of the ability to control animals and humans to some degree. There is a natural ability to relate with everyone on some level. There is an instinctive ability to develop rapport. It is important though to control any tendency toward manipulation, as there is a great ability to do so—even without realizing at times.

Those with this predominant letter in the name are able to link with the most subtle energies of an individual and should trust their instincts along these lines. They understand the influence of the spirit of the individual. They have begun the process of consciousness control so as to be able to align with other beings, angels, humans, etc. It is this ability which when fully developed awakens tremendous healing and pure clairvoyance with no possibility for error.

There may be weaknesses to overcome for those of this letter as well. Overcoming temptations—along with helping others overcome them—may be part of the life task. A fear of trying the new and an oversensitivity may prevent the individual from following his or her intuition. There can arise a fear of choosing and an inability to synthesize. There may be signs of irresponsibility, coarseness and false exaggeration.

If these are balanced, there arises a strong self-sufficiency and a great sense of personal responsibility which influences all around them. There is an openness to the new, and especially to self-discovery. There is always a silent boldness about them and a straight-forwardness that is sensitive and refreshing.

The lives of those with this letter is a search for wholeness. Theirs is the task of understanding their own personal myth and learning to express it creatively. There is always a strong life force which inspires others and an ability to recharge down to the cellular level. Once fully developed, they can also use this to recharge others. There is a deep reservoir of energy to be drawn upon. Theirs is the fire of humility, expressed through motivation. The serpent power within them can become a shield of consciousness that creates and maintains wholeness around them! They become a crystallized light in the lives of those they touch.

## THE CONSONANT T

> KEYNOTE: Inspiration for spiritual warriorship
> COLOR(S): Greenish yellow and reddish amber
> ASTROLOGY: Leo

*T* is the letter of inspiration and aspiration. It is a letter tied strongly to the ego and the task of balancing it—so that true soul force can manifest. This is the letter of self-mastery, of spiritual warriorship.

This is a letter with strong ties to the warrior spirit of Teutonic lore. In the myths of the Norse and Germanic peoples, honor and personal dignity are major lessons. Personal responsibility and dignity within one's life are the keys to true honor—to winning a place within the abode of the gods. One must approach life with a warrior spirit, a spirit of facing one's tasks with courage and honor and responsibility to the best of one's ability.

This is the letter of self-mastery, which once achieved will awaken great aspiration. It is reflected within the glyph of the letter itself. It is one of the many forms of the cross. The *T* takes the form of what is called the Tao cross—a cross that has no upper vertical bar to it. It is upon such a cross that Moses raised the serpent of wisdom, and upon which each of this letter must raise his or her own wisdom.

The cross is a symbol upon which we can be slain or resurrected. It is determined by the degree of self-mastery that is developed. The horizontal bar is the feminine aspect of intuition and creativity which is being met and activated within the individual's life. The vertical bar is the masculine aspect. It is also the drawing down of the feminine into the physical life expression.

Another way of looking at it is that the individual must activate (vertical pole) the wisdom aspect of the soul (horizontal bar). In this manner one can resurrect himself or herself from any situation. It is the feminine aspect of intuition, nurturing and wisdom which must be strived for by the individual. Thus there may be some "warring" within the ego—often in the early years—as to how best incorporate the feminine energies within one's life circumstances. The individual has the capacity to link with the Sophia of the Christian Gnostics and the Shekinah of the Hebrews.

This feminine aspect is strong within all of those with this letter, but there may be difficulty in moving the personal ego out of the way so that it can manifest. The personal ego can block the feminine wisdom through such attitudes and weaknesses as dominance that can border on dictatorship, a putting up of false fronts, an avoidance of trials and growth, vanity, indecisiveness, false pride and even cruelty. If these are controlled, the individual will manifest an ability to keep the peace and an intense energy to right wrongs (a reflection of the warrior spirit). There is the ability to defend the weak and a strong sense of protectiveness can surface within the individual's life. There arises a dynamic ability for inner alchemy and a strength to face reality—however it confronts the individual. It is key that those of this letter follow their own paths, their own aspirations and their own soul prompting, for it is only then that they can know their true individual power!

This is also reflected in its astrological correspondence. Leo is the eternal flame of the individual, but can only come to life when the inner heart is truly awakened. It is the energy of courage, and those of this letter must find the courage to be who they are and to express the feminine within their lives. This means there are often lessons in gentle strength. The individual must decide whether to allow the fires of the ego to shine through or allow the eternal fires of the soul's individuality to shine forth. Leo is also symbolized by the lion, the feline, and the felines fall under the rule of the feminine forces. One achieves his or her true power when the inner feminine is integrated into the personality.

Again the lessons of self-mastery are the key. Until such is acquired, contention and strife—internal and external—will manifest, especially in the early years. There will arise doubts which will force investigation. Personal will and discrimination will be tested, for this is the letter of the battle of self. It is the letter for learning to carry one's own cross. It is a letter which reflects that the individual is learning to become a son or daughter of the "flaming sword" of truth and discrimination.

Any conquest requires pointed focus, and these individuals must learn to look within to their own deepest needs, they must examine their motives and then follow their highest aspirations. They must learn to express self-sacrifice, strength of will and discrimination in all things. As these abilities are developed, the archetypal force behind this letter manifests as a beacon of inspiration somewhere within the lives of these individuals.

This is a letter which stimulates great inspiration in some area of the individual's life. These people know they have come to do something—even if they do not know what it is. They realize that they have access to divine inspiration and intuition in respect to everything arousing interest and attention. The inventive faculties are strong within them and there is usually a strong influence of past memories within their lives which must be discerned and balanced appropriately.

There can be developed the ability to understand and make use of the laws of analogy and correspondence within the lower realms. Thus there is an innate ability that is being developed to carry through "astral magic." This is the ability to work with the laws of suggestion and sympathy. This is a letter which can open one to the knowledge of all spiritual activities of the body—reflected by the raising up of the serpent of wisdom. There is also great ability for true comprehension of the spiritual laws as they are operating within one's life and for the development of higher forms of hearing, *i.e.* clairaudience. Through this letter and its archetypal influence there is developed an ardor of life that can make one sovereign within his or her own life circumstances. There unfold opportunities to assert the creative individualism with the fires of inspiration and the strength of the spiritual warrior.

Those of this letter are rich in human sympathies and have a capacity to lend their hearts to any who are suffering. They hold strong the creative urge within humanity, and they will work to bring about an environment that reflects those inner urges. There is often an inner confidence, which manifests most strongly when the individual finds his or her own place in the environs. The warrior spirit is generous, loving and open, but it can also be ruthless to those who are seen as enemies. There is always an aspiring toward dreams, and all must come to realize that we are never given a hope, wish or dream without also being given opportunities to make them a reality, and the only thing that can shatter such dreams is compromise. These individuals hold within themselves the inspiration of universal love and the strength of the warrior. It is these qualities which will help them unfold the inner potentials that allow them to light and warm the lives of those they touch.

## THE CONSONANT V

> KEYNOTE: Fruitfulness and openness
> COLOR(S): Red-orange and rich brown
> ASTROLOGY: Taurus

This is the letter of fruitfulness and openness to the fruitfulness of life. It reflects the spirit or will of the individual coming to life with greater abundance. It is the drawing down of the spiritual into the physical life. It is a letter which indicates the individual has begun the preparatory process of opening him or herself to new opportunities.

This aspect of fruitfulness is reflected strongly within the glyph and form of the letter itself. It is comprised of two diagonal lines, drawing downward to meet within the physical. This reflects the male and female forces coming together in some form of abundant manifestation within the physical life. The *V* is a cup, a cup that is open to the forces of the spirit while within the physical. Whether seen as the cup of plenty (as in the cornucopia) or as the womb of life from which new birth may arise, there will be abundance in some area of the individual's life.

This glyph also reflects an openness to higher inspiration, and thus dogmatism and narrow-mindedness can hinder the abundance of fruitfulness within the life of those with this letter predominantly placed. Poise is the key, a poise also reflected within the form of the letter as well. Each half of the letter is equal and balanced, a reminder to those of this letter to treat all things with equanimity.

This is the letter of linking and connecting. It is the merging of the higher with the lower, the male with the female. It encloses and joins, while being open to the new. It is a letter which instills a love of poetry, art and music, and it indicates that the individual has developed the capability to be an excellent judge of character, even though such judgments may be ignored.

Those of this letter may have certain lessons and weaknesses to overcome—either within themselves or in those that are closest. There can be a wishy-washiness to the individual and an ability to develop a false sense of security. There can be a lack of fertility or an inability to manifest. This can be reflected through the characteristic of always planning and never following through. Stubbornness and overindulgence may manifest as well and need to be balanced. In the early years, behavior may be impulsive and erratic, and in the latter years there can develop a fixity of opinion that should be balanced.

The Hebrew counterpart for this letter is called the "vau" which means nail. A nail is driven into something to affix it to something else. The diagonal lines of the letter are the "nails" binding the spirit to the personality. This aspect is also revealed through its astrological correspondent.

The Taurus activity and life is one of gathering energy in material form so that the individual can grow to even greater depths. The V is like the upturned horns of the Taurus bull. The downrushing force of life is honed and brought to specific expression by one of strong Taurus influence. This is also symbolized by the shape of the letter.

This is one of the most fertile signs of the zodiac and the V is one of the most fertile letters of the alphabet. It is also a very creative letter, but the individual should dig his or her talents out and open them to the sunlight so that they can grow. The shape of the letter can be viewed as a flower beginning to open up. Seeing oneself as a flower opening to the sunlight is a powerful meditational image for those who have this letter predominantly placed within their name.

As the individual learns to open him or herself up, there unfolds a capacity for understanding and loyalty that touches new heights. Kindness and compassion are inherent within those of this letter, and its archetypal force will stimulate a revelation of creative talents within some field of endeavor. There can manifest a tendency toward sensuality and overindulgence, but there is also tremendous power to affect productivity in all areas of life.

This is a letter for recovering the joy of life and all its processes. This occurs through producing in some area. These individuals need to feel productive and be able to see the results of their efforts. They have an innate ability to bring joy into the lives of others as long as they keep the joy within themselves alive.

Those of this consonant have entered into incarnation to become like the fruit-bearing tree. They have the opportunity to receive many blessings, but they will not always come in the manner expected. They will come in the manner most beneficial to the individual.

These individuals have come to learn to access greater sources of energy and learn to utilize them within their day to day life circumstances. As they overcome blocks within life, there follows an onrush of new energy which in turn stimulates fertility and inspiration. They learn to recognize that within every problem is hidden a special gift, once the problem or blockage is overcome. This is a letter of perseverance and rewards. It is a letter of consideration and deliberation, followed by action which produces! This is the letter of one who has opened the soul to the eternal, and now the work begins to take the new flow from that eternal source of life and find deliberate ways of applying it. This is the letter of one whose spirit has come to life. And where the spirit is alive, there will be fruition!

## THE CONSONANT W

> KEYNOTE: The uniting of consciousness
> COLOR(S): Green and silver
> ASTROLOGY: Venus and Moon

This is a letter that has similarities to the *V*, but it also is one which activates the archetypal forces behind it uniquely. In the letter *V*, Taurus is the astrological correspondence. In the letter *W* the astrological correspondences are the planets Venus and the Moon.

Venus is the ruler of Taurus in astrology and the Moon is exalted in the sign of Taurus. Many sources treat the W as simply a double-V, and although there are similarities, there are also distinct differences in the way they influence an individual's life.

The W is shaped like an inverted wave of the ocean. This is significant when considering the astrological correspondences to it. The Moon has rhythms and cycles, and governs the waters of tides upon the planet. It has a depth of influence within our lives that many fail to recognize. This reflects that there is always a depth to those of this letter that may not always be apparent on the surface. This can stimulate strong emotions in the individual, as well as a depth of intuition and creativity and artistic capability.

Venus and the Moon stimulate sensitivity and great imaginations. This is also reflected in the glyph of the letter, with it dipping down into the depths, up again, down again, and then pulling up to great heights. Learning not to become immersed and lost within one's own depths will be part of the task. Involvement in something practical and mental will prevent depression and the possibility of becoming lost.

This is a letter which can give an attraction to the opposite sex, as long as the individual does not get lost within his or her own emotions and mind. It is a letter which instills an awakened sentiment of love and sharing. There is a great draw to nature and the primal elements within it. Storms often frighten (touching a primal nerve) or energize those of this letter.

Venus is sometimes considered the daughter of the Moon and reflects one of the many forms of life which can emanate from the Great Mother. Those of this letter have an ability to pursue many avenues of work.

The Moon is the Great Mother, and many myths speak of the Great Mother being part of the Great Sea of Life from which we all came. This is reflected in the glyph of the letter itself. The W is a drawing up out of the waters of life into new and varied expressions. Just as the Moon changes constantly, so can the expressions and energies of those of this letter. The task is to remain constant while moving through change. The personality may change, but the individuality and soul expression through that personality must remain constant. (Studying the astrological aspects and influence of these two planets will reveal, to those who have this letter strongly placed within their names, much about one's characteristics and potentials.)

This is a dynamic letter of intuition and mediumistic capabilities. It is a letter that has the capability of stimulating the uniting of consciousness on all levels (reflected also within the form of the letter itself). It is a letter for integrating the spiritual influence with one's day to day consciousness. The archetypal force operating behind and through this letter can assist the individual in touching and communing with various realms and dimensions—inside and outside of oneself. It can open one to true "cosmic intuition." It awakens mental mediumistic talents, but requires that the individual develop strong discriminatory abilities or there is the potential of becoming lost within the "inner realms."

Concentration, discrimination, especially in the ability to recognize deception, are important in the use of the mediumistic talents. This is a letter which when touched on deeper levels awakens a great sense of mysticism and an arousal of religious feelings. There will unfold, for those wishing, a talent for mystical exploration. This includes strong and accurate perceptions of the past (including past lives), and accurate perceptions of events occurring at great distances—if concentration is developed!

This is a letter which indicates that the individual is learning to bring him or herself up and out into new light of awareness. It stimulates an understanding of the old through perseverance. This is a letter which asks the individual to trust in one's own life process, even if it cannot be defined.

To those who touch the archetypal force of this letter will come a depth of joy never before experienced. It is a joy that can never be shaken as it is one that is illumined by the light within. It is important for those of this letter's influence not to look for some light from without to shine down upon them, but to seek out the light within to shine out from them! As the individual learns to separate self from the woes, there occurs a harmony of life elements, and the individual can learn to bind the forces of life to his or her own benefit. This requires but three things of these individuals: (1) a vitality, best stimulated through techniques of breath, (2) a sense of purpose and meaning and (3) a health of body, mind and spirit. With these elements, the individual can link with the higher consciousness in ways that influence the life elements of all within their environments.

## THE CONSONANT X

KEYNOTE: The force and power of duality
COLOR(S): Deep indigo and dark grays
ASTROLOGY: Sagittarius and Jupiter

This is a powerful and abstract letter of the alphabet. Few names actually begin with it, and it is a letter found more within the surname of individuals than within the creative first name. This is significant in that it reflects much learning through family relationships—be it the blood "kin" or a family of friends.

This is also another of the letters which has no distinct sound of its own, when transcribed into the English language (and other languages as well). It is important to note though that it is a symbol—regardless of sound correspondences—that has been used in most ancient societies in varying forms. It is one of the most ancient of symbols available to humanity.

Its two lines are diagonals which intersect midway between each. This is a powerful point of reference for those with this letter strongly placed somewhere within his or her name. It indicates that the individual will have lessons of balance to deal with. Learning to hold the point of intersection, without slipping down or becoming lost in the upper is the key. Theirs is the task of developing true mediatorship without it falling into the trappings of lower forms of mediumship.

This is the letter of polarity, the lessons of the astral plane. This involves learning to balance the male and the female, right and wrong and the physical with the spiritual. It manifests the task of harmonizing opposites. This requires a new perspective. Hot and cold may be seen as opposite—even though they are not. They are just varying degrees of the same concept known as temperature. It is relative.

This is a letter which has within it the archetypal forces of creation. It represents the point in the Great Void where the formation of life begins to manifest, drawing down toward the physical. It endows the individual with a capability of manifesting good or bad to any degree. It is the symbol of the microcosm, reflecting the power of the macrocosm through physical life circumstances.

It is important for those of this letter to work with the Laws of Correspondence. Learning to recognize how all things are related will assist them in avoiding mistakes and in manifesting dreams.

This is the letter which endows great force for activities of sympathetic magic and control of the formative forces of the astral. This is the activating force of shapeshifting—the molding of energies of the void into expression within one's life—in accordance with one's desires.

This letter holds the mystery of "two." It requires learning to activate and merge the masculine and feminine aspects in all areas of life. It requires development of strength of will and concentration. It is often this which is most tested in the early years. This is the power of joining together two separate forces in order to produce a creative might greater than the sum total. This is the power of sexual magic that can be applied to all realms. This kind of power though always has tremendous repercussions that are quick and harsh when misused because the person is operating at a point of primal force. It can lift one to great ecstasy or great suffering and sacrifice.

This letter has ties to the planet Jupiter. Jupiter is a planet of abundance, and those of this letter have the capability of manifesting such within his or her life. Remember that the *X* is the point in the void where the formless takes form. When this letter's energies are perverted, greed, lust and avarice will result, but when its forces are activated positively, the result is a strong sense of philanthropy and an intuitive understanding of life. It is important for those of this letter to have a higher purpose and cohesiveness to their life or it will lead one toward being a wanderer or dilettante—which is also a Jupiter trait.

Jupiter is the ruler of Sagittarius which is also associated with this letter. Chiron was the great centaur teacher, gifted in philosophy and the arts, and he was master and teacher of some of the greatest Greek heroes. He served as a mediator of higher knowledge to those of the physical realms. This is reflected within the glyph of the letter itself—the point of intersection where the higher meets the lower. Many of those of this sign and of this letter choose to expand horizons below their belt, having not learned the difference between need and greed. Thus, caution and self-assessment need to be regular. If one of this letter's influence is not sure, a quick test is to draw a large *X* in the middle of a piece of paper. If the upper portion of the *X* is larger, then the higher qualities are being emphasized. If the lower portion of the *X* is larger, then the more physical and base qualities are being stressed. A balanced *X* indicates a balanced individual.

This is a letter which will endow the individual with a vast and inspirational mind, as long as the mental activity is balanced with the material life. Although there may be tendencies toward false exaggerations and an appetite (of different kinds) that is never quite satisfied, it can awaken a tremendous artistic nature and an ability to teach with a new kind of boldness that expands with each passing year.

This is the letter for walking between the worlds. It requires great balance, concentration and complete control of the will. When these are developed there arises a true shamanic ability to work with the forces of all that we relegate to dreams and myths. One will live the mystery of the occult within the reality of physical life!

## THE CONSONANT Z

> KEYNOTE: Lightning force of intuitive knowledge
> COLOR(S): Pastel orange and pale mauve
> ASTROLOGY: Gemini

This is the letter of the primal force of lightning. Individuals with this as a predominant letter within the name are usually very quick in their responses to situations. Once the mind is made up, they act immediately, not liking to delay at all. Most strong with them are the intuitive flashes to which they are prone. Some occur so frequently that it may appear as if everything in their life is endowed with intuitive insight. These individuals have opened themselves up to receive quick insight at a moment's notice.

The glyph of the letter is shaped like the zigzagging lightning flash through the sky. It is comprised of three lines. The upper bar of the Z is parallel to the lower. This reflects the spiritual forces which imprint themselves in a physical manner. The diagonal line connecting them indicates that the individual has the capability of recognizing these imprints and thus can draw correspondences and act accordingly.

There have been many correspondences made between lightning and the "flaming sword" within the mysticism of some ancient societies. The flaming sword is the sword of discrimination and comprehension of spiritual law. It is double-edged, endowing the individual with great power—an ability to draw upon inner resources with strength and speed. In the Hebrew Qabala, the world manifested along the path of the "Flaming Sword"—a path that drew forth the energies of the spiritual consciousness culminating into the physical consciousness of the individual. This letter thus can endow the individual with the ability to draw forth great intuitive insight with great speed at any time.

Gemini is the astrological correspondent to this letter. Gemini is the sign of polarity, working from several realms. The symbol for Gemini is shaped like the Roman numeral II. It is comprised of two sets of parallel lines. The two horizontal lines are representative of the spiritual and the physical realms. The two vertical bars connecting the horizontal are the sources of flow that enable the individual to draw down the force or raise oneself up. It is the reflection of the male and female aspects that are operative equally on both levels. In the glyph for the letter Z the vertical bars have changed to a single diagonal bar. This is a more dynamic activation of the flow from one level of consciousness to the other. It accelerates that flow and intensifies it within the life of those with this letter predominant within the name.

Those with this letter have great psychic gifts which can strike out of the blue. There is not only a great desire toward the psychic and the occult, but there will be great expression of it within the individual's life. The individual has opened the doors to the higher through the past, and have come to draw upon it more actively within the present life.

This letter endows the individual with a diversity of energy, but he or she must learn to follow through on it. These individuals will develop a strong ability to create and instigate, which can be expressed either positively or negatively. Thus the greatest lesson for them to learn is that of discrimination and discernment. When to listen to that flash of insight and how to act upon it will provide the greatest difficulty. As this ability is developed, events will flow smoother, and there will be less opportunity to offend others or to intrude upon their own free wills.

With a Gemini influence through this letter—its ruler being Mercury—the individual will be endowed with higher intellectual abilities which can open tremendously the more the individual attunes to the archetypal force behind the letter. There will occur, as the individual matures, a recall of past life abilities, along with the opportunity to renew the gifts from the past. Dreams should be worked with, as much will come to the individual through them.

There is also a propensity for one or more languages. If nothing else, the individual will be fascinated by other languages. There is an innate ability to adapt quickly to new situations, along with a strong potential for endurance.

This letter can require though that certain weaknesses be overcome before its highest energies are experienced. There can be a lack of communication and a lack of humor. Any rigidity can be a hindrance, as lightning is a force which cannot easily be locked into a particular mode of expression. Any insensitivity will prevent the innate versatility of the individual from unfolding. There is though the capability for having a strong inner voice—bordering on higher forms of telepathy. (The individual has the potential of using the air waves, rather than the brain waves.)

This is a letter which requires control of the emotions and learning to handle transitions properly. Events may often take the individual by surprise, so it is important to learn to handle such "surprises" constructively. It means developing a sense of the right time and action.

This is a letter which indicates that the individual has prepared him or herself to make new progress and movements. The individual will attract such movement, but must learn to use temperance within it. This gives an inherent ability to link with others on psychic and mental waves, but such a linking must be controlled or it will manifest bringing people into one's life that may not be beneficial. Those of this letter must learn to generate a "magical" will to control the psychic resonance with others.

This is a letter which endows the individual with a powerful force of protection within all areas of life, once the archetypal energies behind it are activated. When the individual has learned to align with the divine, all upon a personal level will be protected, because it effects a manifestation of that sacred lightning which protects with divine power.

This is the letter of genius, of the alignment with what has been called one's daimon, fetch or valkyrya. It is a letter of alchemy which can endow one with control of weather and storms, and they are often energized tremendously by such. They are lightning!

## SPECIAL CONSONANT BLENDS

The following consonant blends are important. Some alphabets are comprised of sounds which are not translated by a single alphabetical character. Many of the ancient alphabets are comprised of sounds which in English are consonant and vowel blends. Names that have such need to be aware of their significance as well.

It is important for the individual analyzing his or her name to examine first the individual elements of the consonant blends and then any paired significance that exists. The following section deals predominantly with those consonant blends comprised of consonant plus an *H: CH, PH, SH* and *TH*. There are many consonant blends other than the ones described below. The ones below were chosen for two primary reasons. The first is that they are frequently found in many first names, and the second is that they are sounds that were important in one or more of the ancient sacred alphabets. In examining them, refer to the individual letters comprising the blend first, and then use this section to enhance your understanding as to how they are manifesting within your life. Keep in mind that for those blends involving the *H*, it was often added to an individual's name at a point of initiation. (Refer to the letter *H* for more details.)

The other consonant blend discussed is that of *TZ*. This is a blend that when it appears in a name, often appears as the capstone. I have included it to help you understand how the energies of the consonants can form a powerful capstone of achievement to one's life, when it is activated. Meditation and analysis of your own will provide great insight.

## THE CONSONANT CH

KEYNOTE: Higher vision
COLOR(S): Amber
ASTROLOGY: Cancer

The first of the blends, *CH* is predominantly a blend that forms a cornerstone within a name. It is linked to higher vision, a vision when the inner sun and its amber rays begin to shine.

This is a blend that indicates there will be a need for equilibrium and a greater conquering of emotions in some area of one's life. It also indicates though that any limitations that one finds will be those which are self-imposed.

This is a blend of unity, requiring the individual learn "that of themselves they can do nothing." These individuals work best with other people, even if it is only one. There is a capacity for developing strong working relationships with those of the opposite sex.

The astrological sign is Cancer, a feminine sign, but comprised of two spirals, reminding one of the yin and yang of Eastern philosophy. This reflects the ability to relate with those of the opposite sex. By learning to do so the individual gives birth to higher vision.

This is a letter which can manifest the energies of instability, particularly within the early years. Physical energy can become depleted easily, unless care is taken, and there may be susceptibility to irritability and lack of self-control. When the archetypal force of this blend is touched, there occurs a balanced response to life and a release of hidden knowledge about one's capabilities. It strengthens psychic energies.

This is a combination that implies purity and clarity of purpose. By eliminating that which is obscure, a greater perception of one's purpose will manifest.

This combination has powerful potentials on spiritual and magical levels. It can awaken an ability to understand spiritual beings, humanity and even animals. It awakens an inherent understanding of languages operative on realms often obscure or invisible. The power and significance of symbols and their uses becomes available. This combination also awakens an understanding of the rhythms of the universe and how to place oneself within them. It thus facilitates the opportunities to make great transitions. It opens one to understanding the esoteric processes of life and death and its significance within all our lives.

## THE CONSONANT PH

KEYNOTE: Touching the ancient wells of knowledge
COLOR(S): Orange-brown
ASTROLOGY: Pluto

This is the consonant blend of transformation and initiation. It is the tying of the past to the present so that a new future can be created. It is the regenerative process of involution and evolution.

For those of this consonant blend, there is a deep need to place the present into a perspective based upon the past. It reflects that the past is as important and as relevant to the evolution of the individual as the present. This is the blend of those upon the "Quest for the Holy Grail"—the search for one's true essence and how best to manifest it within the environs of this present incarnation.

This is a combination which requires that the individual not annihilate the past or destroy old forms. It is the task of these individuals to re-express the old in a new and beneficial manner. This is a combination of great power which, if not controlled, will become explosive within the individual's life. These individuals have a capacity to become agents of the evolutionary forces—even when such agency goes unrecognized. Their influence upon others is subtle and yet very distinctive.

Pluto is the astrological correspondent to this blend. Pluto provides energy for breaking down psychological blocks that otherwise would prevent individual growth. Its influence upon those of this letter combination can indicate a difficulty in breaking out of certain fears in the expression of one's true self. It gives an explosiveness, although the eruption usually requires time to gather momentum; but once erupted, it can take out anything and everything around it.

On the other hand this Plutonian influence with those of this letter combination endows them with a unique ability to re-synthesize and re-vitalize old philosophies and ancient doctrines. These individuals have a capacity for discovering unsuspected information from surprising sources. It may be an old book or it may be the "accidental" crossing of an "old soul" teacher who provides a new insight and re-vivification.

Books, ancient teachings and philosophies are important to those of this blend. For those who access the archetypal forces behind it, it will open the ancient records registered upon the ethers of time—that which is called the Akashic Records. These individuals need to turn to the past to re-discover and re-express the ancient wisdoms. It is important for them to do so without getting lost within the glamour of "past life exploration." Such endeavors can easily splinter the personality of those with this letter blend. They must keep in mind that it is all right to re-awaken those aspects, but only so they can be re-expressed within the synthesis of the present incarnation. When this is accomplished, the past becomes a foundation upon which the new can unfold with great power and tremendous healing transformations.

## THE CONSONANTS SH

KEYNOTE: Awakening the inner fires
COLOR(S): Glowing orange-scarlet
ASTROLOGY: Element of fire

The blend of *SH* is aligned with one of the elements—much in the manner of the vowels, but in this case, it reflects an inner fire that will build throughout the life of the individual, until expressed as a true flame. There is always something unique about individuals with this blend, but that "specialness" is not always definable. The fire and warmth inherent in those of this combination have a capacity of resonating with all. It is a combination of sociability and warmth that has been developed within the individual's past, and which will enable the individual to discover the means of bringing the fires out powerfully to heal, enlighten and warm with great intensity.

In the Hebrew alphabet, its counterpart is called "shin" which is primal fire. It is one of the "mother letters" of the Hebrew alphabet, and that mothering nature and warmth is strong within those that allow it to be.

Fire provides heat and light, and many are the myths associated with fire and its theft for humanity. It was always considered something mystical and holy. The manner in which the smoke from the fire melted into the air was magical. There reaches a time though when the individual needs to begin to look at the spiritual aspects of fire, and how it operates for the physical transmutation of our being. There is so much more to it than just its physical properties or even its mythical significance.

Fire is both creative and destructive. It burns away the old so that the new can form. Those of this letter combination have the ability to see through the smoke and fire of others. Fire also stimulates thought, and without thought nothing can manifest. Thought forms the matrix of all physical form. Fire consumes and changes those that it touches. It propels the individual along the path of self-discovery. Those of this blend have come to begin to recognize and tap the infinite potential that resides within. They have come to burn out the dross of their lives through the discovery of their true relationships with others and what they teach about themselves. Each individual teaches us something about ourselves, and it is important for those of this blend to recognize it.

It is important for those of this blend to maintain emotional balance and a strong sense of responsibility—especially to oneself. A fear of change and self-imposition can hinder most of this blend if care is not taken to counter it. If done so there will manifest a process of self-discovery—particularly in the post 40 era of life. There is usually great strength of will and even greater kindness.

This is a letter which can allow the individual to breathe fire into his or her own life and those closest to them. The individual needs to become the great imperial dragon of their lives. When the archetypal force is tapped, there will occur a breaking down of limitations—self-imposed and otherwise. There must be freedom within this individual's life or the fires will be smothered. Thus there must be care not to always take the responsibility for other peoples' lives and circumstances.

These individuals have a capacity for recognizing the truth of knowledge. It sets a flame loose deep within the soul which registers upon the consciousness. This is the blend of the outpouring of divine light and fire, both of which those of this blend will be in the lives around them.

This is the blend of the fires of the inner sun, and it instills a natural and instinctual enlightenment and spirituality—even if there may be no "knowledge" to support it. This is a blend which will enable the individual to find "faith" as a true power and force, rather than a belief. It gives the individual the ability to transmute any life conditions and to help others find the light and fire to do likewise within their own circumstances.

## THE CONSONANT TH

KEYNOTE: The opening of the gateway
COLOR(S): Deep indigo
ASTROLOGY: Saturn

This is the blend of the laws of cause and effect. It has ties to the planet Saturn which is considered the teacher of those within this solar system. Saturn is sometimes considered a malefic planet, but only because it will not allow itself to be short changed. It pays due reward for effort, no more and no less. It is a planet of learning and responsibility.

In Hebrew this is known as the Tao cross—the cross of crucifixion or of resurrection. It is entirely up to the individual. It is a blend that reflects that the inner realms have opened up their flow of energies, but it takes great control and responsibility to handle them. It endows one with great psychic sensitivity, which can become an unbalanced emotionalism if not understood and handled properly.

The true archetypal power behind this blend is awe-inspiring when touched. It can open one to the true knowledge of the universe and its laws as they are operating within your own life circumstances. Those of this blend have come in to this world to experience a consciousness of a higher universe, but it will require bringing the personality into balance through a higher sense of understanding and perception.

This is a consonant blend that opens the astral plane to the individual. This can lead to out-of-body experiences and tremendously significant dream activities. There needs to be caution though as there can develop a tendency to become "fairy charmed" and lost within the ethereal realms unless one stays grounded.

This is the blend that indicates the individual has learned to cross back and forth through the thresholds of consciousness. It demands a meeting of the "Guardians upon the Threshold"—those aspects painted over, glossed over, shoved to the back of one's closet. They are those aspects of one's personality sometimes referred to as the "shadowselves"—personality traits (from this life time or past) that need to be changed.

Those of this blend may have to deal with idleness and hidden fears, and they must learn not to succumb to depression and despondency. If there is a lack of discipline, the individual will not be able to develop the discrimination necessary to work on the more ethereal psychic realms. This blend though does endow the individual with opportunities to develop common sense and a strengthening of the light bodies, along with a facing of subconscious fears.

Patience is the key to success for these individuals, and it will create a quickening of development. It is important for them to assimilate the experiences of the past so as not to repeat those which would harm.

This is a blend that has strong ties to the Aesir of Nordic mythology—the raw power of the Gods of Asgard. Thunderstorms are extremely stimulating to those of this blend, and it is not unusual to find that as children there was a fear of such. Storms touch a primal nerve, like ringing the doorway to their inner consciousness.

This is the blend for the breaking down of resistance, regeneration and fertility. It is the energy of learning to handle opposition in any form. It teaches the individual to use the energies of stress to propel oneself forward. It teaches the ability to transform one's life through spiritual applications of the sexual force. These individual's are often "late bloomers," but when they do, they do so in a unique lifestyle and individualism that has a force of its own. It is a force which can open the portals of time for those willing to put forth such efforts. These portals reveal all that was, all that is, all that is unfolding at present. Theirs is the initiation of the astral plane and all of the power and energies associated with it. It is the power of control over one's psychic instincts and inspirations. It is the power of movement to new heights, new realms and new expressions of creative individuality.

## THE CONSONANTS TZ

> KEYNOTE: Creative imagination
> COLOR(S): Violet
> ASTROLOGY: Aquarius

This is a consonant blend often found as a capstone within a name. As such, it indicates which avenue of endeavor will ultimately provide the greatest capstone to this incarnation. It reflects in this case that the application of creative imagination—in some avenue of endeavor—will most strongly activate the greatest inner potential of the vowel—doing so in a manner that provides the greatest opportunity for success.

This is a consonant blend that is tied intimately with the forces of creative imagination. The greatest hindrance to this manifesting is a fear of following one's dreams and a doubting of one's own abilities. Dreams are greatly imaginative in those with this consonant blend, and thus there can arise an impracticality which must be worked at and balanced. Once done, the hopes and aspirations soar to new heights. This blend will then endow the individual with a great sense of loyalty, peace and a strength to follow those inner dreams.

Intuition, discrimination and imagination are all part of the archetypal force behind these letters. There will arise an ability to connect with ever new forces and inspirations. There is the ability to merge the normal consciousness with the greater divine consciousness, imbuing the individual with an ability for mediatorship between the planes of life and the personal meditations with great color and vibrancy. Its astrological correspondent is the energies of Aquarius. This gives one the innate ability to be an inspirational visionary and teacher. They can pour forth their creative ideas in great abundance. It endows the individual with an alert and intuitive mind and an ability to love all. It is the sign of new ideas and inventions. These individuals have a great capacity to be a harbinger of light, or in esoteric terms—"A Daughter of the Firmament: A Dweller Between the Waters."

## ALPHABET CORRESPONDENCES

| Letter | Keynote Of Letter | Color | Astrology |
|---|---|---|---|
| A | Higher wisdom & illumination | White/ lt. blue | Ether/ Uranus |
| B | Creative power of wisdom | Yellow | Mercury |
| C | Creative cyclic expression | Red-orange | Moon |
| D | Fertility | Emerald | Venus |
| E | Perception & universal consciousness | Blue | Air/Mercury |
| F | Fulfillment through harmony | Lt. red-orange | Taurus |
| G | Faith and discernment | Deep blue | Moon |
| H | Power of the word, imagination & intuition | Bright reds | Aries |
| I | Divine love | Red-violet | Fire/Mars |
| J | Harvesting cosmic love | Yellow-green | Virgo |
| K | New journeys through creativity | Blue-violet | Jupiter |
| L | Magnetism & power of attraction | Emerald | Libra |
| M | Regrowth and rebirth | Mother-of-pearl | Neptune/ Moon |
| N | Willed transmutation & fertility | Blue-green | Scorpio |
| O | Justice and balance | Black | Water/Saturn |
| P | Power of hidden expression | Scarlet | Mars |
| Q | Intelligence of the heart | Violet | Pisces |
| R | Fires of love, wisdom & freedom | Orange/amber | Sun |
| S | The serpent wisdom | Blue | Sagittarius |
| T | Inspiration for spiritual warriorship | Green-yellow/ amber | Leo |
| U | Birth giving | Earth tones | Element of Earth/Venus |
| V | Fruitfulness & openness | Red-orange | Taurus |
| W | Uniting of consciousness | Green/silver | Venus/Moon |
| X | Force of duality | Deep indigo | Sagittarius/ Jupiter |
| Y | Transmutation & alchemy | Lt. golden brown | Fire & Water/ Venus & Mars |
| Z | Lightning force of intuition | Pastel orange | Gemini |
| CH | Higher vision | Amber | Cancer |
| PH | Ancient well of knowledge | Orange-brown | Pluto |
| SH | Awakening the inner fires | Orange-scarlet | Fire/Uranus |
| TH | Opening of the gateway | Deep indigo | Saturn |
| TZ | Creative imagination | Violet | Aquarius |

# 6

# Activating Energies
# of Name Elements

There is an old occult axiom which states, "All energy follows thought." This is important to understand in activating the power of the consonants to their fullest capability. The more we realize the hidden significance of the elements of our names, the more they are awakened within our lives, but this is just the beginning.

1. Determine the cornerstone and capstone consonants within your first name. Remember that these are the most important consonants. Some names will not have a capstone consonant. Review all the significances associated with these consonants, as described earlier. Do not limit yourself to these, for as you work and meditate and activate them more fully within your life, you *will* see even more correspondences.

2. Examine all secondary consonants. These are all other consonants within in your first name that are neither the cornerstone or capstone. For example, in the name "Phyllis", the *P* is the cornerstone and the *S* is the capstone. The *H* and two *L*'s are secondary consonants.

3. It is a good idea to keep a "Name Journal" in which you can record all the significances of your name, especially those received in your meditation and activation exercises.

4. Make particular note of the colors associated with each of the consonants, as they will be important in the activation process.

5. Allow yourself to relax, undisturbed.

6. Just as you learned to do with the vowels, close your eyes and visualize the cornerstone consonant forming around you, as if you are sitting in the midst of a giant consonant. See yourself as the letter. It is helpful to try and not think of it as a letter but rather as a geometric shape that activates a particular play of energy around you. It is a geometric glyph that is setting up a specific electro-magnetic frequency within your auric field. It is one of great color and vibrancy.

7. When you have established this image firmly about you, in its appropriate color, visualize the potentials of the consonant manifesting more strongly within your life. Reflect on all the ways in which you haven't used its energies. Remember the ways others have blocked your using it to the fullest, and then imagine it coming to life in a manner that empowers you anew. See yourself applying successfully all of its capabilities. See the force of this glyph and its color energy touching you on all realms, releasing you to use your greatest potentials!

8. Remember that the consonants are those potentials we have the greatest capability of manifesting. They indicate what we have already begun to learn to do.

9. At this point allow the letter to begin to change shape, creating a spiral of color force that surrounds you, a layer of the auric field, surrounding the physical body. Make this core layer as wide as you can, in as vibrant of a color as you can, surrounding and emanating from all sides of you. Our auric field is what touches people first in all encounters. The color of your cornerstone consonant is the core of your outer personality—your outer energy field.

10. At this point, feel this core of spiralling energy drawing universal life force down into you and then see it spiralling out from you. You are re-aligning with the universal life force that feeds and nourishes us on all levels. Light and life spirals down to you, and then emanates out from you in powerful creative expressions, unique to the letter and to you. You are constantly drawing from the archetypal forces of the universe and manifesting

them uniquely. You are part of the flow and flux of universal light and life. As you expend, it is instantly replaced.

With practice, the above exercise becomes second nature. You are re-learning the process of activating your higher potentials. As you more fully and consistently activate these energies, it will become easier to bring out the hidden potential of the vowels. The exercise only takes approximately ten minutes. With practice, one can activate it more quickly. You are simply re-activating it, re-training it in what it already knows how to do, but has forgotten. You came into this incarnation with an imprint for its activation. You are now simply setting that imprint into conscious activity.

Within three weeks of performing this exercise, on a daily basis, there will be a noticeable change within your energy on all levels. You will find greater strength and facility at performing all tasks—physical, emotional, mental and spiritual. This exercise realigns you with your basic energy pattern.

There are variations. You can also then take the capstone consonant, and repeat the same process. The only difference is that when you convert the glyph to a spiral of energy within the auric field, it forms a spiral that fills the outer portions of the aura, beyond the cornerstone consonant. The primary consonant, the cornerstone, becomes a spiral of energy surrounding the physical body and extending out as far as you can imagine. The capstone, or final consonant, vibrates and spirals at the outer edge of the cornerstone spiral, extending even further into the universe.

The secondary consonants can be activated and turned into spirals of force that fill and bridge the auric energy of the cornerstone and capstone. See the diagram on page 108.

## TRANSFORMING THE AURA
## THROUGH NAME ELEMENTS:

Ideally, we want to be able to call forth the energies inherent within our names any time that they are needed. Our auric field should be infused with their energies so as to enable us to more fully and productively accomplish what we have come to accomplish within this life time.

Our auric field is a combination of the natural electromagnetics surrounding us, along with biological aspects. When the cells in our body convert the food that we eat and the air that we breathe into

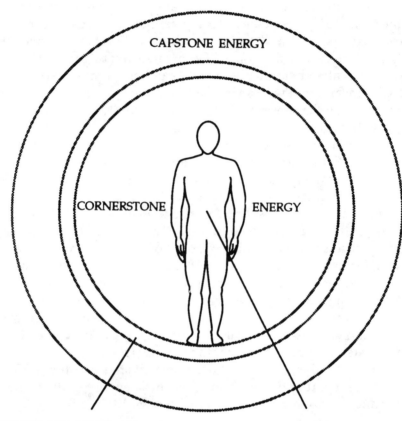

CAPSTONE ENERGY

CORNERSTONE ENERGY

SECONDARY CONSTANT ENERGY

INNER POT ENTIAL OF
THE PRIMARY VOWEL

*Transforming the Aura Through Name Elements*

energy, they give off a by-product known as photon radiation. This is light energy that then surrounds the physical body. This, in conjunction with the electro-magnetism of our true soul essence (and the subtle bodies), comprises the auric field. This light energy is detectable and measurable, and ideally should hold to patterns basic to our soul matrix. It shows up in the form of colors around the individual.

Our emotional and mental states, as well as the spiritual, affect the color of the aura and its vibrancy. And just as we can go through a variety of emotional and mental states in the course of a day, we thus also can go through a variety of colors as well. What we want to be able to do is to maintain a basic energy field—a base coat of color—within the aura that is truly individualistic. This is where activation of the name elements is so important.

As we learn to develop the primal energy pattern we came into life with, then the extraneous changes we go through during the day will have less of a detrimental effect upon our health on physical or on subtle levels. By establishing and maintaining a strong foundation of auric energy that is true to our soul, we can recover from imbalances more easily, along with manifesting our potentials more dynamically. It becomes easier to fulfill ourselves as individuals.

The colors, clarity and vibrancy of our aura tell us specific things about our physical, emotional, mental and spiritual well-being. If these are not harmonious to the colors you have chosen to take upon yourself, problems, physical and otherwise, will arise. Activating the forces inherent within the elements of our name, and infusing our auric fields with them, establishes a foundation that we can then maintain and balance more efficiently. The name—birth or otherwise—is an energy signature we are choosing to resonate with—even if it is only for a short period within one's life. The more we establish its foundation within the auric field, the quicker the harmony with its elements and the easier it becomes to resonate and manifest the inherent potentials. This is particularly important when changing one's name, as will be elaborated upon in chapter three. The following exercise is one which will facilitate establishing an energy pattern within the auric field.

1. As in the previous exercises, it is important to perform this when you will be undisturbed. It will take twenty to thirty minutes, depending upon the amount of preparation one has done with the previous exercises for activating the vowels and consonants.

It is important to keep in mind also that it is the energy that you have brought with you into this incarnation from the consonants that provides the best soil for the flowering of inner powers of the vowels in the manner unique and constructive for you.

2. We begin with the primary vowel. As you close your eyes, relaxing, tone the vowel softly as you previously learned to do. With each toning, feel and see the energy and color of the vowel filling your inner body. Hear the sound of the vowel echoing throughout the body and to the ends of the universe, touching its archetypal source and awakening its reflection within you. Imagine yourself as being vibrant with the potential of this power, as if waiting for the opportunity to express itself.

3. Now take the primary consonant, the cornerstone, and activate it around you. Visualize the consonant forming around you, in its appropriate color vibrancy. Feel the letter begin to shift, turning into a spiral of color that surrounds the physical body and extends as far out as you can imagine. This is the energy you have the easiest capacity to manifest within your life, and which can help you to unfold the inner energies of the vowel uniquely within this incarnation. It is this energy which will help to draw out the power of your inner potential.

4. When you can feel this energy spiralling around you with a vibrant and steady force, focus upon your capstone consonant, if there is one. See and feel it come to life, forming around you in the same manner as the cornerstone consonant. When you can feel its vibrancy, allow it to begin to shift, until it swirls at the outer edges of the first spiral, extending to the ends of the universe. See it drawing energies in and spinning them out all around you. See them touching and blending with the outer edges of the first spiral. (Refer to the diagram on page 108.)

5. Now take any secondary consonants, visualize them forming around you just as you have with the others. As they shift from their glyphic form into spirals of energy and color that swirl around you, imagine them blending and mixing within the cornerstone and capstone spirals. Allow their hues to stay distinct and yet swirling around with the others, creating a unique rainbow spiral of force within the auric field.

6. If there are any secondary vowels within the name, visualize them forming as colored energy within you just as you did with the color of the primary vowel. Visualize them mixing with the primary color in any pattern with which you feel comfortable. Keep its colors though at an intensity and quantity less than that of the primary vowel.

7. You have now created an auric field that resonates with the innate power of the elements within your name. These elements have been translated into colors comprising the energy patterns of the auric field.

8. This is the basic energy (color) pattern of your name when expressed within the auric field. An excellent way of helping you to visualize it is to take the diagram on page 108 and with crayons or colored pencils, color the auric field in accordance with your name. This helps to ground the visualization, objectify it so as to make it more easily imagined. Then each morning as part of your meditational work, look upon the picture to ingrain and re-imprint upon the mind the energy pattern you have chosen. This not only helps activate it, but it also serves to anchor it more firmly within your energy foundation.

9. At the end of days that are more hectic and disruptive, simply take a few moments to re-activate your basic energy pattern. It balances and harmonizes, enabling you to shake off the "debris" of the day.

10. As it becomes more fully established, it is also good to begin to imagine the inner colors (vowels) beginning to spiral and shine outward, mixing with the outer energies (the consonants which enable the inner potentials to flower and grow within your life).

## TECHNIQUE OF THE NAME SONG

One of the most powerful ways of working with our names and activating their energies is through music. Our names can be converted into a musical phrase. There are musical notes which correspond to the letters of the alphabet. Any musical instrument can be used, as long as it is capable of playing the chromatic scale (sharps and flats). Through the technique that follows we can bring the name elements to life with even greater vibrancy within the auric field.

The power of music works with name activation because of a secret content which lays in the expression of the sound. This "secret content" was the pattern of sounds emitted through various techniques. For example, inspiration and intuition occur through a repetition of regular musical structures, tones and patterns. It is the order and rhythm of the tones, the mixture and combining into specific successions of melody that is the source of true magic. Learning to combine specific tones to link energies of the body and soul together for healing, higher intuition, dream enlightenment, communing with the spirits or for invoking a Divine Presence was a part of the ancient teaching of music.

In the Ancient Mystery Schools the teachers and the students sang to absorb their own sounds and vibrations. Once their thoughts and feelings were formulated, they needed to be grounded or focused into the physical realm. Singing—or playing an instrument—enabled them to do so. They recognized that sounds were communicated to the throat by the energies of the soul, and by working with those sounds they could bring more light into the physical.

We are by nature complete. We are each a harmony, but we have learned to separate and create combinations of tones and energies that fight each other. The power of music, when applied to our names, helps us to re-create our original harmonies.

In almost every society, there has been what the ancients called "The Song of the Absolute" or the "Three-Fold Song." Three is the great creative number, the number of the artist, the musician and the poet. The "Song of the Absolute" has three aspects which reflects the manner in which music directs the energies of the universe. These three aspects are also found within our names:

1. Rhythm—from which all motion comes.

2. Melody—from which comes the manifestation of the divine into the physical.

3. Harmony—from which comes individual power that manifests throughout the universe and is reflected within us.

Our names are miniature "Songs of the Absolute." They have a melody, comprised of its glyphs, sounds and musical notes. When all are put together and linked by the individual, we create a melody that bridges the physical with our spiritual essence. The rhythms of our name enable us to employ that melody, to raise and lower the bridge and to travel across it within this incarnation. This rhythm is reflected in the name syllables and the birthdate. When we employ all aspects—when we learn to blend the rhythms with the sounds and the energy correspondences of our name—we create a harmony of life. Giving life to our melodies through our rhythms creates harmony. We create a magical, musical journey through life. We recover our own innate divinity, and we begin to express it with a joy for living and for each other.

1. We will begin with the first name (you can convert the entire name in the same manner). Use the following conversion table to find the musical notes associated with your full first name (at birth). (MC = Middle C)

| MC | C# | D | D# | E | F | F# | G | G# | A | A# | B | C |
|----|----|---|----|---|---|----|---|----|---|----|---|---|
| A | B | C | D | E | F | G | H | I | J | K | L | M |
| N | O | P | Q | R | S | T | U | V | W | X | Y | Z |

2. Begin by playing each name separately. Each name—first, middle and last—is its own musical phrase. The first name though reflects your most individual and creative essence.

3. Experiment with them. Play all the notes of a name simultaneously, as well as separately. Mix up the notes of your first name into a melody that you enjoy. (You can then always transpose that order back into specific letters—giving you a possible "magical name.") Pay attention to what sounds good to you and what doesn't.

4. Give the tones associated with the vowels longer stress. Don't worry if some sounds are discordant. The more you work with it, the more you become familiar with it, the less discordant it will sound.

5. Hum or sing the sounds as you play them. This activates their energies powerfully around you. Simply playing or humming the sounds within your name for five or ten minutes will balance your energies. This is especially effective at the end of a long

day. One of the most effective ways of restoring homeostasis to the body is through sound and music.

6. Experiment. Begin with the first letter and tone. Play it upon an instrument or pitch pipe. Then sing your first name in that note. Repeat two more times. Then take the second note of your name, play it upon the instrument and then sing your name in that tone. Do this with each note of your first name. It is very energizing, and it activates the intuitive aspect of your consciousness. This is an excellent prelude to meditation, as it helps induce an altered state of consciousness, relieve stress, strengthen the aura and also helps to promote healing.

7. One of the best methods for using the tones is in conjunction with the exercise on transforming the aura, just described within this chapter. As you visualize and activate the color of the letters associated with your name in your auric field, play or sing the musical note that is also associated with that letter. This will enhance the visualization. It will strengthen the color energy within the auric field, and it will more quickly re-establish your primal energy foundation.

These exercises re-awaken your "name-song." "The song-word is powerful; it names a thing, it stands at the sacred center, drawing all towards it . . . The word disappears, the poetry is gone, but the imagined form persists within the mind and works upon the soul!" (Halifax, J. *Shamanic Voices*. p. 33. N.Y., Dutton 1979.)

PART II

# CREATING THE
# MAGICAL NAME

# 7

# The Significance of the Magical Name

Our names are direct links to our soul. The spoken "word" or name—when employed with potent thought—becomes a creative power which can fix the play of soul energy within one's life in any manner that he or she desires. The assigning of a name is no longer given the consideration and care that it once was. The taking of a name—whether at birth or at any other occasion—involved an empowering ritual so that the name would reflect the highest potential of the soul into the life of the individual.

To the ancient mystics and shamans, the assigning of a name was a process to be reverenced. It was much more than just choosing a label by which the individual could be called. Names were viewed as the spiritual essence behind the physical form and consciousness. Names were chosen and created uniquely for each incoming child and for major changes within one's life and consciousness.

Our name and its elements resonate with specific archetypal forces operating throughout the universe. When we align ourselves with a name, we are also aligning ourselves with the forces behind it. This is why it is so important to understand the significance of the elements within our names and how they may play themselves out within the circumstances of our individual lives. If we don't understand this resonance, we may never understand the significance of the events within our lives.

The name is a physical link to our spiritual essence. Ancient incantations and forms of high magic depended upon the exact knowledge of a name—particularly those of the gods and goddesses. The name(s) we use reflect energies of our soul essence that we have come to develop and build upon uniquely within the course of this lifetime. They help to define the expressions of our energies for this incarnation. If we change our name, we change the expressions of our energies.

There are no good names or bad names, as the energy they all manifest is neutral and impersonal. However, there are names whose elements are more compatible with your life environs and development than others. (It is this reason that we will explore aligning one's name with one's astrological aspects.) The name, if understood and used correctly, summons forth the energies and essences that it represents and identifies. It invokes a play of those universal energies into your life, influencing your physical, emotional, mental and spiritual states. We are not controlled by them, anymore than we are controlled by the kinds of foods that we eat, but we cannot deny that they do influence the quality of our physical, emotional, mental and spiritual states.

We are the microcosm, reflecting *all* of the energies of the macrocosm—the universe. This implies that we have the capability of resonating with any and all energies existing. The names we take activate that resonance so that particular archetypal forces will play more strongly within our lives than others. We can resonate with the forces behind any name, but yes, there are some to which we have a much greater resonance than others. Factors, such as previous learning and developments from other incarnations, provide us with the ability to resonate with some archetypal forces more easily than with others. These can be reflected within the consonants of one's names, but more influential are the astrological elements which will be discussed further in this chapter. Learning to identify the elements to which one can more easily resonate is the key to assigning a true birth name and to taking upon oneself a new magical name.

There really is no way to take upon oneself a "bad" name. Any name can become powerfully magical, if the individual learns to access the forces behind the elements within it. We can develop resonance with any name, but there are some in which this can be accomplished more easily. That is the task of this chapter—to facilitate resonance with any name, particularly those termed MAGICAL NAMES.

In more ancient times, the naming of a child was conducted by the mother, as it was believed that she had the greatest attunement to the soul that would be incarnating. Even though the father and the priest or priestess had a major role, ultimately, the mother had the final word. The ancients recognized that the time of pregnancy was a mystical and sacred time, and if utilized correctly, it could be a time when the parents—father and mother—could attune to the soul to which they were to be the channel. They could discern the energies and purposes of the soul, and thus they could choose or create a name that would assist the soul in manifesting its highest potentials.

This kind of reverence toward the "naming" process has been lost. The only hints of it are found within initiatory rituals in which new names are taken on by the individual or in groups in which the individual chooses or creates his or her own magical name. We must remember though, that regardless of the naming procedure, once assigned and aligned to, the name will activate a play of archetypal energies uniquely into the life of the individual.

Many dislike the names they have been given, and it is important to understand that we can change them. Before such a change occurs though, it is necessary for the individual to discover the hidden significance of his or her name. No name is bad. Each has its unique characteristics. Each is aligned to certain archetypal forces. EVERY NAME IS MAGICAL!

"Name Magic" or "Name Enchantment" is the discovery of the attributes of the supernatural or archetypal forces within the significance of the individual's name. Beyond the superficial images and stereotypes that can exist around a name, there is a magic that lies within its essence. It is a magic which can tie one to the spiritual paths of the past and can open one to a life of magical light and abundance in the present. What has been lost is the ability to realize the true power within one's name, a power that goes beyond and can shatter all stereotypes, all preconceptions and all thoughtforms. What has been lost is the way to use our name as a key to the doorways of magic and wonder. What has been lost is the means to create a name of light and magic.

Because humanity has lost the ability to re-connect with the esoteric power within any given name, there is great emphasis put on changing one's name. This has both positive and negative effects. Any new name will require time for the physical consciousness to attune and resonate with the energies behind it. There is always a period of adjustment. Techniques to establish resonance with any new name taken by the individual will be discussed further in this chapter.

Changing one's name has repercussions. People do make judgments about names. Some names sound older, more mature. Some names give a perception of youth and adventure. Our name can reflect nationality, religion, etc., which can affect personality behaviors.

We can either choose to allow such assumptions and preconceptions about a name to limit us, or we can explore it and all its elements, learning from it so that we can grow. We can allow our names to label us, or we can tap the archetypal forces behind them to break all old labels and conceptions to create new perspectives and new expressions of individuality.

People need to rejoice in their names. The magic of the individual is first manifested through his or her name. We are our names, and they do reflect our true essences—if we are willing to look at them. It is much easier to unfold the magic within the name we now have than to change it. Changing names is not like changing tires that are worn out or don't seem to fit. Names are intimate links to our highest essence. They are an outer reflection of an inner essence.

I once counselled a woman who had changed her name legally five times in about as many years. Every time she heard a name she liked, she changed it. As a result she had so many energies playing within her life, with none being firmly established, that her life was filled with chaos and disruption.

Our name at birth provides a foundation for us. It is a matrix of energy which helps to stabilize the expression of our soul energy within our daily life circumstances. This is not to say that we should never change our names, but it is something that should not be taken lightly. There are ways of effecting changes within our energies other than tearing down a foundation that has been established. We need to reconnect with the core of that foundation by first learning the significance of the elements of our name that we have been ignoring. We need to strip away the prejudices, and reconnect with the archetypal forces behind it. We can then begin a process of intensifying the manifestation of that soul energy.

## THE SIGNIFICANCE OF THE MAGICAL NAME

Any name can be magical, as we have already discussed. Changing one's name should be a last resort because names are living and changing anyway. As you grow, mature and unfold, so do the perceptions of others concerning your label. You are constantly breaking old patterns and opening new. If you must change your name, work towards it by taking a "magical name."

The magical name serves a variety of purposes:

1. It greatly empowers our birth name.

2. It can be a tool for smoothing the resonance of the play of archetypal forces within our lives.

3. It can facilitate the manifesting of one's true inner potential.

4. It can help awaken you more fully to the innate power of your birth name and its purpose within this incarnation.

5. It serves as a bridge toward the outer expression of the archetypal forces and their true effects upon the soul.

6. It can facilitate instituting a process of change in your life.

7. It can be used to manifest the archetypal forces of the universe more effectively within the outer world.

8. It can provide a tremendous reservoir of energy to access and draw upon in your day to day life circumstances.

9. It can be used to help institute initiatory processes or "rites of passage." It helps you in the transition from one state of life to another, by activating forces that help move you through the changes more effectively and more dynamically. It helps to institute and ground a rebirth into manifestation within the physical. This often entails a symbolic death—the death of the old you (and the old way of working with your energies) to be reborn into a new expression of energy—symbolized by the ritual and the magical name; enabling you to more fully access the true soul energy and its expression within your life.

10. It can be used as part of a process of self-dedication—a name which both reminds you and activates energies around you to manifest greater dedication and effort toward unfolding one's soul essence more creatively and productively within one's

outer life—as reflected by the outer (birth) name.

11. It can be used to institute a series of changes within one's life, more in line with one's personal, professional or spiritual goals. Any name change brings with it corresponding changes in the outer world—not only how people respond to you, but also with the energy you have to respond to outer situations.

12. It enables you to choose and build an energy around you with a name you like. It enables you to more consciously pick the energies you want to have at play within your life. Keep in mind, though, that as long as your birth name is your legal name, it will affect you. Combining the magical name with your birth name facilitates harmony on all levels. A process for this will be discussed later within this book.

13. Choose your magical name carefully, being fully aware of all the elements within it. This will also be elaborated upon. Let it reflect your personality, interests and/or feelings.

14. The magical name can also help awaken the individual to a realization of the SOUL NAME—the name that resides behind all names that we use in all incarnations.

15. The magical name can be used to strengthen the "body of light" so as to provide a vehicle for consciousness upon other planes and dimensions. It facilitates the development of the "magical body"—the energy that comprises the ideal you in all your forms. The magical body is the new, more conscious, you that is created through aligning with the forces in your name.

    The magical name assists you in assuming the manner, the powers and the aura necessary for whatever your individual task may be. In order to do so, you must first have those energies, abilities and powers to assume. By taking a magical name, you begin the process of creating a new you, an empowered outer you. You are not changing the old, but you are helping to further empower it with the forces of the new. It requires that you focus upon the ideal, archetypal forces operating within your life, and making them more vital and strong.

    The formation of the magical body begins with the formation of a magical name in association with an "imagickal body." What is the highest, brightest, most successful image of yourself that you can create? What characteristics would you ideally have? What abilities and energies would you be freely able to express whenever you desired? How would you ideally like others to see you? What name elements (vowels and consonants) most align you with such abilities? What elements in your first name already align you with this ideal? All this must be kept in mind when changing one's name.

16. The magical name can help stimulate greater resonance with astrological influences within your life.

17. The magical name can assist in keeping you upon your own life path and help you to maintain your innate rhythms of balance.

18. We are physical beings, and our primary focus should be within the physical world. We can use other dimensions and levels of consciousness to create greater productivity within our physical lives. The magical name can help us to access other levels of consciousness for that purpose. It can enable us to bypass the preconceptions and prejudices and limitations we may have built up around our birth name, until we are capable of shattering such hindrances and touching the archetypes within it.

19. The magical name helps us to more fully activate our capacity for creative imagination, or imaginative cognition. This helps open the doors to our true spiritual energies and to those beings and energies on the more ethereal realms. It helps activate the intuition so that it can manifest more fully within the outer world. It helps to translate the archetypal energies of the intuitive consciousness to outer expression and images.

20. The amount of energy available to each of us is limited *solely* by our capacity for realization. If we increase our awareness concerning our name, and then use the "magical name" to amplify it, we begin a process of initiation that will remove our inhibitions and limitations in all areas. Every aspect of our nature—whatever we are or are becoming—is intensified in accordance with the magical name. *We learn to activate that soul essence within us, to shapeshift our energies, to increase our capacity to realize and express that which within us is forever divine!*

# 8

# Considerations
# in Creating
# the Magical Name

It is most important to understand that there are no right or wrong ways of either choosing or creating your magical name. There are, of course, guidelines which can serve to enable your magical name to work more effectively for you. There are ways of harmonizing it more productively with your birth name. It must be assumed that if you are looking for a magical name, you either are not satisfied with the forces inherent within the birth name, you just may not like the birth name itself, you are wishing to find a name that will help manifest your inner potentials more effectively than your birth name, or you may have any number of reasons for doing so.

Whatever the reason, the process of creating the magical name is much easier when you understand the full potential of your birth name. This is because there are a number of ways of deciding upon a magical name—all of which can be influenced by the actual birth name. In all of them there are three special considerations which can enhance the effects of the magical name:

*1. Choose the Elemental Force and Its Appropriate Vowel*
Our name is a formula for releasing certain forces, manifesting certain potentials and realizing certain lessons. It can be seen as a magical formula that activates the play of archetypal energies into

our lives. To help activate this play of energies more consciously, we can take upon ourselves a magical name, whether we call it a secret name, initiatory name or whatever. Because it can most powerfully be used to help activate those archetypal energies more directly and consciously, it is always beneficial to align the elements of the magical name with the elements of the birth name.

This does not mean that they must duplicate the elements, but simply re-enforce. Previously, we discussed the elements (ether, fire, air, water and earth) that are associated with the vowels. This is the first aspect that should be decided upon with any of the ways of creating a magical name. What element do you wish to emphasize and activate more strongly within your life? Keep in mind that each element has its own peculiar qualities and energies. *The primary element should be in harmony with the primary element of your birth name!*

All elements can work together. The charts in chapter 2 will help you in determining which element(s) and the corresponding vowel to use within the magical name. Some basic guidelines are:

—Use an element (and its vowel) within your magical name that is also within your birth name. This amplifies the effects and more intensely will activate its play of energy within your life, both inner and outer.

—Use an element that is more harmonious, if not a duplicate of the primary element of your first name. Although all elements do work together, some combinations are more easily controlled and directed. For example, fire and water can be a tremendously powerful combination, but it is also one that can be one of the most difficult to control and direct. Meditation and reflection upon the elements will help you as there is no hard and fast rule for combining them.

—You may also want to consider including within your magical name any vowels (elemental forces reflected by them) that are not part of your birth name. When your name (the full name) has a certain element missing from any part of it, it can indicate a possible imbalance of the forces to which you have access. Including a vowel within the magical name that is tied to an elemental force missing from your birth name will help harmonize and stabilize the energies playing within your life. It sets in motion an energy that allows you to round out your universal life experience. It gives you a wider range of energies. For some people, this can be too scattering, so caution is advised. When one has all the elements active within one's life, it can make things hectic, setting more in motion than can be handled by the individual.

—One other means of working with the elements is through the astrological correspondence. This was also touched upon in part one. (Refer to the chart on page 15.) The astrological sign in which you were born has a predominant element. The astrological sign also reflects much of what you have come to unfold and learn within this incarnation. Choosing a vowel for your magical name that is associated with the element of your astrological sign will help manifest those energies more fully, especially if it is not already within your birth name.

—Keep in mind that the magical name is as much a formula for activating energies as your birth name. The only difference is that you are more consciously choosing which forces you are wishing to set in motion by this formula. This brings us to the second special consideration which will enhance the effects of any magical name.

*2. Consciously Choose and Infuse with Power*

It is most important when creating the magical name to infuse it with as much power as possible. This is done through a variety of methods. First, and foremost, is the need to consciously recognize, create or choose the name purposefully. Every aspect of its energy needs to be ascertained. You must recognize that each character, each letter, each sound has significance. You must learn to keep in mind that significance at all times. The greater the significance and meaning that you can read into your magical name, the more it will do for you.

Secondly, you must develop a strong thoughtform around the name itself. This is closely tied to the process discussed earlier, concerning the development of the "imagickal body." The more we focus upon an image, an idea, the stronger the energy around such an image or idea will become.

All energy follows thought. If you change your imaginings, you change the world. What we are working to do with the magical name is to initiate a process of changing the energy centered around us or an aspect of our lives. The more we focus upon what we want to manifest, the stronger the energy of it becomes. This energy is sometimes looked upon as simply the electrical brain-wave pattern we emanate in our thinking process. With magical work, it becomes amplified and infused with the more universal energy that surrounds and permeates all life and all dimensions. This has been termed everything from prana to life force, but it is a "free floating" energy that we are binding together in a particular frequency in accordance with the direction of our concentrated imaging and thought patterns.

This means that you need to focus upon all the qualities that you will manifest as a result of taking a particular name. These, of course, do not instantly materialize, but the more you can consciously awaken and focus them, the quicker they begin to manifest. Meditating upon the ideal you, as reflected by the characteristics and energies associated with your magical name, is extremely important. It develops an energy matrix within the auric field, and ultimately a "magical body" of energy that can be called upon as needed.

This is what is often termed a thoughtform. Thoughtforms are thoughts and ideas which will take on a particular shape, form, color or vibrancy when strengthened with enough energy by our thinking, concentration and meditation. This thoughtform can become a separate vehicle for consciousness and can be drawn upon as needed.

Thoughtforms can be used for good or ill, as they are simply matrices of energy. Their strength is determined by the intensity and focus of your thoughts and imaging—and the length of time such thoughts and images are perpetuated. They may exist in the aura to be drawn upon, or at a time in which they develop strong enough energy, they can be used as vehicles for consciousness and directed outward into the various realms and dimensions.

The quality of our thoughts will determine its color, and the nature of our thoughts determine its form. This is why when you decide upon a magical name you want to image yourself in the highest truest manifestation of the elements associated with that name. This involves creative visualization.

Creative visualization and imagination is the process of setting energy in motion through what and how we visualize and imagine. You must remember though that you are not trying to change the old, but rather the images you use associated with the elements and energies of your name are part of creating a "new" you—one that is more empowered in life. You must "see" yourself as if you are already empowered. If you see it as something that will be coming to you, it remains forever in the future. We live in an ever-present moment, and one must visualize and imagine accordingly.

The mind is at the heart of what energies form around the

magical name. There is a level of our consciousness which takes all of our thoughts and words and responds to them in a very child-like and literal manner. If you tell yourself that you catch two colds every winter, that level of consciousness kicks in and begins working with your physical energies so that when winter arrives, you are more susceptible to catching those two colds. If we imagine and tell ourselves that we have certain qualities and energies, and then take on a name that helps to activate such, they will begin to manifest. We create a self-fulfilling prophecy. We infuse the magical name and thus our own selves with greater strength and force.

When a thought goes out strongly towards an object, you are pouring out a very real, albeit subtle, force. Focus upon the elements within your name—birth or magical—elicits a play of that force, strengthening the play of the name's energies within your life. If we can cause dramatic mental images and ideas to rise within the mind, concentrate them and focus them, that outpouring force becomes a thoughtform. When we set up such an energy matrix within our auric field, it will begin to give off vibrations (for it is also electro-magnetic energy). This then has the potential of eliciting effects upon those circumstances and people with whom we connect.

As you develop this magical body of energy, this thoughtform, we have greater opportunity to change our life situations in accordance with its particular realm of influence. Again, this is why it is important to understand the intricacies of the energies activated by one's name. That name serves to anchor that thoughtform of energy within the auric field. It grounds it, preventing it from just dissipating over time.

We are, of course, held karmicly responsible for any thoughtform that we create and must eventually correct anything negatively influenced by it at some point within our evolvement. Since it is our creation, there will come a time, when we must reabsorb its energies back within ourselves and dissipate it or transmute it. This is something that should be done each time you change your magical name. This process will be elaborated upon later within this work.

The thoughtform around your magical name is built up of continually visualizing, imagining and concentrating upon something to which you can attach strong emotion. The emotion gives impact and power to the formation of the magical body, and serves to ignite the energies associated with the magical name. This thoughtform then becomes charged with the emotions associated with it and thus serves to bridge the inner to the outer, linking the normal consciousness to the universal.

### 3. Align with Your Life Path Rhythms

Our names have a rhythm that also ties us to specific archetypal forces and lessons within life. There is at the core of our existence a rhythm, which can be translated into a single numerical correspondence. Understanding that numerical correspondence can be extremely beneficial in creating a magical name. We can align the rhythms of the magical name to the rhythms of our life path and thus enhance the opportunities for learning, achieving and manifesting what we have most come to do.

In the metaphysical science of numerology we can convert our names and our birthdate to numbers. These numerical correspondences can reveal aspects of our personality, inner potential and life path. Most of the ancient mystery systems taught the science of numbers and their metaphysical correspondences. These numbers provide clues to specific rhythms and forces of nature to which you can more easily align. We can take our magical name and construct it so as to harmonize and intensify our alignment with the more universal rhythms operating around us.

The first step in this process is to convert your birthdate to a single number. There are various ways of doing this, but the most common will be elaborated upon here. A study of numerology will elicit greater insight along this avenue. The birthdate is a dominant vibration, and provides a keynote to your basic life essence. It can reflect which rhythms and forces that you must stimulate and bring into play within your life in order to realize true happiness and success. It can indicate which path in life, with all of its tests and initiations and energies will most help you to achieve mastership within the course of this incarnation.

The birthdate corresponds to your life path, your destiny, your school of life lesson—what you have most come to learn within this lifetime. It is a lesson that the soul wants to complete here on earth. It is the force and power and rhythms that the soul has chosen to work more strongly with during this incarnation. You are, of course, not bound by this, but it will manifest certain expressions of energy and lessons within your life. It reflects the path of experience, the rhythms of nature, needed to be aligned with for your further evolvement. It indicates the path you walk, the virtues and vices you will frequently encounter, what you are ultimately striving for and which forces and rhythms of nature can best assist you in your endeavors.

To discover the basic numerical correspondence to your birthdate, we convert your birthdate to numbers and add them. For example, if you were born on June 27, 1962, you will treat each aspect of the birthdate individually. June is the sixth month, so it has the #6 assigned to it:

June 27, 1962 = 6-27-1962 = 6+2+7+1+9+6+2 = 33

When the total has been achieved, we reduce it to a single digit, by adding them together:

3 + 3 = 6.

THE 6 IS THEN YOUR BIRTH NUMBER!

This indicates that the basic rhythmic force and life path is aligned with the associates attributed to the number six. On page 132 is a brief table of rhythmic correspondences to which you can refer. Ideally, one's name—birth or magical—should harmonize with the rhythm or number associated with one's birthdate. Why is this so? Because while we may change our names, our birthdate will always remain the same. It is a basic foundation of energy that we have come to build upon and enhance. It also reflects a basic energy signature aligned with archetypal forces.

Once the basic rhythmic correspondence has been established—based upon your birthdate, there are a number of ways of determining and aligning one's name with that primal rhythmic pattern:

A. Our names have a predominant rhythmic pattern. Our full names at birth can be broken down into syllables. The number of syllables can indicate the most *obvious* rhythm pattern to which you have access.

For example:     Mary Joanne Walker
Ma-ry Jo-anne Walk-er
1    2   3    4     5     6 = 6 syllables.

If Mary Joanne Walker were born on the date we used earlier (June 27, 1962), her name would have a rhythm identical to her birth rhythm.

| TABLE OF RHYTHMIC CORRESPONDENCES | |
|---|---|
| **Rhythms** | **Energies, Effects, Lessons, etc. of Rhythms** |
| 1 | Aligns one to archetypal male energies; initiator; strength of will; discrimination; inventiveness; self-centeredness; laziness; fearfulness or fearlessness; lessons and energies of confidence; search for answers; independence & originality. |
| 2 | Aligns to rhythms of astral plane, archtypal feminine energy and dream consciousness; co-operative; kindness; psychic sensitivity; hypersensitivity; can be scattering; need to focus on details; vacillating and lessons of divisiveness; passion. |
| 3 | Aligns one to rhythms of saints and blessed souls; energies of art/inspiration; creativity; lessons of wastefulness and repression; spirituality and the awakening of the inner child; expressiveness (good or bad); optimism. |
| 4 | Aligns one to the rhythms of the Devas and Divine Men; energies of harmony/balance; building with patience; restricting and insensitive; narrow-mindedness; impracticality; solidarity; integration of energies/learnings from 4 corners of earth. |
| 5 | Aligns one to rhythms of Mother Nature herself; awakening of the microcosm of soul; lessons of freedom and purity; versatility; scattered; resists change and imposes rules; healing; adventuresome; freeing from limitations; psychic powers. |
| 6 | Aligns one with the feminine/mothering energies of the universe; nurturing energies; healing; birth-giving energy rhythms on all levels; rhythms of the educator; cynical and worrisome lessons; responsibility and reliability. |
| 7 | Aligns one to energies of all people and all planes; rhythms of healing for all systems; lessons of self-awareness and truth; rhythms of strong intuition; lessons of criticalness, melancholy & inferiority; wisdom and knowledge. |
| 8 | Aligns one to the energies of the gods & goddesses as they worked through nature in the past; unites physical rhythms of individual with spiritual ones; confidence; occult power; lessons of carelessness & authority; awakens true judgment of character. |
| 9 | Aligns one to *all* healing energies and experiences; rhythm of empathy and transitional forces in the universe; lessons of being hurt and overly sensitive; pessimism and indifference; intuitive love; rhythms of at-one-ment. |

This indicates harmony. If a name matches or can be found within the same triad of numbers, then there is harmony. The following triads are usually harmonizing and beneficial to each other: Rhythms of 1,5,7 / 2,4,8 / 3,6,9. Odd numbered rhythms and even number rhythms are harmonious.

If you find that your name is not in harmony, it can be adjusted to more easily align with the birth rhythm. For example, if Mary Joanne Walker had a birthdate rhythm of 5, there would be difficulty harmonizing the energies of her name with the energies of her birth. Her name has a syllabic rhythm of 6. One is odd and the other is even. Since she cannot change her birthdate, she can change her name. Such a change does not have to be legally done, but can simply be the name used to sign papers, etc. She could call herself Mary Jo Walker, which has a rhythm of five syllables, bringing her name into greater rapport with her birthdate rhythm.

Determining the syllabic rhythmic correspondence is one of the easiest, and it does give a starting point, even if it is not as specific in regards to alignment. It is a way for the individual to adjust his or her name more consciously to attune with the energies that are the foundation in which they are working (reflected by the birthdate). These next few ways of aligning your name with the birth rhythms will be more specific.

B. The letters within our name also have specific numerical correspondences. There are many methods of assigning numbers to letters and vice versa. Probably the greatest source is that known as the Pythagorean. Instead of approaching the name's rhythms from a syllabic perspective, we approach it from a numerical perspective, assigning a single digit number to each letter. The most common transposition of letters to numbers is through the table below:

| 1 | 2 | 3 | 4 | 5 | 6 | 7 | 8 | 9 |
|---|---|---|---|---|---|---|---|---|
| A | B | C | D | E | F | G | H | I |
| J | K | L | M | N | O | P | Q | R |
| S | T | U | V | W | X | Y | Z | |

It is especially important to understand this when attempting to harmonize with one's birth energies. We can take our full name at birth and convert it into a numerical expression, which can reflect specific universal rhythms predominant within your name.

In numerology there are three numbers derived from the full name of an individual which most reflect specific abilities, potentials and lessons. One of these is derived from the vowels, one from the consonants and one from their combination. What we are most concerned with are the influences, not of the entire name, but rather the first name—our most creative and individual aspect.

In working with these rhythms, again we begin with the predominant vowel of your first name. Using the above chart, you can see that the vowels have an association with specific numbers, and thus specific universal rhythms. In the name *MARY*, the predominant vowel is an *A*. *A* corresponds to the number one and the rhythmic forces associated with it, as described on the chart on page 132. Thus we can align all the vowels with specific rhythms and forces of nature, which is even more significant when we remember that the vowels are symbols of specific elemental forces as well.

A  =  Rhythm of #1
E  =  Rhythm of #5
I  =  Rhythm of #9
O  =  Rhythm of #6
U  =  Rhythm of #3
Y  =  Rhythm of #7

This not only helps us to understand even more of the significance of the individual characters and elements within our names, but it also helps us in aligning our names with the predominant birth rhythms and forces. If our birth rhythm—which is our primary energy foundation—has a rhythm of 5 and our primary vowel is a *U*, then there is harmony, as they are both odd number vibrations.

On the other hand, if our birth rhythm is a four and our primary vowel is an *E* with its numerical equivalent of 5, then there may be difficulty harmonizing the energies. This is where the import and significance of a magical name enters in. We can choose a magical name that has a vowel element, that resonates with our birth rhythm. We choose or create a name that has the same numerical correspondence as our birthdate. We thus initiate a process of creating harmony and alignment with our life purpose and drive.

If nothing else, we must begin to realize that there is much more playing within our lives than we may realize, affecting much of what works and what does not. Through the process of creating a magical name, we begin to re-establish more control over the events and energies of our lives. It is by no means an exact science, but it is a process that leads to greater self-understanding and a greater sense of personal control over one's life circumstances.

Many times, simply employing a name that has a vowel with the same force as the birth rhythm will correct much. It creates a smoothing of life's events and situations, and there occurs a sense of well-being. It is often like having a great pressure lifted. This is why there is really nothing wrong with changing the spelling of one's name to suit yourself. Teenagers are often teased about changing some of the letters around within their names in school. They are simply demonstrating an intuitive awareness that they are more in tune with the change than the old energy of the name. Betty with an "ie" rather than a "y" changes very strongly the rhythms to which the individual resonates. Simply shifting, changing or adding a vowel can do so much to restoring a harmony and resonance with one's foundation and birth energy pattern.

Taking a magical name, that is a variation of the true first name—as is described in the first technique of "Creating a Magical Name"—and then adding a vowel to it that is aligned to the rhythms of your birthdate, is a powerful means of activating tremendous inner forces and potentials.

C. It is also a good idea take your birth name and convert it into a numerical correspondence and assess its compatibility with your birth rhythms. As mentioned, you can explore this in one of three ways—any of which will reflect that there is harmony with the birth number and its forces.

The vowels within the name reflect the inner potentials, as has already been described. We must first transpose them into numbers, add them and then reduce their total to a single digit.

$$
\begin{array}{llll}
\text{M A R Y} & \text{J O A N N} & \text{W A L K E R} \\
\quad 1 \quad\;\; 7 & 6\;\; 1 & \quad\;\; 1 \quad\;\; 5
\end{array}
$$

$$1+7+6+1+1+5 = 21 = 2+1 = 3 \text{ (vowel rhythm)}$$

Compare this number to the birthdate number. Are they the same? Are they at least both odd or both even numbers? If there is not harmony here, do not be discouraged. The harmony with the birth number may show itself through the consonants or through the entire name at birth when they are converted to a numerical and rhythmic correspondence.

The second way of exploring the harmony of the birth name with the birth rhythms is by comparing the numerical symbol for the consonants to the number of your birthdate. Using the previous table, you add the numbers for each consonant within the name, reduce the total to a single digit and compare to the number of your birthdate:

$$
\begin{array}{lllll}
\text{M A R Y} & \text{J O A N N} & \text{W A L K E R} \\
4 \quad 9 \quad 1 & \quad 5\ 5 \quad 5 & 3\ 2 \quad 9
\end{array}
$$

$$4+9+1+5+5+5+3+2+9 = 43 = 4+3 = 7$$

Compare this number to the number for your birthdate. Are they the same? Are they within the same triad? Are they both odd or even? This allows you to discern how much harmony there is between your outer personality and those qualities you have brought with you from the past (reflected by the consonants) with the life goals and rhythms you have set in motion by your date of birth.

The third way is by comparing the number for both the vowels and consonants of your birth name and comparing it to the number for your birthdate. This is often known as the soul's expression in numerology. It reflects the archetypal energies of the inner and the outer, as they work together within this incarnation. It reflects the rhythms you have the best opportunity of expressing within the environs that you have chosen to incarnate within (time, date, place, etc.).

$$
\begin{array}{lll}
\text{M A R Y} & \text{J O A N N} & \text{W A L K E R} \\
4\ \ 1\ 9\ 7 & 1\ 6\ 1\ 5\ 5 & 5\ 1\ 3\ 2\ 5\ 9
\end{array}
$$

$$4+1+9+7+1+6+1+5+5+5+1+3+2+5+9 = 64 = 6+4 = 10$$

$$10 = 1+0 = 1$$

In this case the soul expression has a rhythm of #1, which should also be compared to the birth number. Are they the same? Are they within the same triad of numbers? Are they both odd or even? By comparing these aspects of the birth name with the birth date number, we can determine a great deal about the harmony between the archetypal forces of our name and the archetypal forces set in motion around the time and date and place of birth. While we can't change the latter, we can change the former to harmonize with the latter more effectively.

It is also important to do this with just your first name. Compare all of the rhythms of it with the rhythms of your birthdate. Keep in mind that of all the names, it is the first which holds the strongest key to your most individual creative aspects.

D. It is also important to compare the rhythms of your magical name to your birthdate as well. When you have chosen or are creating your magical name through any of the techniques within this chapter, test their compatibility with your birthdate rhythms and forces. Compare the number for the vowels with your birthdate. Compare the number for the consonants with your birthdate, and compare the combination of the vowels and consonants with it.

If there is not a harmony between them (as determined by being identical, in the same numerical triad or at least being both odd or even), then adjustments might need to be made in the magical name. We can add a letter—vowel or consonant—or combination to smooth it out. Decide what number would need to be added to the magical name's number to harmonize it with the birth number. Insert it within the name. This not only makes the name even more unique, but it does so with greater harmony. It also gives you extra potentials to work with and manifest—all of those associated with the added letter(s). This particular method will be explored in the first technique for creating a magical name.

# 9

# Transforming the Birth Name to a Magical Name

This chapter explores two very basic and easy techniques for transforming the birth name to a magical name. Remember in working with them to apply your own creative imagination to the processes. That is what brings alive the true magic.

## 1. Transforming the Birth Name into a Magical Name

The first is by way of using an ANAGRAM or a form of it. In this method, you rearrange the elements of your name to create a sound that is foreign and unique. You are in essence creating your own word out of your name.

    A. For example, you can take the name ROBERT, and by re-arranging the letters you have the name TERBOR. It becomes exotic sounding, depending upon the pronunciation you give it. It could be pronounced "Tayr-bor." And in this particular case, the *E* becomes the primary vowel and the *O* becomes secondary. The *T*, which in the name ROBERT is the capstone, now becomes the cornerstone consonant and can manifest more quickly.

    B. It is necessary though to determine exactly which elements you may wish to emphasize. You must understand the inner significance of your first name.

C. It is important also to meditate upon the new name, infusing it with the ideals associated with it, and creating a thoughtform around it that will ultimately empower the outer you.

D. You can alter this, adapt it and add on to it in any manner you desire. It is important to remember though that each element will reflect energies that will play themselves out somewhere within your life.

—If there is a particular element (fire, air, water, earth or ether) that you wish to have more access to within your life, simply add the corresponding vowel to your re-structured name. Refer to chapter one, and the information on the vowels to assist you. You can also add the vowel or consonant in order to harmonize this magical name with the birth rhythms and energies, as has been discussed.

—If you wish to emphasize them all or intensify those already within your name, simply add the *A* (element of ether) somewhere within the name. Using the name we created from ROBERT, we add an *A* and we have the name ATERBOR or TERBORA.

E. We can also add consonants, if we so desire, creating a new cornerstone or capstone as you see fit. Simply be as much aware as possible of the significance and the archetypal energies you will be setting in motion around you when you align with that letter by employing it within your magical name.

F. In this manner the birth name, and its inherent energies, becomes an outer reflection of the inner name or essence you are bringing to life. The names we use or create reveal only what we wish them to reveal. By creating a magical name based upon the birth name, we change the energy of the birth name. We initiate a process of empowering it. It will begin to reflect certain inner qualities that are not always discerned because of usual name prejudices. As we come to use and understand this new magical name, we are also activating more of the archetypal force in our birth name, for they are intimately connected. They have the same elements and qualities, but now we are beginning to breathe new life into them. The outer name becomes a microcosm of the inner magical name or the macrocosm. The outer birth name begins to dynamically reflect the new inner magical name. Inner, outer. Physical and spiritual. They are intimately intertwined, but now they are becoming empowered. The outer birth name is now no longer a label that you have to simply endure. It is a dynamic reflection of the magical inner you!

G. What is most important is that you consciously decide on the structure and sound and elements of your name. In forms of Hermetic Magic, it is important to imbue every thought, word, gesture and act with significance. There is a reason for doing so. *Nothing is insignificant! Everything empowers!*

H. This is also one of the most effective means of creating a magical name, because there is already some degree of harmony with the primary elements, forces and potentials within it. Because we have lived with the forces associated with the birth name, there is some degree of resonance. By employing them in a new, more conscious manner we take on the responsibility of activating them and controlling them more constructively. We are telling the universe, "I am ready to handle all the power with which I was born!"

## 2. The Intuitional Realization of the Magical Name

It is not unusual for an individual to discover a magical name simply through his or her own intuition. This name may take many forms, some of which will be elaborated upon within this text. It may be foreign and exotic, a name of a god or goddess that reflects an energy pattern that the individual is moving into, or it may even be a name associated with nature and the nature kingdom. It may be a familiar name or it may be one in which the individual feels "uncannily" drawn.

One of the best means of uncovering an intuitional awareness of a magical name is by exploration of and meditation upon one's birth name. Quite often, as you come to understand the significance of your name, its meaning, sounds, rhythms and symbology, it will bring to light an aspect within you that has its own name. It is the author's opinion that many of the "exotic channelings" currently experienced, and the names of those beings "channeled" may in fact reflect a magical name from the individual's past whose

thoughtform has been re-awakened. The personality being channeled, may be a past life personality, complete with name and energy, developed in that lifetime. (This is not to say that channeling is
not what it is presented to be or that there is conscious misdirection.
It simply means that we have to try as much as possible to discern
the energies operating in and around us at all times. There are many
forms of channeling, and many possible explanations. Knowledge
and discrimination are of key importance, and begin with one's self.
"KNOW THYSELF" was not a precept of the ancient mystery
schools for inconsequential reasons. Our name opens up a "channel" for our highest potential and awareness to manifest. This is the
key importance of name enchantment.)

Part of the intuitional realization of our magical name can
come through the meanings of our names. In the index of this work
is a list of names, their basic meanings, along with two variations of
affirmations as applied to those names. The basic meaning of the
name, when meditated upon, often may trigger a name or a quality
that is most capable of being manifested by you.

As you meditate upon the elements of your name, you may
find that certain qualities and characteristics are more prominently
associated with your name than others. It is not unusual for an individual to take that quality as his or her magical name. For example,
the name ELIZABETH means "house of God or consecrated to
God." An individual with the birth name of ELIZABETH could take
on a magical name associated with the quality inherent within the
meaning of this name. In this case, a magical name for ELIZABETH
could be "CONSECRATION."

We can use abstract qualities and characteristics as our magical
names. This is even more empowering if the quality we choose as
our name aligns with a quality reflected within the birth name, although we are not limited to such qualities. We may wish to choose
a quality that we want to develop and manifest more strongly in
dealing with our life situations and in meeting our personal life
goals. We must keep in mind though to treat it like any name. This
means that the vowels and consonants of the "quality" we are using
as our magical name must be explored as well. Together those aspects work together to create an expression of that quality. For example, if your magical name is JOY, you must look at the significance of the J, the O and the Y. Together the energies of all three letters will activate an energy within your life so that you can manifest

a unique expression of joy!

Another way in which the intuition may reveal a magical name possibility is through meditational imagery. Some names have ties to powers in nature. When such names are meditated upon, that force behind the name may reveal a specific image of something in nature. It may reveal a tree, a flower or even an animal. These are totems, images reflecting specific forces operating around you. Most common are names associated with trees and flowers. This nature aspect will be explored in detail in part four.

An aspect of it though must be touched upon in regards to intuitional creation of a magical name. Some names have meanings that align them with nature in some form, as well as with an abstract quality. "Bruce" is a name which literally means "dweller in a thicket or grove." "Iris" means "the rainbow."

Many names have a tie to the nature realm, even if not recognized. Many names have an origin that is obscure, but as one meditates upon the elements within it, its source may be re-connected. This may manifest in images of specific animals or plants. The name is tied to archetypal forces. Those forces may translate themselves in meditation as specific images, images to which you can relate. This image of nature can become the basis for a magical name and a corresponding thoughtform.

You must first come to discern the qualities of the nature image. Those of the plant kingdom will be explored in great detail in the next chapter. Others may have to be discerned by you as an individual. Study the totem animal. What are its primary qualities and behaviors? Go to your library and check out a book upon that animal. There is usually one or two primary qualities associated with every animal. Incorporate those qualities into your magical name and image. For example, the name "Byron" means "bear." A bear is strong. Thus a possible magical name for someone named Byron could be "Strong Bear."

If there is a quality that you feel a need to manifest more fully, incorporate that with this name. Maybe gentleness needs to be expressed more fully. In this case, Byron may wish to use as his magical name "Gentle Bear." A bear is innately strong, but in this case the quality of gentleness is also being activated, thus such strength has a greater potential for manifesting in a gentle manner.

Some names may not have ties to specific forces of nature, but as you meditate upon your birth name, you may find that it elicits certain images of nature. The subconscious mind serves as translator and mediator between archetypal energies and how they reveal themselves and play out within the physical life and the physical consciousness. The image received in meditation is one that reflects the archetypal energies as they are playing currently within your life. The image is one that reflects those same energies. The subconscious mind translates them into imagery to which it can relate. Thus as you meditate upon your name, you may discover a "totem" that can serve as the basis of your magical name.

Often there are aspects of nature—animal or plant, etc.—that we relate to more than others. One way of discerning or choosing an animal totem of nature is by aligning yourself intuitively with the element of the primary vowel within your name. If the primary vowel is an *E*, you may wish to align or discover a totem that is associated with air. This could be a bird of any kind. Meditating upon your name, looking for a bird to reveal itself is an excellent way. Then you assign a quality. For example, if your name were MEG, the element of air (the vowel *E*) would be the predominant element. Maybe during meditation a sparrow was seen. Also maybe MEG wants to brighten her own life and the lives of others more effectively. She could use as her magical name "Bright Sparrow."

Much is being presently explored concerning shamanism and the finding of one's own spiritual totem. This is a way of doing so, by working with one's own name. The next step is to then build a thoughtform into the aura of that image. Seeing oneself as a "Bright Sparrow" or a "Gentle Bear" or whatever you decide will start the process of change. This totem—especially if connected to the potential and the elemental force of the primary vowel within your name—will grow each day. You are translating an abstract force into a more substantial image that can effectively ground and direct those archetypal forces productively. It is always easier to call upon a specific image, rather than an abstract force behind an image.

The following meditation can be used to discover your name totem which can then be used as part of a magical name if you desire. Remember that it is an image that reflects the archetypal force associated with your name. This is especially effective if your name has no discernible ties to something within nature. In chapter four we will look more closely at names associated with the plant and mineral kingdoms.

## *DISCOVERING YOUR NAME TOTEM*

As you allow yourself to relax, making sure that you will be undisturbed, pull your energies and attention within yourself. Begin some rhythmic breathing. As you inhale, sound your first name silently within your mind. As you exhale sound it softly, but audibly. Continue this for several moments. Think about the meaning of your name. Think of the primary vowel and the element associated with it. Think about what you have read concerning the energies of your name. Allow yourself to relax, and visualize the following scene as best you can.

You are standing within a wide open field. The air is still and there is calmness around you. It is dusk, that powerful time between day and night. The sun is still visible, although it is setting. The moon has also risen. It is the time when the sun and moon share the sky. It is the time when the physical meets the spiritual, the inner meets the outer.

Before you stands a tall oak tree. Its bark is gnarled and twisted, and its roots extend far into the heart of the earth—connecting with that which is not visible. Its branches block the view of the sky as you stand beneath it. Somehow you know that it is like your name—it hides much from your view.

At the base of the tree is a small opening, just large enough to squeeze through if you bend over. Carved above the opening is your name. It is an open invitation. With one last look toward the setting sun, you step carefully into the darkness within.

There is the smell of old moss and moist wood. It smells as ancient as it appears, and as you squeeze through the narrow opening, you find that you are soon able to stand erect. You breathe a little easier. You pause, catching your breath and summon your courage to proceed. It is then that you hear the whispers.

At first it is faint, barely discernible. You hold perfectly still to insure that the sound is not your own movement. The sound is soft, but clear. It is the soft whisper of your name coming from in front of you, as if inviting you. In the darkness of the inner tree, it is a haunting sound. Others have used your name in the past—some have shouted it, some have used it in anger or irritation. It has been spoken in love, but never has it quite had this sound or effect. It seems to touch a primal nerve. It touches the core of you, at once stimulating you and yet somehow it is a little frightening, as if touching an aspect of you that you have neither seen nor recognized.

It coaxes you through the dark, deeper within the tree itself. It is hypnotic, and you know that it is sounding forth that which you have awaited a long time. You are not sure what that is or what it will be. You have never been sure, but you do know that you will recognize the reality of it when confronted by it.

You notice that it is growing lighter. You are not sure whether it is due to your eyes adjusting to the dark or whether something new is being introduced into the environment. Then you see ahead of you a torch burning, illuminating the path you are on.

The path is narrow, and the sides are steep and ridged with the inner veins and arteries of the tree. You touch your hand to the sides of it, and surprisingly it feels warm. As if in response, you hear your name again—still a whisper and yet more distinct.

The torch rests at the top of a steep, descending path, illuminated by sporadic torches. The path twists and turns, hiding its destination from your sight. You hesitate momentarily, and then you begin your descent. You place your feet carefully for the path is covered in spots with slick moss. The further you descend, the brighter the light becomes. All the while you hear the periodic whispering of your name.

The path slowly spirals down, as if leading you into the heart of the earth itself. You feel as if you are following the roots of this tree—your tree—to the center of your life. You know that you are being led to a primal point of life and energy within yourself.

It is then that you see the end of the tunnel. Ahead of you is a cavelike opening through which you step out. You find yourself in a meadow of bright sunlight and all the greens of nature. In the distance is a river of crystalline waters running through the meadow to a distant yet visible ocean.

Wildflowers of every color fill your senses. The grasses are emerald, and at the edge of the meadow is a forest of rich dark greens—the colors of primeval life at its purest.

Across the meadow on the other side of the river is a mountain of pines, extending upward into the clouds. The rays of the sun reflect off its crest like radiant fires . The warmth of the sun fills your body with a fire that soothes and heals, chasing away all remaining fears. A soft breeze carries the exotic fragrances of the meadows to you, stimulating images and memories of far away places and times. The sound of the river calms the emotions, relaxing you. The feel of the soft grass is comforting and nurturing. You feel so much at home, and you hear your name whispered once more.

Next to the river is a stone, carved into the shape of a chair. You settle yourself comfortably within it. It fits your form perfectly. From this position you can see all areas of the meadow—the grasses, the forest, the tall mountain, the river and the distant ocean. There is a sense of peace, and you close your eyes to absorb it.

As your eyes close, the whispering of your name comes from all directions. It is as if the river itself whispers your name. The winds carry its sound to you as well. From the meadow grasses and the forest, and even down from the mountain comes the sound of your name. And then it stops.

You slowly open your eyes. You scan the meadow, the forests and the distant ocean. You look toward the crest of the distant mountain, and you tilt your head to the wind. You look down into the waters of the river. And as you look about, your breath catches. There is movement. It may come from the river or the ocean. It may move across the meadow out of the forest. It may wing across the sky or circle the mountaintops. It may be large or small.

There is before your eyes an animal of great beauty. It moves quietly, simply. Its eyes seek you out and hold your gaze. Never have you seen anything so wonderful, so unique—so magnificent! There is no fear. There is only recognition and wonder.

As if in response to your thoughts, you hear your name whispered once more, and the animal moves. It is a movement which indicates its unique power and strength and then it disappears before your eyes.

You stand up, looking about you. Had you been dreaming? Had it all been simple imagination? You scan the skies. You search the edges of the forests. You look to the waters. Nothing.

Had you done something to offend it? You stand confused and unsure. It had been so beautiful, such a unique expression of life! It deserved to be honored and respected. And you hear your name called.

You turn towards the tunnel through which you came. There in the opening is your totem. You run towards it, and as you stand before it, its eyes holding yours, it melts into you, becoming part of you. You shiver with the feel of its energy coming to life within you, and your laughter and joy fills the meadow. You understand. As you give honor and respect to the energies within you, they will serve you as your guide and companion. As you claim your own power, you connect to your true self.

You step into the tunnel to find it now brightly lit. The path is short and straight, and you find yourself stepping out through that opening within the oak tree. You close your eyes and you see within your mind's eyes your name totem strong and alive within your energy. And you understand that it is there to be claimed and called upon for all time.

## 3. Choosing a Name from the Kingdom of Nature

To some degree, this technique for choosing a magical name was touched upon in the section on intuitional realization. This technique actually involves more of an alignment with the archetypal forces operating behind the plant and mineral kingdoms.

Many who are into magical practices, those who work with pagan and Wiccan teachings, those who have strong ties to nature can benefit by taking a name that more closely ties the individual's energy to specific energies of nature. Taking a name from the nature kingdom—especially when it is a name which resonates with the birth name and one's individual beliefs—can serve many functions and benefits.

Humans have a tendency to think that we are the only life form upon the planet. As one's awarenesses grow, so does the realization of beings and energies operating beyond the physical level, and yet intimately entwined with it. Some of these beings are more traditionally known as angels, devas, nature spirits—those which have been relegated to fiction, but which are actual beings of light and finer substance than humanity. They work intimately with the care and maintenance of the earth and its life forms.

Within nature there are forces, physical and subtle, which can be used to heal, balance and enlighten. Aligning with these forces can be initiated simply through the taking of a name that resonates with those forces. Every plant, flower, tree, herb, stone, etc. has an energy field that interacts with us. There are archetypal forces working with humanity through these physical manifestations of nature. Learning to align oneself with them and to harmonize our own energies with them through the use of a magical name drawn from nature itself will be the focus of chapters 16-18. We will explore the healing and magical effects of names drawn from Mother Nature herself!

# 10

# Creating a Name
# Through Astrology

This is one of the most effective techniques for creating a magical name. It does require some basic knowledge of your own astrological chart, but it is a way that can enhance the astrological influences in your life and can assist you in understanding such influences more beneficially.

On page 103 the letters of the alphabet are listed with their keynotes, predominant colors and their most common astrological correspondences. We will use this chart to assist us in determining the foundation letters of a magical name.

In all of the variations that follow, it is most important to be aware of the primary element(s) within your birth name. As discussed previously, each of the vowels is associated with a particular element—ether, fire, air, water or earth. It is beneficial to use that same vowel and its element as the "heart" of the magical name. You are not bound to it, but it will give a starting point. If there is an element that you wish to bring out more fully within your life, you may choose its corresponding vowel. There are specific considerations before you choose the primary vowel for your magical name:

— If it is the same as the vowel in your birth name, it may be easier to develop resonance with it. For example, if your birth name is JANE, you may want to use the *A* as the primary vowel for your magical name.

— If you have secondary vowels within your birth name, you may want to use them as the primary vowel within your magical name, thus activating their energies more fully within your life. Keep in mind that secondary vowels—whether silent or pronounced—do influence us, but not as strongly as primary vowels. Again, using the name JANE, instead of using the *A* as the primary vowel for the magical name, you may wish to use the *E* as its primary vowel, thereby more fully activating the play of its energies within your life. The archetypal energies of secondary vowels can thus become equally or more active than the primary vowel of the birth name.

— You may wish to choose a vowel and its corresponding elemental force that is not part of your birth name. In this way you activate energies to which you may not have ready access, and you help round out your universal life experience.

— Whatever vowel you choose, be aware that it has positive and negative expressions associated with it.

— Having decided on the primary vowel(s) you wish to have within your magical name, you must decide on the pronunciation. The manner in which you pronounce the vowels (with long or short sounds) will affect the way in which they play within your life. Refer to the chart on page 29 for a greater elaboration of the effects of the sounds of the vowels.

— Remember that one vowel is not better or worse than any other vowel. They all have their positive and negative aspects, which will manifest uniquely for each one of us.

— It is also a good idea to compare the primary vowel and its elemental association with the element that is associated with your sign of the zodiac. For example, in the name JANE, the primary vowel is an *A* (ether) and its secondary vowel is an *E* (air). If Jane were born in a sign of the zodiac associated with one of these elements, using that vowel as a basis for the magical name will more intensely activate the energies, lessons and potentials associated with that particular sign. We cannot change the influence of the sign of birth, but we can change the manner in which our name harmonizes with it. We can employ a vowel within the magical name that resonates more smoothly with the astrological sign. (The charts on pages 15 and 16 will assist you in this.) Thus if JANE were born in the sign of Taurus (an earth sign), and since neither of her vowels are earth elements, she might want to consider using the vowel *U* as part of her magical name to create greater harmony and resonance with her astrological sign. Remember that each element has its own peculiar expression of universal energy, as do the various combinations. Deciding upon your purpose, and the kinds of energies you wish to invoke within your life will help you in choosing the vowel whose elemental force must play itself out under the influence of the elemental force of your astrological sign.

— Having decided upon the vowel for your magical name and its corresponding element, we can begin the process of working with other astrological correspondences to create the magical name!

## THE MAGICAL TRIAD OF ASTROLOGY

This first technique for working with your astrological chart in creating a magical name requires that you know what your Sun sign, Moon sign and ascendant or rising sign are within your astrological chart. These three aspects form a triad of power that reflects much about your energy make-up as defined by astrology. These are often considered the most influential aspects within the astrological chart.

The Sun is our individuality our spiritual essence. The Moon is our personality and soul essence. The rising sign is the physical matter and the nature of our temperament. They can be looked upon as the masculine and feminine aspects of ourselves (the Sun and Moon) and the way in which they are expressed within our lives (the ascendent or rising sign). A study of basic astrology will reveal greater insight to their significance.

If the Sun and Moon are placed in signs that are harmonious, the will of the individuality and the feelings of the personality can be coordinated. Studying the elements of the sign in which the Sun and Moon are located will help you to understand their degree of harmony.

Having determined what your Sun sign, Moon sign and rising sign are, it then only requires that you translate them into specific letters. The corresponding letters then can form a matrix or skeletal framework in which you can place the vowel you have chosen to form the magical name. On the chart on page 103, you can look up the three signs and find their corresponding letters.

For example, we will use JANE. Jane has chosen to use the silent *E* of her birth name as the primary vowel of her magical name. Jane was born in the sign of Taurus, her Sun sign. After examining her astrological chart, she found that her Moon was in Aries and Aquarius was her rising sign. Using the chart, we find that the letter for Taurus is *F*, the letter for Aries is *H* and the letter for Aquarius is the combination *TZ*. Jane now has a basis of letters to begin forming A MAGICAL NAME.

> E  = element of air
> F  = Taurus (earth)
> H  = Aries (fire)
> TZ = Aquarius (air)

Jane does not have to limit herself to these four letters, but it is important to know that four is the number of the foundation. It can thus be the foundation upon which we create a magical name. We can arrange these letters and add onto them with other vowels or letters to enhance the innate power of the name. Keep in mind that the first consonant will become the cornerstone of the magical name, and the last the capstone. Keep this in mind in creating your magical name.

There are those who will say that you are just making up nonsense words. Remember that a word has no more meaning and significance than what you attribute to it. It may be nonsense to those who don't understand it. The sounds of foreign words may sound nonsensical to those who do not speak the language. With the creation of this magical name, you are re-establishing the language of your own soul.

## ADDING TO THE MAGICAL FOUNDATION

There are a variety of ways of adding to that astrological foundation. If there are specific letters or vowels that you have always been drawn to, include them in the foundation you just established with the primary vowel and the astrological triad. If there is an element that is missing, you can add a letter to round it out.

In the previous example of "Jane," when converted to letters, her triad comprised an earth sign, and air sign and a fire sign. The vowel she chose was also an air elemental vowel. The only major elements she does not have are water and ether (which is comprised of all the elements). Jane may thus wish to include within her magical name, a letter that is associated with the element of water. This could be the vowel *O*, or it could be the letters *CH* for the water sign Cancer, the *N* for the water sign of Scorpio or the *Q* for the water sign of Pisces. She thus has a balance of the four major elements.

Another way of adding to this basic astrological foundation of four letters is by adding the letter(s) for the Sun progression. The progressed Sun within the astrological chart reflects the growth of the personality and personal evolution. We move forward in our growth, moving through the chart at a rate of about one degree a year. If we were born at zero degrees, every thirty years we would move into the influence of the next sign of the zodiac. If you know the degree and sign of birth, count ahead one degree for every year you have lived. Each sign of the zodiac occupies thirty degrees. For example, if you are 35 years old and you were born at twelve degrees Pisces, starting at 12, you count ahead thirty-five degrees.At thirty degrees Pisces, you move into the sign of Aries. If you continue counting, you will find yourself at seventeen degrees Aries. Your Sun has progressed into an Aries influence.

Having determined your "progressed Sun," determine its corresponding letter, and add it to your magical name. This method particularly helps you to activate those energies influencing you astrologically at the current time.

## PLANETARY INFLUENCE IN THE MAGICAL NAME

Every sign of the zodiac has planets that are its rulers or are exalted. To keep your magical name even more mystical and hidden, you may wish to use the letters for the planetary rulers of your triad rather than the letters for the signs themselves. Keep in mind that the planets are not always found within their home "port" or sign, and thus using their letters may activate the energies of the sign within your astrological chart.

| Sign of Zodiac | Mundane Ruler | Exalted | Esoteric Ruler |
|---|---|---|---|
| Aries | Mars | Sun, Pluto | Mercury |
| Taurus | Venus | Moon | Vulcan |
| Gemini | Mercury | Uranus | Venus |
| Cancer | Moon | Jupiter | Neptune |
| Leo | Sun | Neptune | Sun |
| Virgo | Mercury | Uranus | Moon |
| Libra | Venus | Saturn | Uranus |

| Sign of Zodiac | Mundane Ruler | Exalted | Esoteric Ruler |
| --- | --- | --- | --- |
| Scorpio | Mars | Pluto | Mars, Pluto |
| Sagittarius | Jupiter | Mercury | Earth |
| Capricorn | Saturn | Mars | Saturn |
| Aquarius | Uranus | Mercury | Jupiter |
| Pisces | Neptune | Venus | Pluto |

Using our example of Jane. Her Sun was in Taurus, her Moon in Aries and her rising sign was Aquarius. Rather than using the letters for these signs, she may wish to use the letters for their esoteric rulers instead. Since the magical name is an awakening of the hidden forces within ourselves this can be a very powerful variation. The letters would then be:

Taurus (F)—Moon = C (We are using the exalted planet for Taurus since there is no letter assigned to Vulcan.)
Aries (H)—Mercury = B
Aquarius (TZ)—Jupiter = K

Jane thus can use an even more esoteric transposition, creating a very intricate and secretive magical name. The secretiveness of it is very important as will be discussed later.

Along this same line, we can take any planetary aspect which is compatible and beneficial within the astrological chart and activate it more fully within our lives through transposing it into the magical name. This does require that the individual understand the various astrological aspects. If there are specific planetary influences that the individual wishes to stimulate more strongly, employing the letter that corresponds to it is an excellent way of doing so. Any house in which there are three or more planets is a dynamic influence and is well worth considering transposing into components of a magical name. Working with the astrological chart in this manner enables us to choose the forces we want to have active in our lives.

# PART III

# MAGICAL NAMES
# OF MYTHOLOGY

# 11

# Choosing a
# Mythical Name

It is not at all unusual to find individuals using mythical names, names of gods and goddesses, names of heroes and heroines from other cultures and times, as magical names. This is especially common in various magical groups and those of pagan and Wiccan influence. In the latter two, there is often a name chosen to align oneself with the feminine goddesses being worshipped by the particular group or individual.

A major complaint about Christianity by the followers of what is often called the "Old Religion" is that the feminine aspect of the universe has been excluded. Many are thus drawn to the ancient religions in which there may be many of the same "Christian precepts and ethics" but which also place the feminine aspect on equal footing with the masculine. We are all a combination of male and female energies—whether we define them as electric and magnetic, yin and yang, positive and negative, assertive and receptive, etc.

The ancient mystery schools taught that the one god-force manifested in various forms within various societies. The teachings were often quite identical, only expressed in a manner that could be related to by those of that particular society and that particular time. The re-emergence of the ancient teachings and the general purveyance of metaphysical knowledge has greater numbers exploring the ancient teachings, that they might be re-expressed in a manner beneficial to the individual at this particular time within the individual's evolution.

There are those who would condemn anyone who aligned him

or herself with ancient teachings and the so-called pagan gods and goddesses. What is important to realize is that quite often this can help individuals to open to their own creative aspects, and thus discover the divine within themselves. Whether this occurs through Christianity or through the ancient religions is inconsequential. It is important though that the individual find a means of activating his or her own creative aspects and become more productive. Truth comes in many guises, and people need to look beyond the surface to what lies beneath. The archetypal energies express themselves—translate themselves—in many ways.

There is an ancient tale about a man who was successful in all things. He had a fine wife, a loving family, a craft for which he was famous, but he was not happy. He wanted to know Truth. With his wife's permission, he went forth to find Truth. He searched the hills and valleys. He went to small villages and great cities. He searched the forests and crossed wide seas. Then one day, atop a high mountain, in a small cave, he found her.

Truth was a wizened old woman with but a single tooth left in her head. Her hair hung down her shoulders in greasy strands. Her skin was brown and yellow and dry—taut over the bones of her thin body. With a crooked finger, she motioned for this man to step forward, and she greeted him with a voice that was low and pure and lyrical, touching a chord within his heart. The man knew then that he had found Lady Truth.

The man stayed a year and a day with her, until he learned all that she had to teach. And when the year and a day was up, he stood at the mouth of the cave to say his farewell.

"My Lady Truth," he spoke, "you have taught me so much and I wish to do something for you before I leave. Is there anything you wish?"

Lady Truth tilted her head to one side, puzzled upon it for a moment, smiled and raised her ancient finger. "When you speak of me," she said, "tell them I am young and beautiful!"

When we begin to align ourselves with our true soul energies—through something as simple as a magical name—we become young and beautiful again. We learn to express the ancient energies within us anew. Aligning oneself with the ancient mythical beings is a powerful way of doing so. They each not only have their own unique energies, but they also have strong thoughtforms associated with them. The prayers and worship of the past has developed powerful energies around them. When you align yourself with these beings, you are also aligning yourself with the thoughtforms around them. Thus it is very important to choose such a name carefully, for they can be very powerful and overwhelming at times.

When working with the ancient names of mythology, it is important to first grasp a good foundation of the teachings and energies associated with the entire mythology, and not just one individual character's part within it. That one being is part of a grander thoughtform, that will also affect you, as you align yourself with that name.

Myths presented certain mysteries of the universe in a manner unique to the society in which they were taught. There are certain premises underlying the individual energies of the gods and goddesses. What follows is a brief outline of four major mythologies— Greek, Egyptian, Celtic and Teutonic—from which individuals often take magical names.

### SPECIAL CONSIDERATIONS:

— You are by no means limited to one of these four groups. These are often the most popular sources for magical names.

— Choose a mythology toward which you have always been drawn. If it is one of these four fine, otherwise research and explore others to find a name to which you feel some resonance.

— Consider that the name of the god or goddess activates energies just as any name will do. These names also have energies unique unto themselves, going beyond the archetypal forces reflected within the characters of the name itself.

— As you read the myths and tales associated with the one whose name you have taken, you will discover that it may involve energies foreign to those in the physical world. This means that there may be a longer period of adjustment before harmony and resonance is established with the thoughtform and power of the name.

— Most of the gods and goddesses were fallible. They may have expressed very divine characteristics, but many also had human qualities as well. This is quite evident within the Greek and the Teutonic myths. By taking their name, you open yourself to their strengths, as well as any weaknesses they may have as well.

— While many of the followers of the old religions worship the feminine in one of three forms—virgin, mother and wise woman—you do not have to limit yourself to just those forms of the gods and goddesses. Depending on your personal goals, it may be more beneficial to take as your magical name one of the opposite sex.

— Choose the god or goddess name according to your personal goals and not according to which one seems the "most powerful." Complete resonance and alignment with a lesser god or goddess can do more for you than partial alignment with a major god or goddess.

— Most of the gods and goddesses had working relationships of varying sorts with the others of their pantheon. Learning how they related to each other can help you to call upon the others if needed.

— Many myths are tales of great beings who may have actually walked upon the earth at one time, serving as teachers and helpers to humanity. Do not confuse myth with unreality. The tales may be a blend of both. Discrimination is always important. There is often more going on within these myths and tales than what appears upon the surface. There is more going on within our own lives than what appears on the surface. Name enchantment involves the process of uncovering those energies and activities.

— It is also a good idea to familiarize yourself with the beliefs of the people who worshipped these gods and goddesses. Remember that you will be tapping into the thoughtform around them— this can include any energies of misuse.

— Learn about any magical symbols associated with your god or goddess, as these become excellent tools for meditation to activate the power of this being within your own auric field.

— Learn techniques of "assumption of god-forms." In essence, this is the development of the magical body, but in the image of the god or goddess. Learn to be able to visualize this being overshadowing you any time the name is whispered—audibly or not. Every time you hear your birth name called, mentally follow it with the name of the god or goddess you have taken as your magical name. This helps to link their energies, uniting the inner and outer you.

— Do not be in a hurry to manifest their energies. Allow them to enter into your life gently and smoothly.

# 12

# Magical Names from Greek Traditions

The Greek mythology is the mythology of individuality. It is the mythology of becoming the hero or heroine of one's own life. It holds a magic of often standing alone and facing whatever monsters may appear within one's life—human or otherwise. It is a mythology of the quest to overcome one's own weaknesses in order to attain a spiritual goal.

The gods and goddesses of this mythology work intimately with their human counterparts and provide the weapons and tools necessary to the task at hand. As long as proper respect is paid the deity, including appreciation, the individual will have awakened the powers necessary to overcome that which would hinder.

This is a mythology of the interrelationship of the divine with the human. The deities play as much within human lives as humans do in the lives of other humans. Its philosophy embodies individual responsibility and a personalizing of the deific forces of the world. The deities of this pantheon were often very "human" in their responses to the world around them. On one level, it serves to sever the distance between an abstract divine force that operates stoically within the universe, and it enables a more personal and intimate relationship to be established between the divine forces and humanity. It is a mythology that places the divine within reach of the human, and provides directions for the human to discover the divine within him or herself.

A reminder is necessary at this point, and it holds true for all of the pantheons described. When you align yourself with a deity of a particular mythology, you may activate within your life circumstances similar to the events within the mythic lives of the deity. Also, keep in mind that there are other major figures within the myths and tales that are not part of the pantheon of deities. In the Greek myths there are figures such as Heracles, Orpheus, Theseus, Perseus, Odysseus, etc. whose names can be taken as your own magical name as well. They also have unique qualities and characteristics, but you may also manifest circumstances within your own life that are similar to the circumstances of these characters.

## ZEUS

Zeus is the god of thunder, the air and the sky. He rules the winds and thus can be beneficial to anyone with an *E* within the birth name. He opens knowledge of law and order, justice and proper leadership. His energies may lead to being overly paternal. There may manifest tendencies toward chauvinism, domination and dictatorship as well. His magical symbols are the oak tree and the eagle, and the color purple resonates with his energies.

## HERA

Hera is the goddess of marriage and all feminine energies. She awakens an innate sense of the noble beauty of oneself and others, and her name is tied to the powers of fidelity. Unbalanced, her energies may manifest in one's life with jealousy, bickering and over-dependence. Her magical symbols are the scepter and cuckoo and the peacock. The color she resonates with and may activate within one's aura is emerald green.

## ATHENA

Athena is a warrior goddess, as well as a goddess of wisdom. She protects the brave, and activates innate bravery within the individual. She is a virgin goddess, and stimulates inspiration and ability at all domestic crafts. Her energies may stimulate over- assertive tendencies and jealousy. It may activate the "battle-axe" syndrome, but it stimulates some dynamic primal feminine energy, which may never have been experienced before—at least with this intensity. Her magical symbols are the helmet and aegis, as well as the spear and the shield. The owl is also associated with her, and red and gold are her colors.

## APOLLO

Apollo is the Sun god, the god of prophecy, music, art and

beauty. Awakening one's own healing nature through creative inspiration can often be achieved by alignment with this being. This name and energy may require a balancing of the male aspects of the psyche, and it may stimulate a rebelliousness that must be controlled. There are often lessons involved in balancing youthfulness and aging as well. The magical symbols associated with Apollo are the Sun, archery and the lyre. Yellow-gold is the color activated by alignment with him.

## ARTEMIS

Artemis is the goddess of the forest and the Moon. She is also a virgin goddess, and she protects all children and animals which are sacred to her. If these are important to your own goals, then you can do no better than to align with her. She provides an energy for mental healing abilities, awakening such within the individual. These are energies associated with both the air and water. She awakens a new sense of purity and reliability. The safety and welfare of all women fall under her guise, and she strongly activates an energy of protection against psychic attack. Those who take this name should be cautioned against suppressing their sexuality and resisting growing up. Her energies may also manifest a disapproval of others. Her magical symbols are the bear and the dog, and the color she activates within the aura is amethyst.

## HERMES

Hermes is the god of communication, initiation and magic. Movement of all kinds, the element of air, learning and healing are activated within one's life by alignment with this name and the being that uses it. This is one of the gods of medicine. The energy of this name can manifest in inconstancy if not guarded against. Insecurity and too many transitions may also manifest. Any tendency toward insecurity could also reveal itself so that it can be dealt with by the individual. The magical symbols which help activate the archetypal energies of the name are the winged hat, the winged sandals and the caduceus. This name will activate the energies and color of silver within the auric field.

## ARES

Ares is the god of war and passion. To the Romans (who borrowed their gods from the Greeks), Ares was also a god of nature and fertility, a protector—especially of new ideas and new projects.

His is the energy of discipline, and the power to overcome violence. This name and the energies associated with it will stimulate opportunities to develop discipline, to overcome any sense of combativeness and can be used to awaken the ability to slay one's dragons. The magical symbols which assist in manifesting the energies of this being are all weapons. Once activated, it will manifest with an energy and color of scarlet-red.

## HEPHAESTUS

Hephaestus is the god of craftsmanship. Alignment with his energies will activate one's own creative skills. He was the fire smithy of the gods, and thus there is resonance with anyone who has fire within his or her name. His is the energy of finding oneself—regardless of outside circumstances. He activates the energy of pride in one's own abilities regardless of outside appearances. His is an energy of overcoming childhood traumas, and it can activate any tendency toward being overly critical of oneself. Thus the opportunity to deal with low self-esteem and to rise above it by discovering one's own unique talent(s) can be activated by this name, and alignment with this being. The symbols and images which facilitate alignment with this name are the net and the hammer and tongs. Once activated, the energies will manifest through the color bronze.

## APHRODITE

Aphrodite is the goddess of love and beauty. She awakens the passions, and she helps to align one with the forces of nature, especially those active within gardens and flowers. Her name and the energies associated with it awaken proper balance and open one to developing proper expression of the sexual energies. Those who take this as the magical name must learn to see their own self-beauty and the beauty that lies within all people. Jealousy, shyness and/ or promiscuity may be tendencies to overcome by aligning with this name. The symbols and images which help call forth the energies of this name are the dove, the porpoise, the girdle and the rose. Her color is turquoise.

## POSEIDON

Poseidon is the great god of the waters, and thus anyone with a strong water element within their name will resonate at some level with his energy. This name—this being—awakens the intuition of great depth. He stimulates the power of dreams and the ability to control and direct them. He is a tie to the primordial depths. Those who take this as a magical name may find themselves overwhelmed by the unconscious mind and all that lies within it. It can be easy to get lost or to drown within its waters. The symbols and images which help to manifest its energies within the auric field are the conch shell, the trident, the white horse and all marine life. This name often activates the color coral within the aura.

## HESTIA

Hestia is the goddess of home and the home fires. She guards and protects the family and awakens a greater sense of dutifulness to the family within one's life, be it blood family or a family of friends. She awakens an energy for feeling secure and safe within the environment one calls home. Hers is a combination of the mother energy and the wise woman energy, for there occurs the ability to assist others with their problems. There may manifest though a tendency to take ownership of others problems which must be guarded against. There may also arise an unwillingness to step out of the security of one's home and try new things. Alignment with this name can awaken the energies to assist in overcoming problems of the ego. Her symbols are the veil and the fireplace, and she will awaken the color white within one's auric field.

## DEMETER

Demeter is the mother goddess of Greek myth. She is the goddess whose energies help the soil and assist all growing things. This is a name whose energies enable you to connect with the forces and rhythms of Mother Earth. She brings the potential for fulfillment and the development of a life philosophy. The energies of this name may have a tendency to make one overly maternal if care is not taken. It is a name whose energies require letting go of the past , and it may also manifest a tendency toward scolding. Her magical symbols and images are the cornflower and corn. The color energy activated and resonating with this name are the earth tones and the yellow of corn.

## PERSEPHONE

Persephone is the daughter of Demeter who is taken from her by Hades (Pluto). From her comes the Mysteries of Eleusis. Her name and energy awaken the process of death and rebirth. It can awaken the ability to cross both kingdoms—those of the physical and the invisible—and back again. It is through her that one can touch the hidden feminine energies within and bring them out into the light. It can lead one toward unpredictable mood changes and a discovery of the dark side of the feminine aspect. She brings the seeds of new life in cyclic rhythms. Her symbol is the pomegranate, and the colors activated are citrines, russets and olive greens.

## HADES / PLUTO

This is the god of the underworld who snatched Persephone and carried her off. This is an extremely powerful name as its energy can easily overwhelm. It has the potential for manifesting great wealth, drawing from the deep resources of the subconscious (underworld). It activates an energy that will require the individual learn to navigate and work within the astral plane safely. Any tendency toward jealousy may have to be controlled. This is a name with ties to the energy of a being who oversees the lower kingdoms of the subconscious. It may awaken opportunities to learn the mystical secrets of death. The symbol is the helmet of invisibility, used for astral projection that is consciously controlled. The color is black, which like white has the full light spectrum within it.

## HECATE

Hecate is the goddess of the Moon, most often represented as a crone or the wise woman. Her name and essence open one to powerful forms of magic and mysticism, and can manifest sudden and powerful psychism, which if not handled correctly can easily create imbalance on all levels of one's life. This is a name that has a potential to awaken wisdom with opportunities to gain wealth. It may manifest a "dabbling" in the magical arts that if not used properly may have strong repercussions. This is a force which can easily overwhelm, resulting in self-delusion and even a loss of personal identity. Her symbols and images are the black, hooded cloak, the dark of the Moon and the hellhound. Her color is black with silver flecks.

## DIONYSUS

This is the god of magic and healing. It is a name whose essence and energies bring great opportunity and potential for transforming energies. It awakens a psychic sensitivity. It has strong associations with the wise satyr Silenus. This is a name which activates the opportunity to face and conquer personal weaknesses and obsessions. It can stimulate an over-enthusiasm and the need to develop proper forms of expressing oneself. The magical symbols are the staff of ivy and the thyrsus which is effective for awakening the alchemical process within one's own life. The colors are the red burgundy of the grape and the green of ivy.

## PAN

Pan is the god of prophecy and the awakening of the healing forces of nature. It is a name whose essence can stimulate powerful forms of physical healing within one's life, as well as awakening the opportunity to learn to use the healing remedies derived from nature itself—herbs, flowers, stones, etc. Its energy is unpredictable in how it manifests for the individual. It may make the individual overly independent and mistrusting of others, creating a kind of "drop-out" attitude. The symbol is the syrinx or the pan flute. The colors are the greens of the forest.

## THEMIS

Themis is a lesser deity within the Greek pantheon, but the name itself is very powerful. She was the goddess of justice and counseling. It is a name that can be quite beneficial to those involved in any form of counseling. This name awakens the energy that requires the individual to maintain order. It is also a name that is tied to awakening the ability to achieve more from ceremonial rituals. It can make one stoic to varying degrees and, if not balanced and expressed properly, its energies may lead to being overly critical and dogmatic. She awakens inner wisdom and clairaudience. The colors are the deep purples of ceremony, and its symbols and images are all ceremonial robes and symbols of justice and counseling.

## IRIS

Iris is considered a lesser deity, but it is a name whose essence can be powerfully evocative within one's life. It awakens the energy of telepathy and hope. She was a messenger to the gods and thus could travel on all realms. This same potential can be awakened in those who take her name. The name means "rainbow," and the rainbow is a powerful symbol of hope and good news. It is a name whose energies can assist the individual in linking the inner with the outer. Her name holds an energy that brings illumination and solace. It may place the individual in a position of assisting others, often at inopportune times. Its energy assists the individual in getting beyond the initiatory storms, or to perceive the light that will come when the storm is weathered. The symbols are the rainbow and golden wings upon the shoulder. The color energies activated are those of the seven colors of the rainbow itself.

## ILYTHIA

Ilythia is the goddess of childbirth. The name is both beautiful and powerful, and the essences behind it serve to relieve women who are in pain. Ilythia presides over all births, physical and otherwise. Through her energies, you can give birth to the child within you. Her energies bring relief to the pains of labor, including the labors of new endeavors within our lives. These too are births. She activates an energy which helps one to see the child within that needs to be born, and she provides the energy to enable the individual to go through the pains of labor to a successful birth. Her symbols are the torch light and the encouraging hand extended. The colors are those of the soft, baby grass greens of early spring.

There are, of course, other gods and goddesses—great and small—within the Greek pantheon. By exploring the myths and their characters, you find that certain ones will stand out more strongly for you. Meditate upon them and remember that the energies associated with them and their name may manifest positively, negatively or even in an entirely alternate form. It all depends upon you.

# 13

# Magical Names from Egyptian Traditions

Egypt was the center for the dissemination of great mysteries to the world. It influenced and was influenced by most major societies. Its own distinct spiritual cosmology often appears quite complex. It is the seat of much of the "magic" that has come down to us in modern times.

The Egyptian pantheon and mythology have similarities with others, as they all do in varying degrees. The Egyptian mythology teaches us about the process of alchemy, the transmutation of energies through a greater understanding of birth, death, resurrection and rebirth. Much of its premise comes to us through what is known as the Book of the Dead, which more literally translates as the Book of the Coming Forth. It teaches us the state of our soul and what happens to us after the transition known as death.

The Egyptians have a mythology that is balanced in regard to the activities of male and female deities. Both are highly regarded, each with its own distinct energies. The magic involved with them, if invoked properly, would be done in a manner of great control. Theirs is often a magic of "mind over matter."

The gods and goddesses of this pantheon are not easily categorized. A prominent theory exists that explains this as the result of them existing as beings not originally part of this solar system. Still they seem to have an understanding of the human weaknesses, and they demonstrate a higher spiritual ability in their desire to assist humanity in spite of such limitations.

## RA

Ra is a major Sun god of the Egyptian mysteries. Some sources speak of Amun and Ra as being the same. Others tell us that all of the gods of the Egyptian pantheon are simply different manifestations of Ra. His name and essence invoke energies of new life. It opens the elements of the air—especially the wind. This is a name which can stir the primal creative forces within the individual. The magical symbols which help to manifest his force within your life are the obelisk, the hawk and the uraeus. The color force activated is that of the golden sunshine.

## OSIRIS

Osiris is the king priest, and his name can help one to unfold any capability towards such. The energy associated with his essence is that of higher wisdom, justice and true spiritual strength. Osiris awakens a realization of the vivifying powers of nature, and helps one to attune more closely to the forces of nature in assisting one's own growth. The energies of Osiris—whether invoked through the use of his name or in any other form—are very powerful, requiring great control, self-sacrifice and self-discipline. If these qualities are absent then the energy invoked may stimulate delusion and unreliability. His symbols are the crook and flail, along with the tet (a tree). The colors activated are white and green.

## ISIS

Isis is the goddess of the Moon and of magic. She is a mother goddess and a protectress of the young. Her name and essence invoke greater compassion and can open one to being able to look beyond the veil which separates the physical from the spiritual. She awakens psychic energies within the individual, and the ability to work with them for "magical manifestations." This, of course, must be balanced and controlled carefully, or it will be easy to cross that thin line which separates white from black magic. It may also stimulate a manifestation of any tendency toward superstition and an over-active imagination. Anyone working with name enchantment can do no better than to invoke her influence. One legend tells us that she acquired her tremendous magical powers from Ra himself, by tricking him into revealing his name to her—thereby giving her full access to *all* of his magical knowledge. Her symbols are the throne, the buckle, the veil behind the throne and wings. Her color is that of sky blue.

## HORUS

Horus is one of the savior gods. He is a Sun god whose energies awaken artistic abilities, musical knowledge (for health and light) and general healing capacities. His is the energy of the patron of families. Great strength and an ability to protect oneself and that which is held dear is awakened by this name and its corresponding energies. Horus also stimulates any prophetic tendencies as well. The energies of Horus may also stimulate any tendencies toward vengeance and insecurity so that they can be balanced within one's life. His magical symbols are those of the hawk and the all-seeing eye. His colors are bright yellow and gold.

## BAST

Bast is the sister of Horus, and is the goddess of joy. Her energies can help attune one to the animal kingdom, particularly the cat family. The energies of this name awaken any mental healing abilities, intuition and the opportunities to express grace and experience joy. She is the patroness of marriages. An imbalance in working with her energies may awaken an insensitivity or indifference towards others. It may manifest the opportunity to deal with the influences of others within your life. The sistrum and the cat are her symbols (including the lion). The color her name may awaken within the auric field is usually a combination of yellow-gold and turquoise.

## THOTH

Thoth is the master of medicine, learning and magic. He was the scribe of the gods and goddesses, and many of the ancient mysteries are ascribed to his teachings. Alignment with his energies will awaken the opportunity to develop intellectual and mental forms of magic. His energy can help you to understand the laws of fate and time. The energy of this name can link you to new opportunities in education and communication. If not balanced properly, it can create misfortune. "Nothing is more dangerous than a little bit of knowledge" is a warning to be heeded by those who take this as their magical name. False intellectualism may manifest, and interference with the laws of time and karma. The primary symbol for Thoth is the caduceus, and the color forces activated are violet and amethyst.

## HATHOR

Hathor is a goddess that is sometimes known as the "cow of heaven" as she nourishes the gods and goddesses—along with humanity. It is through her energy that the comforts of life can more easily manifest. Her energy is very protective of women. When used as a magical name, it can activate those same qualities within the individual. It awakens a greater sense of beauty and strength. She is also the patroness of astrology and thus her energies can help the individual understand the influences of the stars. It endows one with great ability to fight—especially in defense. If not activated and utilized in a balanced manner, the energies activated by her name can manifest in vacillation and a need to learn to draw upon one's own spiritual strength. Her symbols are the mirror, the sycamore tree and the cow. The color force that resonates most strongly with her is coral.

## NEPTHYS

Nepthys is a goddess of intuition and tranquility. She is one who is sometimes known as the revealer. In many ways she is comparable to Aphrodite. Her name and energy stimulate psychic sensitivity. She guards that which is hidden, and alignment with her energies can make such more accessible, this includes not only psychic gifts but dream consciousness as well. She can be associated with the dark aspects of the Moon. If her energies are expressed in an unbalanced manner it may open the individual to self-delusion and deception. Anonymity often can result, and the individual who aligns with her energies must learn "strength through silence." Her symbols are the chalice and basket, and the color forces of her energies are pale greens and silver grays.

## PTAH

Ptah is the Egyptian god of craftsmanship and science. Alignment with his energies can open one to understanding and applying the laws of science. He stimulates invention and ingenuity, and he is the patron of builders. He was also known to manifest miracles within the lives of humans. His energy awakens a gentle masculinity, often quite contrary to what is normally associated with the masculine life force. His energy will teach the individual to labor for the joy and sake of itself, and he requires the individual to build from a new solid foundation. His symbols are the mason tools and his color force is violet.

## ANUBIS

Anubis is the son of Nepthys and Osiris. His energies are those of guardianship and guidance, particularly through the lower astral realms and the realms of sleep. Alignment with his energies awakens inner guidance and opens the opportunities to develop an ability to control dreams and navigate the inner dimensions. He is also considered the patron of lost things. Alignment with this energy may manifest lessons on the dangers of foolhardiness and the need to keep one's humor. His symbols are those of the jackal and sometimes the sarcophagus. The colors are black and silver.

## MAAT

Sometimes considered a feminine aspect of Thoth, Maat is the goddess of truth. Her energies awaken an ability to develop truth as a power within one's life. She is associated with affairs of the heart and manifesting discriminating justice. She helps the individual put his or her own life karma into perspective. Unbalanced, it may manifest a need to discern and hold to one's own truth. This name and the energies behind it can open the individual to discerning the true intentions of others. Her symbols are those of the scales and the feather by which she balances the scales. Her energies may manifest within the aura as violet or even as lapis lazuli.

## SEKHMET

Sekhmet is often seen as the other side of Hathor, although some traditions put her as the wife of Ptah. She is a warrior goddess whose energies can either heal and nourish or break and destroy, depending on whether the individual aligns with them in a positive or negative manner. Hers is an energy of great protection and the applying of wisdom to force. Her energy is such that it manifests opportunities to right wrongs, but unless handled properly and used discriminately, it could bring upon the individual an intensification of force that could easily rebound. Her symbols are the lioness and the mirror, along with the sun disc. Her colors are copper and deep yellows.

# 14

# Magical Names from Celtic Traditions

The Celtic pantheon embodies a magnificently romantic, creative and intuitional mysticism. Although predominantly a matriarchal system, it does not neglect the masculine aspects. It can be quite complex as it was influenced by various races of people.

The Celtic mysticism is that of awakening one's own intuitive and creative aspects and expressing them in a uniquely individualistic manner. This is not only found within the pantheon of gods and goddesses but also within the adventures of the heroes and heroines within the legends and myths. The tales of Arthur, Merlin and Guinevere and the Knights of the Round Table still inspire and intrigue.

The Celtic myth and mysticism is that of the discovery of the innermost fires of the individual. It embraced the feminine in all three of its aspects—virgin, mother and wise woman. It embraced and reverenced nature in all of its forms. Trees and flowers were given names and personalities, reflecting the archetypal energies recognized within them. It was a religion of the Mother Earth.

The Celtic pantheon is one of numerous deities, drawing from the Irish, Welsh, Scottish and English peoples. To try and describe the energies and influences of the names of all the deities associated with the Celtic and Druidic religion is beyond the scope of this work. Fifteen have thus been selected in order to show how this pantheon can be used to activate the play of archetypal energies within one's life by taking upon oneself the magical name of the deity, the hero or the heroine.

You also do not have to limit yourself to just the names of the deities. The characters of the tales of King Arthur and the Knights of the Round Table are powerful names to use as your own magical name. These tales are filled with mysticism, magic and archetypal symbolism, and many occult groups have used their names as means of establishing a collective consciousness within the group. The Arthur and Grail legends are steeped in a symbology both magical and educational and for those drawn to the Celtic tradition, some study of these legends and tales—and their inner significance—should be given. It is in fact one of the best tales for enabling an individual to bridge the ancient teachings with modern Christian concepts.

The Celtic tradition is one rich in the magic of music and words, predominantly through the bardic tradition which was briefly mentioned earlier. The bardic "magicians" were skilled in the use of words and names as a powerful tool for healing and teaching.

The Celtic tradition is one of allowing the intuitive feminine and creative forces to reveal themselves in the manner appropriate for the individual. Preconceived notions must be gotten rid of as the gods and goddesses of this tradition are extremely individualistic and approach the individual as is needed more than when called upon.

Green is the predominant color of the Celtic tradition. It is the color of Mother Earth and the ties to the creative feminine as expressed within the physical. According to Murry Hope, *Practical Celtic Magic*, "In the Celtic system one simply tunes into the 'Green Ray' and waits. Of course, one studies all of the relevant literature, meditates on whatever aspect one feels drawn to...but as regards the deity, he or she will come to you when they deem fit, and it may not be exactly what you expect, so dispel any preconceived ideas to start with."

The gods and goddesses do have specific characteristics as in other pantheons, along with their own "magical" symbols. The difference between their symbols and those of other pantheons is that they are not invoking of the specific deity as much as they are an attuning device to the entire Celtic tradition. They play upon your energy to attune it so that you are more receptive (the feminine aspect as worshipped by the Celts) to a specific influence as is suited to you and your own energies. Along this same note, the colors associated with the Celtic deities vary from individual to individual. When they do present themselves, they often do so in a color whose energy more closely resonates with your own. Using the color green as a general meditation color is the easiest way to approach them and send out the message.

The Celtic system is one of great creativity, strength and the magic of the fairy realms. It is one for the development of strong character and responsibility, with an openness to one's inner voice. It is the system for learning to draw upon the Great Unconscious mind of the universe—whether expressed within the individual or within nature.

## DAGDA

Dagda is sometimes considered the patriarch of the Celtic gods and goddesses, although he has not been considered the actual father, as one might find in other mythologies of those in similar positions. His task was more of nourisher. His appearance was always described as common and even gross, but withstanding the appearance there was a tremendous force and power of great beauty and strength around him. For those who need to re-discover the inner beauty and strength within themselves, this is one to begin to align with. If Dagda comes into your life, the force of his name and essence protects and can even destroy enemies if necessary. On the other hand, his energy awakens the music and magic of the soul. His symbols are the harp, upon which he created his magic, and a cauldron that could never be emptied of its resources.

## DANU

In some myths, she is considered the daughter of Dagda, and she is considered by all the greatest of the Celtic Mother goddesses. She is the founder of the tribe of the Tuatha de Danaan. Hers is the energy of wisdom and teaching. Her essence is found within all waters of the world—again representative of the feminine found throughout the universe. If Danu enters your life, she brings a dawn of new life with her. Her name and essence is that of awakening the inner feminine forces of the individual. Her symbols are all symbols of water and newly planted seed. She awakens through these the seeds and waters of intuition, understanding and wisdom—although the awakening of these may come in the guise of situations where you must draw upon those inner resources to succeed. She can come as child, mother or old wise woman.

## MORRIGAN

Sometimes seen as a destructive aspect of the old wise woman, Morrigan brings tremendous primal force to bear within the individual's life. Balance must be maintained. She can be compared to Circe and Hecate of the Greeks. She had a capability of opening one to the energies of prophecy, as she herself was an enchantress. To those whom she appears, great care must be taken for it can become easy to "enchant" oneself without realizing. She brings an energy that demands self-assurance. Anything less can create problems. Her energies may require that you learn not to be the undoing of others within your life—consciously or otherwise. Her name and essence may also awaken deception—in self and others. She brings assertiveness, and she is sometimes seen as both war goddess and enchantress. Her symbols are crossed spears and the raven.

## CERRIDWEN

This is a name which has become the magical name of many individuals in the past. Often considered a witch herself, it is not unusual to find her name taken by many within the pagan and Wiccan religions. Her name translates as "the cauldron of wisdom." She is powerful in magic and prophecy. She helps the individual to awaken his or her own divination abilities. Hers is the energy and ability to shapeshift as suits the occasion . She is possessed of great wisdom. Those aligned with Cerridwen must learn not to let their anger get the best of them or their powers may be stolen, such as in the tale of Cerridwen and Gwion. She brings to birth the innate power of magic and prophecy within the individual, but such an individual must be "ever watchful" in all details and expressions of his or her energy. The individual must be conscious of all life and magical operations for complete success. Her symbol is the cauldron of great wisdom.

## MORGAN LE FAY

Morgan Le Fay is the "Lady of the Lake," found within the Arthurian legends. She is the fairy queen, the queen of the Isle of Avalon. Sometimes seen as separate, it is often easier to see them as really being one and the same, finding their origins in an earlier goddess. To many she was the brother of King Arthur and the one who gave him the sword Excalibur. Others have aligned her with the goddess Bridget. Regardless of the source, this name and essence evoke great power and magic. She is often found as the guardian of groups of women dedicated to expressions of higher wisdom. Her energies require purity and sanctity for its true force to be experienced. She brings knowledge of healing and magic. Tradition tells us that she tricked Merlin into revealing his store of magical knowledge to her. Hers is the energy of responsibility, and her symbol is the hand extending the sword of sovereignty out of the waters of life.

## BRIDGET (BRIGID)

A very strong and enduring goddess, she often served as a bridge between the old traditions and the rise of Christianity. Her energy and essence are both soft, benign and abundant in their manifestation within the individual's life. She is sometimes considered the guardian of the Daughters of Flame—nine women of initiation who protected the sacred fire of life. These nine women helped to distribute the wisdom of Bridget to the rest of the world, assisting the individual in discovering his or her own flame of life. Herbal healing falls under her guidance. Hers is the inspiration for poetry and the hidden music and magic within it. She teaches compassion to all whom she touches. Hers is the great wisdom of fire. Torches and fire are her symbols. The well of healing waters is also one of her most powerful images.

## TALIESON (MERLIN)

Talieson is an ancient poet, often thought of as the greatest of the Celtic prophets. Known by many names, the most common associated with him is Merlin. This great person's energy is one that can open a wealth of knowledge and the power of the bardic tradition. Tradition tells us that Talieson was actually Gwion who stole the magic and knowledge from Cerridwen's cauldron of wisdom. His energy can open one to awareness of the entire Celtic wisdom, poetry, magic, shapeshifting and an understanding of the riddles of life. At the same time, it teaches the laws of cause and effect or the "Law of Rebound" as it is often called within the Celtic magical traditions. His symbols are the harp and the staff.

## RHIANNON

The goddess Rhiannon is tied to ancient Celtic horse cults. Her name and energy awaken assertiveness within the individual, one that must be balanced with justice. She is sometimes considered the queen of the underworld, and yet able to move through the country at a speed that could not be matched. She awakens a great pleasure in things of nature—the forests and woods and the life that lived within those realms. Her energies can assist individuals in learning great knowledge of even the tiniest and seemingly most insignificant foliage. She awakens strong wrath toward arrogance and cowardice which must be expressed appropriately. She brings kindness into one's life. Her symbols are the pale gray horse and three sacred birds which sing lullabies and sweet melodies. She possesses a bag of abundance which she can also share. Compassion is always rewarded by her.

## LUGH

Lugh was a solar deity associated with the Celtic tradition. There are ties in legends and myths between Lugh and Gwydion, a heroic deity of the Welsh tradition who raised and guided Lugh much in the tradition of Merlin and Arthur. Lugh has ties to the energies of the Sun, and was called the "many skilled." He imbues the individual, not only with magical power, but he inspires great energy associated with artistic endeavors, enabling the individual to find a unique expression within his or her own life. Alignment with this being may require that the individual learn to deal with deception—in self or in others. His symbol is the spear.

## GWYDION

Gwydion is a deity of heroic proportions with many tales and legends of his exploits. He is depicted as a guardian and guide to Lugh, raising him—even though he was not Lugh's father. His influence is the energy associated with law, justice and science. If aligned to, his energies awaken a dynamic ability to work with natural and spiritual laws instilling an almost magical ability to work out legalities according to one's desires. There must be caution though, as the misuse of knowledge and occult power has its repercussion and should not be used to give unfair advantage over the less fortunate and talented. Gwydion opens the doors to the science of alchemy as applied to the physical realm. All images of science and law are symbols that can help align to his energy.

## NUADA

Nuada is one of the few male deities associated with the Moon. There are many lunar associations within the tales of Nuada, but predominant is that of his being a keeper of the fairy gift of the Tuatha de Danaan. The fairy realm is often represented in esoteric lore as part of the etheric plane of life, a plane of life closest in vibration to the physical. The Moon is the astrological sign associated with the etheric realm. The gift was the invincible sword that was so powerful that no enemy could ever hope to withstand it. He is one of the deities of the Celtic tradition that seems to have a consistency concerning a color association. Silver is that color, which is quite appropriate when you consider that it is also the element and color associated with lunar energies. His energy and essence awaken a strong sense of security and the ability to overcome the foes within one's life—be they other people or attitudes and thoughts. This, of course, has ties to other mythologies and the imagery of the double-edged sword of discrimination and spiritual law.

## CERNUNNOS

Cernunnos is the horned god, a lesser deity of the Celtic tradition. Some legends tie him to that of Gwyn and even Herne the Hunter. Cernunnos is the lord of animals and the forests. His is the energy of uniting and becoming one with the forces of nature. Alignment with his name and energy awakens shamanistic energies, and the horned figure could be either male or female. Animals were sacred to Cernunnos. He can awaken a shapeshifting ability, which if not guarded carefully could lead to deception. His is the energy of earth magic, and spirit totems in the guise of animals. His color is always green, and his symbols are the stag, antlers and the torch—all symbols of the creative feminine force expressed through the male aspect.

## GWYN

Gwyn is most often seen as truly Herne the Hunter, one who hunts at night and must catch his prey before the dawn's light. He is a guardian of dark doorways of the mind and the world. His energy can open one to "see in the dark"—to move easily through the lower astral realms, to navigate those areas not readily seen while awake. He thus can help stimulate the awakening of dream consciousness and astral travel. He is the initiator of the individual who must first learn to negotiate the lower realms before the higher will be opened. He rules the underworld, and provides an energy that brings opportunities for the individual to learn to rule his or her own "underworld"—the lower and baser emotions and energies. Symbols of the night, shadows, darkened doorways are those aligned with his essence.

## BRAN

Bran is the "Blessed Giant." He is the brother of Branwen. He awakens the innate good-nature and its expression within the individual. Alignment with his energies may signify that there is mischief about and even treachery which must be dealt with firmly—without losing one's good nature within the process. His energy enables you to hear the inner quiet voice of calm. It opens one to prophecy. Much of the tale of Bran has correspondences to the Greek tale of Orpheus. Both lost their head, but the head continued talking after death, prophesying. His energy awakens the strength of poetry and the ability to use one's voice as a healing instrument. His is the energy of self-sacrifice for a higher and greater cause, and alignment with his energy will awaken such within the individual. His symbols are those of the harp and the singing voice.

## BRANWEN

Branwen is the sister of Bran. She is considered the love goddess, and she dies of a broken heart within the Celtic legends. Branwen was married to an Irish king so that Britain and Ireland might become one force. It unfortunately did not work out, and her brother had to sacrifice himself to save his country. The wedding had become a catalytic opportunity for those who would sow treachery. Hers is the energy of gentleness, beauty and love. Her symbol is that of the white cow—that which can nourish and nurture—not only the body but the soul as well. She awakens love and warmth within the individual. She teaches the lessons of learning to love, in spite of outer circumstances. Her symbols are the white cow and the gillyflower.

# 15

# Magical Names from Teutonic Traditions

Teutonic myth and lore are filled with awesome power, beauty, magic and violence. These great myths of the Teutonic peoples come down to us through the Scandinavian and Norse poets. Three major groups comprise this tradition: the Goths, the Teutons (who settled within the Scandinavian countries) and the West Germans, ancestors of the present German people and Anglo-Saxons.

The deities of this tradition are powerful and strong, but they are by no means immortal or omnipotent. They have failings. They have weaknesses. And they are also subject to the Norns—the Fates who spin the length of life for all. They have vulnerabilities, and it is these vulnerabilities which endear them to humanity and contributed to their extended worship and reverence. The Teutonic tradition was one of the last to fall to "modern Christendom." (Inherent within these tales are teachings extremely similar to the teachings of Christianity.)

On the surface, the Teutonic myths and beings are violent and harsh, but the energies of this tradition teach personal responsibility and personal recompense in all things. All is achieved according to one's own efforts. All is rewarded in accordance to the degree it has earned. All is punishable or accountable as well. Good or bad, justice is swift and true and equal to the energy of the deed.

This is a tradition that teaches the individual spiritual warriorship. This is a mythology for teaching how to awaken the warrior aspect—not in outward acts of aggression, but through inner confrontation. This is the mythology for those wishing to confront the "dwellers upon the threshold"—those aspects of ourselves that we have painted over, pretended didn't exist, shoved to the back of the closet, etc. that we must confront and transmute in order to cross that threshold into higher realms of consciousness.

This is the mythology of the transmutation of energies. It is learning to transform ourselves, by taking task in hand responsibly and drawing upon the innate force of our inner magic and light. It opens one to the abilities to work from many realms (there are nine worlds within this tradition) and many levels of consciousness.

The deities of this tradition are many and varied. The predominant ones come from two particular groups of gods and goddesses. The Aesir are the warrior gods. They epitomize many of the masculine aspects of energy within the universe—whether the deity of this group is male or female. The second group is the deities of fertility known as the Vanir. They are representative of the feminine energies. Initially the two groups fought each other, but neither could gain an advantage or win over the other. They thus chose to live together in the realm of beauty and gold known as Asgard.

Inherent within this is much of the significance of all their tales. Neither the male nor the female is more powerful. Neither the male nor the female can overcome the other. The only manner in which the forces can truly build a universe of light is by bringing both together into harmony within oneself. Then the gold of new life is achieved. It is the gold of the alchemical process.

It is this richness of symbolism which makes the Teutonic tradition a powerful source of individual magic and light. In association with the process of name enchantment this mythology can be powerful for an individual. "Skaldcraft" was the Teutonic method of using names, words and poetry for magical purposes. The energies and essences behind the mythical characters of this tradition easily come to life when invoked. One who takes a magical name from this tradition should be prepared for confronting that within themselves that would hinder growth and should be prepared to meet the energy and essence behind the name from the moment it is taken. The gods and goddesses of this tradition are quick to respond to the call of humanity and to provide opportunity for growth and expression.

## THE DEITY NAMES OF THE TEUTONS

The Teutonic tradition is one in which the meaning of the names of the gods and goddesses still remain rather clear and definable today. While in many mythologies the "meanings" of the specific names often become obscured, it is not true of this one. This is also part of the reason it is still easy to invoke their energies at a very strong level. The following is a list of the major gods and goddesses of this tradition and the literal translations of their names. On the pages that follow we will examine twelve of these in particular.

1. Odin—"air of heaven; spirit"
2. Frigga—"lady mistress"
3. Thor—"thunderer"
4. Freyr—"foremost"
5. Feyja—"lady mistress"
6. Balder—"shining god; lord"
7. Tyr—"shining"
8. Heimdall—"rainbow"
9. Bragi—"song"
10. Loki—"fire"
11. Idun—"rejuvenation"
12. Sif—"kinship"
13. Eir—"air"
14. Ull—"shaggy one"
15. Vali—"terrible"
16. Vidar—"ruler of large territory"
17. Gefion—"giving"
18. Skade—"damage"
19. Gerd—"fence enclosing tilled land"
20. Modi—"courageous"
21. Magni—"great; strength"
22. Hoenir—"hen-like"
23. Vili—"will"
24. Lodur—"flame"
25. Nanna—"mother of brave"
26. Saga—"story"
27. Forseti—"he who sits in front seat"
28. Hermod—"battle courage"

### ODIN

Considered the father of this pantheon, Odin is the most powerful and most knowledgeable of all the gods and goddesses of the Aesir and the Vanir. He is the "all-father." He sacrificed himself upon Yggdrasil, the Tree of Life, for nine days in order to attain higher knowledge and wisdom revealed to him through the runes. Alignment with his energy and essence opens great foresight and prophecy. He is sometimes considered the patron of poets, which is shared with Bragi. He walked the earth many times teaching humanity in various guises, and he opens the individual to great knowledge. Such knowledge when awakened by alignment with his name and energy can make one over-expectant. The individual must learn to develop a sense of integrity and honor within his or her life, and there may come a time when sacrifice is necessary for special achievements, but if done with honor, it will bring achievement greater than anticipated. His magical symbols are the ravens and the wolves, mighty spear and an eight-legged steed. When awakened within one's auric field, the energy often reveals itself as a deep shade of blue or indigo.

## FRIGGA

Frigga is the wife of Odin. Of all the other gods and goddesses she alone was permitted to sit upon his throne from time to time. Upon this throne, the individual could see what was occurring within all nine worlds. Thus she too was all-knowing, and alignment with her and her essence will open the opportunity for great learning. Frigga is the Queen of the Aesir, and has great power herself. She spun yarn upon a golden staff and spindle, and a gift of a piece of her yarn would create a never ending supply. She guides the other deities from behind the scenes, and she always answers any fervent prayer. She can awaken within the individual the ability to work with the weather and to awaken knowledge of how to heal magically with herbs. She is a protectress. Her magical images are the golden spindle and a sacred necklace. Her energy can awaken within the aura the balancing and magical color force of deep greens.

## THOR

Thor is the mighty god of thunder and lightning. He is the powerful warrior god who comes to the aid of those who call upon him—no matter how far away. Alignment with his name and energy awakens inner strength and the enforcement of laws. His is the energy of stability and bravery. He is the champion of the common man, and he awakens within the individual an ability to complete seemingly "impossible" tasks. There can arise a tendency to act before thinking and there is always a need to control the temper. Maintaining a good sense of humor is one of the most effective ways of handling the energy of Thor. His magical images are the mighty hammer which never misses its mark and always returns to his hand, the iron mitt by which he would catch the hammer when thrown and a magic belt which enabled him to draw upon greater strength and power. Thor traveled about in a chariot drawn by two mighty goats. His energy manifests in shades of bright red.

# FREYR

Freyr is the Teutonic god of plenty. It is he who brings the sunshine and the rain in the proper amounts for abundant harvests. Alignment with his name and energy awakens opportunities for prosperity and sunshine within one's own life. He is also the ruler of the elves, and thus his name can open one to their world more easily. He brings the energies of human increase and fertility, and he is often considered the patron of the seafarer. Freyr carried a sword that was as bright as the Sun, and Odin gave him a ship that sailed on sea and air and could be folded up and kept within a pouch. He also rode upon a golden boar whose energy would light the darkest valleys and increase abundance. His color energy is that of bright golden yellow.

# FREYJA

Freyja is the foremost goddess of love of this pantheon. Her beauty is unmatched. She is one of the mother goddesses, and she taught magical songs to women to enable them to look into the future. She is the patroness of women prophets. Alignment with her name and essence can awaken such opportunities for the individual. Her energy brings love and friendship and, like her brother Freyr, she too rode upon the golden boar which brought abundance. She also had a strong relationship with the elves. There may awaken a tendency to not relinquish past loves once they are out of one's life, so care must be taken with this. Her magical symbols are the Necklace of Brising, a chariot drawn by cats, the falcon wings which enabled her to fly swiftly and the golden boar. Alignment with her energy activates soft reds and pinks.

# BALDER

Balder was the "shining god." He was the one deity in whom there was no guile or deceit, and one can only think pure thoughts in his presence. Not even the gnomes and the jotuns (giants) could dislike him. He was the wisest, sweetest and most merciful for he could see whatever good there was in an individual, no matter how deeply buried and how despicable the outer actions were. Alignment with his energy awakens greater forgiveness and gentleness. Anyone drawn to the healing remedies of flowers can do so more easily through Balder, for flowers would spring up in his presence. His energy awakens charisma and is excellent for situations where there may be antagonism. There may arise an inability to take a stand, as the individual's ability to see the good in all things may prevent proper action. His symbols are all flowers, especially the balderblum.

## TYR

Tyr is the son of Odin and is considered the bravest of all the deities of this pantheon. It was Tyr who sacrificed his own hand so that Fenris the wolf could be bound and controlled. Alignment with the energy and essence of Tyr awakens the courage to do what must be done. His is the energy of sacrifice for the good of all or for beneficent causes. He teaches that sacrifice is sometimes necessary, but one never really loses, for Tyr still maintained great strength in spite of losing his right hand. He helps the individual to draw upon all the inner strength and courage necessary to accomplish one's purpose and to overcome the "monsters" within our lives. His symbol is the sacrificed hand, and his color is the dark red of great strength.

## HEIMDALL

Heimdall is the son of Odin and is the watchman of Asgard, the home of the gods and goddesses. He guards the rainbow bridge that links heaven and earth. He is extremely handsome with blue eyes so clear that he can see to the end of the world. His ears are capable of hearing wool growing upon sheep, and he needs no more sleep than a bird. Alignment with his essence awakens farsightedness and clairaudience. It provides opportunities for the development of stamina and highly developed senses. He is sometimes recognized as a fertility god and is associated with various tales of the proper ways of using our creative energies in the alchemical marriage. He awakens opportunity for development of spiritual discernment and discrimination. His symbols are the trumpet horn by which he warns the deities of Asgard and the rainbow. The colors activated by alignment with his name and essence are the colors of the rainbow itself—red, orange, yellow, green, blue, indigo and violet.

## IDUN

Idun is the goddess of rejuvenation and youth. She possesses the golden apples of youth and immortality which she distributes to the other deities. She is the goddess of youth and beauty, and alignment with her energy assists the individual in manifesting opportunities to re-awaken the "child" within. She brings an energy of youthful zeal. Her name and essence also require that the individual learn to protect that which is most sacred and those things that help to keep one young at heart. She inspires creativity. She is the goddess of fruit, and thus there are archetypal ties to fertility. She assists the individual in bearing fruit within his or her life. Her symbol is the basket of golden apples which never empties. Her colors are gold and the pastel blues of youth.

## BRAGI

Bragi is the husband of Idun. He is the god of poetry and eloquence. He is the true god of the bards and of skaldcraft—the magic of word and song. He was given the mead made by gnomes which enabled the individual to lift high the spirits of others and free them. He was also taught the magic and power of the runes. Alignment with his energy can open one to finding his or her own "sacred word." It brings stimulation and inspiration for poetry and song which can touch the hearts of others. Name enchantment falls under the rulership of Bragi, and he brings an energy that enables the individual to awaken the throat chakra—the center for creative expression and will force. His images and symbols are all poems, songs and musical instruments, and his color force is the rich blue of the sky, sparkled with gold.

## THE NORNS

The Norns are comparable to the three Fates of Greek lore. They spin at will the fates of men and women. It is their task also to sprinkle the great Tree of Life, Yggdrasil, with mead from the Fountain of Life so that the Tree stays ever green. It is the honey dew that drips upon the world and is stored by the bees. Urd, the first of these three sisters, controls what is. Working with her are maids performing various tasks and who are the guardians of humanity through their lives. They bring counsel from Urd into dreams and award good fortune to those who are favored by Urd. They attend families and care for unborn babes and find them kindly mothers within the world of men. Verdande spins the past, what has been. She can reveal it to the living so that the course of life can be changed or set or merely understood. Skuld spun the fate of the future, that which is to be. Alignment with any or all of these opens one to great knowledge, but that knowledge may reveal more than what is desired, for once the fate is spun, it cannot be changed. The symbols are the spinning wheel, the bumble bee and the two mystic swans of Urd's pond who are the ancestors of the swan race of Midgard (Earth). Their colors are varied, depending on the thread that they choose to spin for the individual.

## LOKI

Loki is not really one of the deities from either group that comprised Asgard—the Aesir or the Vanir. He was a jotun, but unlike the others of his race, he was graceful and handsome. Odin met him before he received his wisdom from hanging upon the Tree, and he took a strong liking to Loki, making him a blood brother. Loki was a master shapeshifter. Unlike many who may have had the ability to change into one other shape, Loki could become almost anything he desired. He is quick-witted and cunning, with the wonderful ability to make even the coldest heart warm with laughter. Alignment with his energy and essence can bring opportunity to develop this within oneself. On the other hand, Loki became bored very easily, and he was extremely mischievous which created much trouble. He is an ambiguous figure, a combination of positive and negative. His energy is dynamic, catalytic and unpredictable. Alignment with him can stimulate this same energy within the individual, and any propensity for unbalance will become exaggerated. Control and discipline are required to handle this energy properly. Loki could display control when absolutely necessary. This energy can also awaken within the individual a tremendous ability for communication. Loki could smooth talk almost anyone. His gifts of persuasion were great. Fire is a symbol for him—a force that must be controlled or it becomes destructive. The color force activated by this name will vary, as Loki was a great shapeshifter and could appear in any manner he desired. Fire shades can manifest though as a result of alignment with this energy and essence.

PART IV

# NAMES FROM THE
# MAGICAL KINGDOM

# 16

# Creating a Magical Name from Nature

It has been said that the way to heaven is through the feet. This implies that the spiritual student must learn to connect with the energies of the physical world to give propulsion to his or her growth. We are living in a time where there is occurring a return to the explorations of the forces of nature and all the energies associated with it. The Native American tradition and other forms of shamanistic studies are growing in popularity. Individuals are working to attune and resonate more harmoniously with nature and all of its rhythms and expressions.

By learning to work creatively and constructively with the energies of nature, we are given propulsion to bridge to heaven. We can learn to work in such a manner in some very simple ways. The first is by recognizing the element of nature to which you most closely resonate. We discussed briefly in chapter two, the elements associated with the vowels within the alphabet. These five elements—ether, fire, air, water and earth—help define the energies of nature. This resonance is reflected by the vowels within the birth or the magical name.

Each of these elements has a group of beings associated with them. Thus the vowels in our name tell us which beings of the nature kingdom we may have the greatest facility with and what we must learn to an even greater degree. Knowing which part of nature and the elementals associated with it that our name-sounds link us to serves to begin the process of attuning more to nature and can provide much insight into the hidden significance of our name—birth or magical.

| Vowel | Element | Beings of Nature | Direction in the World |
|-------|---------|------------------|------------------------|
| A | Ether | All elementals | All four directions |
| E | Air | Sylphs | East |
| I | Fire | Salamanders | South |
| O | Water | Undines | West |
| U | Earth | Gnomes | North |

These elementals are the building blocks of nature. The angels or devas are the builders. Most of the elementals act unconsciously, instinctively, while those known as the angels are the more conscious creators operating through nature. This celestial kingdom is as hierarchical as that of humanity.

There is also often confusion as to the difference between the elementals and those beings known as the nature spirits—those more commonly known as the fairies and elves, etc. They are all part of the "angelic" hierarchy, but they serve different purposes. Those we know of as nature spirits are more likely to display "personality." The elementals are more "characteristic." For example, in any family there may be a characteristic or trait that all members of the family possess—tendency toward baldness, thinness, dark hair, etc. Each member of that family—even though he or she may have a similar characteristic—will display a unique personality.

The energies of the elementals and nature spirits are expressed and experienced through all facets of nature. This is why a second way of attuning to nature is by discerning which expression of it you are most drawn to. Every flower, plant, tree and animal is a reflection of archetypal energies. These archetypal energies are expressed in nature in a physical form through the assistance of the elementals and nature spirits. Thus when an individual takes a magical name—drawn from nature—the individual aligns not only with certain elemental forces and beings but with the archetypal force that lies behind it.

One of the most powerful and popular means of creating a magical name is to draw upon the magical kingdom of nature for inspiration. Previously, we learned how to discover the nature animal totem that could become the foundation of the magical name. We learned to employ the name of a particular animal with a particular characteristic (*i.e.* "Gentle Bear"). In this chapter we will learn to draw from the plant kingdom as a source for one's magical name. We will learn how to align oneself with the archetypal force operating through and expressed by the individual plant(s).

When you choose to use as a magical name any name drawn from nature, you are aligning yourself, not only with certain archetypal forces, but you are also aligning yourself with certain beings of nature who work with and through those expressions of nature—be they plant or animal. In choosing or creating a magical name associated with nature in any of its forms, it is always beneficial to know which element in particular you most strongly resonate. By choosing an expression of nature that is aligned with that element, it is often easier to access the play of archetypes within one's own life. If your name is TOM, the vowel is an *O* which is tied to the element of water, and thus the individual named TOM may wish to draw from those plants and animals associated with the element of water (*i.e.* water lily, whale, etc.) as a basis for a magical name.

It is not a law that states you must choose or create a magical name associated with the element of your birth name. It is just one of the easiest methods to create rapport and resonance with the archetypal forces behind it. If you choose an expression of nature from an element different from the element within your birth name, it is good to know how the two elements work together. In chapter 2, is a chart (page 16) in which various elemental combinations are explored. It is also important to understand more fully how each element operates within our lives and within nature itself. As we come to a greater understanding of this, it becomes easier to understand the archetypal forces behind the names of nature to which we are aligning.

For most of the elementals there are basic energies and characteristics which have been passed down by both myth and legend. Meditation upon them, and study will bring to light more of their aspects—particularly as they are applied to one's own life. What follows is just a brief description of the four basic elemental groups of beings.

## GNOMES

More a generic title than a reference to our usual conception of the gnome, this group of elementals is associated with the element of earth; all elemental work with the physical world through what is more commonly known as the etheric. They are all four-dimensional with nothing to restrict their movements. They thus move through matter as easily as air.

Various entities fall into this category, each with its own degree of consciousness. An individual that takes a magical name from nature that is aligned with the element of earth can learn to commune with these beings at various levels.

The gnomes maintain and work for the physical body and its composition—our own and that of the earth. Without them, we could not function in the physical. There is usually one that has been assigned to help us maintain the physical body.

All of the elementals are affected by what we do, especially those who have chosen to work directly with our energies. Thus, if we abuse the body, we abuse the elemental that is assigned to us. If we respect the body, we give respect to that one who is assisting us and even greater can be done with the body itself.

The gnomes are needed also in nature to build the plants, flowers and trees. It is their task to tint them, to make the minerals and crystals within the earth and to generally maintain the earth so that humanity has a place to grow and learn. Those with a vowel of *U* have a strong ability to resonate with their energies.

## UNDINES

These are those beings of the elemental kingdom of nature associated with water. Wherever there is a natural source of water these beings will be found. These beings are also associated with the astral body of humanity, and there is usually one in particular who has chosen to work with the formation and maintenance of it within our own energy structure and to assist with the functions of all bodily fluids.

All water upon the planet—rain, river, ocean, dew, etc.—has tremendous undine activity associated with it. The assimilation of water by plants and trees is part of their function as well. Any one with a vowel of *O* within the name has the ability to develop resonance with them and all life associated or affected by their elemental activity.

## SYLPHS

The sylphs are more closely aligned in consciousness to those we call the angels than any of the other elementals. They often work side by side with them and serve as messengers between them and humanity. They are part of the creative element of air, and they are part of all expressions and functions of it—from the tiniest breeze to the mightiest tornadoes.

Many of the sylphs are of high intelligence, and have much to do with humanity, particularly in assisting with pain and suffering. They often serve as "temporary guardian angels" until we draw to ourselves the one which will be our teacher and guardian.

Certain sylphs are also assigned to the individual human. They help in the maintenance of the mental body, and thus our thoughts—good or bad—can affect them. They work for the assimilation of oxygen from the air we breathe and with all functions of air in and around us.

They work for the plant process of creating oxygen and for maintenance of the atmosphere of the earth. They work to cleanse and uplift the thoughts and intelligence of all. Those with the vowel *E* within the name have the ability to develop resonance and communion with these beings more easily.

## SALAMANDERS

These are the elemental beings associated with fire. They also are found throughout nature and all of its expressions. No fire is lit without their help. They are most active underground and internally within the body and mind. The fire and heat of the Sun—and its influence upon the entire planet—is also part of their domain. Within the physical body they assist the function of the circulatory system and the maintaining of proper body temperature.

Fire is a powerful vibration. These beings have a strong love for music and are a foremost agency of nature. They have the ability to evoke powerful emotional currents in humanity. They stimulate fires of idealism.

Their energies are very stirring and it takes tremendous ability to control and direct them for the most creative results. Those with the vowel *I* have an easier ability to establish resonance with them.

Almost all elemental beings and nature spirits require some contact with humanity, and there are many who require the assistance of humanity to help with their own evolutionary progress. It is important that we learn to establish a more harmonious relationship. It not only assists these wonderful beings, but it opens us to the true magic of the nature kingdom.

Nature has always held an enchantment for humanity. There was a time when the distance between the worlds of humanity and that of the nature kingdom was no further than outside one's own door or the nearest bend in the road. Every cavern and hollow tree was a doorway to another world where beings and energies existed that were mystifying and magical. Humans recognized the energy of life at all times—in all things. The streams spoke and the winds whispered ancient words. Every blade of grass and flower had a story to tell. Shadows were not just shadows and trees were not just wood. Clouds were not just pretty. There was life and purpose in all things and there was recognition of the loving interaction between all worlds.

Taking a magical name associated with Mother Nature is a means of establishing that ancient relationship once more. When we align with nature, we align with the beings and archetypal energies behind it. The forces and expressions of nature within our world can be used to heal, balance and enlighten.

Every plant, tree, flower, herb, stone, etc. has an archetypal force that is reflected by it for us to utilize. There are archetypal forces that work with humanity solely through a physical manifestation of nature. Using the names of the plants and trees and substances of nature is a means of activating and aligning those archetypal energies with our own. It is these energies which we will explore in the rest of the chapter so as to give you the opportunity to decide which—if any—of the forces of nature you may wish to align with and invoke through a magical name.

We will concentrate predominantly upon two aspects of nature—trees and flowers—as these are the most common sources for magical names, and they are often the easiest to align one's own energy with. They also are more universally effective in activating energies that touch us on all levels—physical and subtle. Many individuals will use the names of crystals and stones as magical names (*i.e.* "Amethyst"). If you find yourself more drawn to that kingdom of nature feel free to use them. There is an abundance of material currently available, describing the various energies of stones and crystals. Remember that as you align yourself with the name of anything in nature this also aligns you with the archetypal energies that are expressed through it—any beings that work with it and all thoughtforms and significance that has been attributed to it in the past.

## PRELIMINARY CONSIDERATIONS:
1. Plants, flowers and trees make wonderful magical names as they are sources of great light and healing and can invoke such energies even more dynamically within your own life.

2. A plant's whole life is a worship of the light. Whether a tree, a flower or any other plant, it reaches toward the sun. Plants need sunlight to live.

3. Some plants, flowers and trees invoke more of a healing energy while some may invoke more magical aspects of the soul. It is important to know not only the properties of the plant but your own personal goals so that you can align them properly.

4. Flowers and trees are extremely receptive to working more intimately with an individual. This includes the archetypal energies behind them and any of the nature spirits that work with them. Keep in mind that taking a name from a plant, flower or tree in nature is the initiating of a relationship—not only with the plant but with all of nature. You are beginning to align yourself to its more universal rhythms.

5. When you take the name of a flower or tree as your magical name, you are setting up a psychic rapport with its energies. You are beginning the process of connecting with its vital element.

6. Most trees and plants have Latin names that the scientific community has assigned them in the past. Sometimes these Latin names are quite beautiful and can easily be adapted as one's own magical name, rather than using the more generic name of the tree or flower. For example the Latin designation for sagebrush is *Artemisia*, a very beautiful sounding name. A good book on flowers and plants will list these scientific names. It not only makes the magical name more exotic, but more secret as well!

7. Fragrant flowers and trees, as a general rule, represent a more giving nature and activate such within the individual. They assist the individual in opening up more fully within the world around them.

8. You may wish to join the animal totem you have discovered for yourself with the name of the flower or tree. This gives you access to both the animal and plant kingdoms and makes for an even more unique magical name and a unique expression of archetypal energies within your own life. If, for example, the animal totem is a hawk and your plant totem is a rose, you may wish to use the magical name of "ROSE-HAWK." (Other examples are "WILLOW-WOLF," "BEAR-IVY," etc.) You are limited only by your own imagination and creativity. Make sure that you understand the energies of both aspects. Make sure you can

also perceive how their energies may mix within your own life circumstances.

9. *Honor that which you take upon yourself as your name!* In using the names of trees and flowers, this is especially important and there are a number of ways of doing so:

—Learn as much about the flower or tree to which you are aligning. This means read about it, study it, don't just limit yourself to the brief descriptions within this book.

—Learn something about its growing process. How does it grow? In what kind of climate and soil? Where does it grow more fully? How much sunlight, water, etc. does it require? Keep in mind that part of the process of empowering a magical name is to imbue every aspect of that name with significance.

—Learn about the parts of the plant: roots, stem, trunk, leaves, flowers, bulbs, etc. When you take on a name associated with nature you are taking on energies associated with every aspect of it.

—Make paintings and drawings of it. Find pictures of it and hang them where you can see them everyday. You may even find little charms that you can wear.

—Visiting nature areas in which the tree or flower is found is always beneficial. Meditating upon it in an outdoor area is empowering in that it helps to create resonance.

—Make each aspect of it signify something. *Nothing is insignificant.* The more significance that you can attribute to it, the more effective it becomes as a link between the archetypal forces and your life.

—Plant the tree or flower somewhere where you can watch it grow and honor it on a regular basis. Even those who do not have outdoor yards, can create an indoor plant. Even small trees can be kept in pots indoors. If the flower is not one that you can grow indoors, buy yourself a bouquet of them periodically. The process of planting is a powerful form of "sympathetic magic." What you do on one level affects you on all other levels. "As above, so below. As below, so above." Planting the tree or flower is a way of dedicating the new name and empowering it. You are planting a new energy within your life.

10. Inevitably, someone will plant something and it will not grow or may even die. Death is part of nature's process. We die to be reborn. You do not want to take it personally, as there are many

possible reasons which should be explored before jumping to conclusions. It may be that you are not ready for the energy associated with this new name. It may also mean that you were not giving the plant enough attention. It may mean that you were not aware of all that it requires to live and grow, and thus more study and learning is necessary. It may also mean that the plant was sick when you got it.

If it does die, do not be discouraged. Buy a second one, and take even greater care with it. Meditate upon it and with it. If it dies a third time, re-evaluation is necessary. Maybe this totem and its energies will be yours someday, but it may require earning it and developing oneself further before it can fully be experienced. Meditation and reflection upon it will help you to discern this. There is often a tendency for some individuals to choose as a personal totem energies of the plant and animal kingdom that they believe to be very powerful. They may be so, but their energies may not be suitable for where the individual is within his or her own stage of growth. If the plant dies three times, it is a strong indication often that maybe ego is coloring one's own discernment. It is usually an indication to re-assess your energies and stage of development. Keep in mind that one plant, flower, tree or animal is no better or worse than any other. Each is unique in its own expression. Each has its own strengths and weaknesses, and we should not allow preconceptions to mislead us. This is why study and knowledge of that which you align with is so important. *Know thyself!*

## NAME AND NATURE SYMBIOSIS

When we take the name of something from nature as our magical name, we are instituting a powerful process of alignment with the archetypal forces that work through Mother Nature herself. We, as a race of beings, owe so much to the expressions of nature—not only for the beauty, but for the environment it provides for us to grow and learn. It is a shame that it is so often taken for granted. Aligning with nature and any of its expressions is a re- commitment to reverencing all of life—no matter how small or insignificant it may appear. Flower and tree names are prayers. These prayers—of reverence and joy—we keep alive through the essence of the name.

We must begin to return to nature the respect and service it has extended to us. The more we honor the various expressions of nature, the more time we spend in nature enjoying its beauty and majesty, the more easy it becomes to align with it. We are drawn to a symbiosis with it that cannot be broken. We begin to feel what it feels, understand what it understands and see ourselves and the rest of humanity from its perspective. We must learn to be silent with the flowers and trees and allow them to speak to us. They are not just subjects of study and curiosity. They are expressions of life as unique as we are to each other. Plants draw us to the realization of the divine, expressed through nature. And when we can see it within Mother Nature, we begin to recognize it within our own nature as well!

# 17

# Magical Names
# from Trees

The tree is an ancient symbol. It represents things that grow, fertility and life. To some it is the world axis; to others it is the world itself. Its roots are within the earth, and yet it reaches toward the heavens. It is a bridge between the heavens and the earth, the mediator between the two worlds. This is quite apropos in creating a magical name, for we are trying to bridge the inner energies with the outer.

Consider all that is done with trees. They bear fruit from which we gain nourishment. They provide wood for building of homes and the making of paper—by which knowledge and communication occur. They provide windbreaks and shelters, and they often served as barriers and fencing by early settlers and farmers. They were boundaries, separating one piece of land from another or one world from another. They also provide shade, the cooling and nurturing aspect of Mother Nature.

As children we climb them, finding enjoyment in reaching new heights and new challenges. Leaves fall off many trees in the autumn, only to re-emerge in the spring, reflecting the continual cycle of change and growth—dying to be born again—all of which can be aligned through the name. We rake leaves, gathering that which has occurred in the previous months, and then they are burned or used as a mulch for future plantings.

Trees also bear fruit. This is especially important to consider when taking as one's magical name the name of a tree. Fruit is usually borne but once per year. The rest of the year leads up to that one harvest. Such a cycle of harvest is often manifested in the lives of those who take on the name of a fruit-bearing tree.

The tree has been associated with both paradise and hell—the Tree of Life and the Tree of Knowledge. In Greek mythology the Golden Fleece hung upon a tree. The Christian cross was originally a tree. Buddha found enlightenment while sitting under one. Odin hung upon the great tree Yggdrasil for nine days and nights in order to attain higher wisdom. The ancient Druids recognized distinct energies with various trees. Every civilization has its stories, myths and legends of the Tree of Life.

Trees have always been imbued with certain magical or spiritual attributes. Our superstition of "knocking on wood" was initiated to insure that no spirits were residing within the tree before it was cut down and utilized. The jack- in-the-box was a home for the spirits of trees that were cut down. These wooden boxes were designed to scare children away so that the spirits would not be disturbed again.

We also have a family tree. This tree has its roots with our ancestors, both familial and spiritual. All that we are lies in the roots of the tree, and thus all of our ancestry can be awakened through the tree.

When you choose a tree as a basis for a magical name you are making a conscious choice of the energies you wish to align yourself with in this life—or at this particular time in life. You do not have to know *all* that the tree will reflect; much of it will unfold as you live with it. It is important to learn as much about its significance as you can. It is also important to choose a tree whose energies reflect your own goals at this point in your life. Keep in mind though that trees grow slowly, firmly and need to take root.

Do you want a fruit bearing tree? Do you personally want to bear a lot of fruit in your life? Take into consideration that most fruit trees—as already mentioned—only bear fruit seasonally. It does not mean that growth is not occurring at other times of the year, but there may be periods within a year's cycle in which the tree may not ostensibly show productivity. Also all trees bear fruit in unique ways. Learn about the trees before you choose to align with one in particular. Start with the tree you have always felt closest to. Go out into nature and meditate around trees, allowing for the one which is best for you to reveal itself to you. Don't choose a tree simply because it seems to have more "magical" associations and energies. It may not apply to you and where you are at the present.

One of the best ways of activating its energies within your life is by planting the tree of your choice—indoors or outdoors—somewhere where you can see it everyday. This then becomes a constant reminder that as it grows and blossoms and becomes a bridge, so does the tree within you!

If the tree is planted indoors, at some point you may want to transplant it outdoors so that it can grow free and uninhibited. This is especially effective when you go to change your magical name. At this point you may wish to change to another tree for the inside. Be sure to care for the tree you plant—pruning, watering, etc. As you do so, do it in full awareness that you are also pruning and watering the magical aspect within you, enabling it to take firmer root and reach towards greater heights of expression.

Each tree has its own unique qualities, as does each individual. The tree that you align with and plant is an outer reflection of an inner energy you are activating within your life. If the tree dies, as discussed within the previous section, it does not mean that you are going to physically die. What it often means is that an aspect of yourself, no longer vital, has been changed. We must use discrimination. Maybe the tree you chose was not the best one for you to start with. Many trees are difficult to grow, and maybe it died because you were trying to do much more than you are capable of handling at this moment. Start simply. Allow the tree to grow at the rate that is best for it and for you.

Trees are patient. You cannot force the growth and expression of their energies. When you plant a seed—which is what we are doing by taking a magical name—that seed needs time to germinate, take root and then work its way up through the soil. Do not assume that nothing is happening if there is no immediately noticeable growth. If we wish to truly bridge and unfold our highest potential, we must persist. Everything that we try to grow within our life—whether successful or not—adds to our knowledge and life experience on a soul level.

## ALDER

The alder tree is one whose energies provide protection. It can awaken prophecy and has strong ties to the element of water and its force within the universe. The raven is an animal totem often associated with it, and the raven is a bird of great mysticism and magic. It can awaken the ability to open perceptions to the dark void. It has ties in mythology to the Celtic pantheon and the blessed giant Bran. It is a good tree to align with in order to overcome unawareness.

## APPLE

The apple tree has many magical, healing characteristics and energies associated with it. It is sometimes associated with the Tree of Knowledge. The apple was considered the "Fruit of Avalon" that could endow the individual with magical abilities. The apple tree is also the home of the mythical unicorn. Its energies are such that it can stimulate healing on all levels. It bears a fruit, and its blossoms are powerfully fragrant and can promote happiness and success. Its energies are cleansing to the astral body. It activates the need to make choices within one's life, and to see that there are always options. In Teutonic mythology, the apple stimulates youthfulness and beauty. It also has ties to Aphrodite, as it grew in Hesperides.

## ASH

The ash is the sacred tree upon which Odin sacrificed himself that he may achieve higher wisdom. The Teutonic gods held council under it each day. It has an energy that when aligned to will awaken greater strength and might. It is a universal source of light and life energy, amplifying the innate abilities of the individual. Using this as a magical name will manifest opportunities to link the inner and the outer worlds. There were nine worlds in Teutonic myth, all located throughout the great Tree of Life. The energy of this tree can open us to the perception of how events and people are linked together. Its energy promotes learning to be at one with the self, without cutting the self off from the rest of the world. It awakens the development of sensitivity to great and small influences. It also has ties to Celtic mythology and the one known as Gwydion.

## ASPEN

The aspen is a tree whose name and essence brings upon a facing of fears and doubts. It is associated with the Egyptian symbol of the uraeus. It is a tree of resurrection, and can bring a calming of anxieties around changes within one's life. It releases an energy into the individual's life that facilitates entering the subtler planes of life and greater soul fearlessness. It can open one to greater control of the dream realms of sleep. It can bring fears to the surface so that they can be met. Once met with determination, there occurs a rebirth and the ability to overcome impossible odds. It stimulates communication with the higher self.

## BEECH

The beech is a tree whose energy and essence can awaken old knowledge and new expressions of it. It awakens the soul quality of tolerance, and its name and essence help align the individual with the higher self. It can be a name that is beneficial for all patterns of growth. It can awaken greater opportunity to explore the past (immediate lifetime or past incarnations) and to synthesize that knowledge into new expression. This is the tree of the discovery of lost wisdom, and thus the individual must learn not to discount the knowledge and teachings of the past. It helps soften an over-criticalness due to the individual's past and balances oversensitivity.

## BIRCH

The birch tree is one whose name and essence has ties to ancient forms of shamanism. Staffs of birch were used by shamans to awaken an energy that would enable the individual to pass from one plane of life to another and to balance them as they made such treks. Balance in the awakening of energy is the essence of this tree. It awakens the energy of new beginnings and a cleansing of the past. It manifests opportunities to clear out old ideas, those which are no longer beneficial, as new energy must be purposeful. It is one of those energy expressions of nature whose name was renewed each year in varying ceremonies. Those who take upon this tree as a magical name, must also learn to renew it—re-dedicate it each year. This is best done in the month of November, as November was the start of the Celtic new year. Birch is known as the "Lady of the Woods," and it helps connect the individual to all goddesses of the woodlands. One is never to take its bark without permission of the goddess.

## CEDAR

Cedar is a tree whose name and essence will strengthen and enhance any inner potentials of the individual. Its energy is one of protection, and it can open opportunities to heal imbalances of an emotional or astral nature. This is a tree tied to strong healing energies. Cedar is a tree whose energies work to cleanse the auric field, especially at night while the individual sleeps. It helps the individual to balance the emotional and mental bodies and can stimulate dream activity which brings inspiration and calm. It is a tree of consecration and dedication, and it has ties to Wotan. Tradition tells us also that the unicorn keeps its treasures in boxes made of cedar.

## CHERRY

The cherry tree is the tree of the phoenix which rose from the ashes. One who aligns with its name and essence will find the energy and ability to rise from the fires of their own life in a magnificent manner. It awakens openness in consciousness and assists in the realization of insights. This is a tree whose essence can bring the individual to the threshold of a new awakening. It is up to the individual though to cross that threshold.

## CYPRESS

The cypress tree awakens the understanding of sacrifice within one's life. It opens one to a greater awareness that sacrifice must not always involve pain and suffering, especially when the sacrifice is made for something or someone we love. Its name and essence can awaken the primal feminine energies which reside within us all. It provides a manifestation for the opportunities of healing. It stimulates the understanding of crises, and it awakens the comfort of home and mother.

## ELDER

Elder literally translates as "old" and its energies are sacred to the followers of the old religion—especially those of Druid and Celtic tradition. This is a tree whose essence is that of birth and death, beginning and end. It is the tree of transition. It awakens opportunity to cast out the old and renew the creativity of the new. It is a tree whose energy always manifests changes within the life of the individual, and change is beneficial, even if its benefits are not immediately recognized. This tree and its essence can help open the individual to a greater understanding of the ancient burial rites as forms of initiation. It opens one to contact with the Mother Goddess in varying forms. It provides an energy of protection and healing. Its energies are dynamic and can be overwhelming at times. It is important to understand all the significance associated with this name in order to balance the energies as they manifest within your life. It provides blessed protection and it brings magic to even the slightest wish. Magic with the elder must be controlled or it will manifest confusion. It facilitates contact with the spirits of the woods, the Dryads, especially at the time of the Full Moon. It helps one to awaken a renaissance with the fairy kingdom. The elder tree is the mother who protects her groves and children.

## ELM

Elm is a tree whose name and essence lend strength to the individual. It assists the individual in overcoming exhaustion—especially that which has accumulated over great lengths of time. It helps the individual to awaken to more universal sources of strength so that individual strength will not be tapped and expended. This is the Tree of Intuition. Alignment with it assists the individual in "hearing the inner call." It is a tree strongly associated with the elfin kingdom, and alignment with this tree will assist the individual in attuning to those more ethereal beings of the nature realm. It is important though not to become lost within it or to become "fairy charmed."

## EUCALYPTUS

Literally, the name of this tree means "wrapped, covered." Its oil was used in the Ancient Mystery Schools to wrap the aura in balancing vibrations, for they recognized that knowledge could bring an unbalanced awakening of the psychic energies of the individual. Its energies are highly protective and dynamically healing on all levels. Its influence penetrates both the physical and subtle energies of the individual, and it stimulates an opening of the brow chakra. It can awaken the individual to full consciousness while in the dream state (lucid dreaming). It clarifies dreams and balances the emotions. It helps to bring out healing energies and an understanding of the causes of various illnesses.

## FIG

The fig tree was the sacred tree of Buddha. Under it he found enlightenment. Its name and essence when aligned to awakens the intuitive insight that enables the individual to put his or her life into a new perspective. It releases past life blockages, bringing them out and into the open so that new thresholds may be crossed. It is a tree whose energies help the individual to link the conscious mind with the subconscious and to do so with the correct perspective.

## HAWTHORN

Hawthorn translates as "garden thorn." It is a tree symbolic of the energies of fertility and creativity. It is one whose name and essence will stimulate and manifest opportunities for growth on all levels within the individual's life. It is a tree sacred to the fairies. It manifests opportunities for cleansing and the development of chastity that strengthens the individual's inherent energies and allows them to draw upon greater reserves. It provides protection against the inner magical realms, but the individual will have to learn not to act too hastily or the new doors will not be opened (and life may bring a thorn prick to remind you). It is a tree of magic—often of which those of the fairy realms hold knowledge. Once linked with properly, the individual's life will manifest many opportunities for new expressions of creativity and fertility. It is up to the individual though to act upon them in the appropriate manner.

## HAZEL

This is a very magical tree. It is a tree whose name is also a common name used in society by people. It comes from the "hazel nut tree" and indicates the quality of "quiet spirit." All fruit and nuts associated with trees are symbols of hidden wisdom, and this tree and its energies can bring out the opportunity to acquire and express hidden wisdom in a unique manner. Hazel twigs were often used as powerful dowsing instruments, being very sensitive to the electrical-magnetic fields of the earth and of individuals. Alignment with this tree awakens the inner intuition and insight, and it is a powerful tree for stimulating artistic and poetic skills. It is often associated with "skaldcraft" of Teutonic lore. It awakens one to the true power of meditation, and it helps the individual develop a greater concentration of innate talents.

## HEATHER

Heather is a tree whose name and essence can help the individual to awaken closer contact with the inner world of spirit. It can open one to the healing forces of nature and especially of the power for healing and magic with herbs. It helps the individual understand that healing begins within and not from without. This is a name and tree of fertility that can be expressed in many ways. The task of those who take this as a magical name will be to learn to build upon a strong foundation. Looking for shortcuts or easy ways will create problems and demand correction of the past and the laying of a new—more solid—foundation. Heather represents immortality, and it facilitates seeing the immortal soul. For those undergoing an initiatory path, its name and essence will help to unfold the inner potentials. It brings beauty into one's life.

## HOLLY

Technically, holly is a bush, but it has all the power of a tree. Its name and essence manifest an energy of protection. It has the archetypal energies of love, with its ability to overcome anger and hate. This is a tree whose energies can help the individual to awaken the Christ energies within, and can open one to angelic contact with time and effort. It holds the energy of the spiritual warrior, an energy that can be drawn upon in times of fighting and disruption. It activates the masculine energy of the individual in a creative manner. It is important for those who align with its energies not to scatter their own energies. Any lack of direction may create problems. This is a plant whose energies need to be honed and pruned and watched in order for the highest expression of it to manifest. Once done, it can stimulate a dynamic healing capability, one that can be expressed in many avenues. Holly was sacred to the Druids. They kept it in their homes during the winter to provide a haven for the "little people."

## HONEYSUCKLE

Honeysuckle is a tree with an energy that helps the individual learn from the past (present life or past life) so that mistakes will not be repeated. It may manifest similar situations as have been experienced from the past, to enable the individual to deal with them more productively and to eliminate the karma of such. It stimulates a strong energy of change, and it sharpens the intuition. It will open the psychic energies of those who align with it. It can bring revelations of hidden secrets, and assist the individual in developing a sureness, while overcoming any tendency toward faltering. Opportunities to develop strong discriminatory abilities are awakened—especially in distinguishing the true from the false. It helps the individual to follow his or her own beliefs safely. It awakens greater versatility and confidence, and the fragrance of its blossoms is "attracting" to those of the opposite sex. It helps the individual to balance the hemispheres of the brain for more powerful expressions of creativity. It increases understanding of non-physical realities and has ties to the Celtic goddess Cerridwen.

## LEMON

Lemon is a tree whose energies balance the aura and help to keep it cleansed of negative emotional and astral influences. This is especially important for those who are just beginning to develop and unfold their psychic energies. It draws protective spiritual guides and teachers into one's life, and it is especially powerful for anyone who does work at the time of the Full Moon. It brings clarity of thought, and its essence can make one more sensitive to using color therapy—in any of its forms—as a modality of healing. It stimulates love and friendship and it is strengthening to the entire meridian system of the body.

## LILAC

Lilac is a tree whose name and essence activates a play of archetypal energy within the individual's life that helps to spiritualize the intellect. It is a tree which will align and balance all of the chakra centers of the body, and it draws protective spirits into one's life. It awakens mental clarity, and for one wishing to activate the kundalini in a balanced manner, it is an excellent tree to align with. It has a strong tie to the nature spirits as they use its vibrations to raise their own consciousness. Various orders of fairies have always been associated with this tree. It can open one to a recall of past lives and can help awaken clairvoyance. Most importantly it manifests the energy that helps the individual realize that beauty is sufficient only to itself, and that there is a beauty inherent within all things.

## MAGNOLIA

Magnolia is a tree whose energies help to strengthen and activate the heart chakra, the center of idealism, love and healing. More importantly, its name and essence help to align the heart of the individual with his or her higher intellect. It is a tree whose essence strengthens fidelity and provides opportunities for developing strong relationships. It is an aid in the opening of psychic energies, and can enable the individual to use that intuition to locate lost items, lost thoughts and lost ideas and apply them anew.

## MAPLE

Maple is a tree which helps the individual to bring a balance to the male and female energies within. It balances the yin and yang, the electrical and the magnetic. This tree and the archetypal energies behind it help the individual to ground psychic and spiritual energies and to find practical means of expressing them within their lives. It is activating to the chakras in the arches of the feet, which enable the individual to stay tied to the energies of Mother Earth.

For men, this tree is often beneficial to align to as it facilitates the awakening and proper expression of the feminine aspects of nurturing, intuition and creativity. The flowering maple has the energies of sweet promises and aspirations. It awakens the inner fire which illumines without burning.

## MISTLETOE

The archetypal energies behind this are very powerful. The mistletoe was sacred to the Druids, and it was a predominant symbol of the feminine energy. It can be used to help the individual link with all lunar aspects within the universe. It manifests an energy of protection, particularly toward children or to the child within that the individual is trying to re-manifest. It can open one to recognizing the power and rhythms of change reflected within the lunar cycles, and it also increases dream activity. It has the capability of opening one to the primal feminine energies of the universe, but it may require sacrifice with joy in order to achieve such an alignment of such great intensity. It can be used to develop an "invisibility" or going unnoticed when desired, along with the ability to shapeshift. The mistletoe was a powerful herb of the Druids, used for fertility and as an aphrodisiac. It was a symbol of rebirth and the awakening of vision that could open the secrets of life beyond the physical. Its energy awakens the vision of one's soul life in the future.

## OAK

The oak tree was sacred to the Celts and Druids, and in the Teutonic mythology it was associated with the energies of Thor. It is a powerful symbol of the male energy, the yang or electrical aspect of the universe or individual. It is also aligned with all solar aspects of the universe. When aligned to, its name and essence awaken great strength and endurance—even through the most trying circumstances. It helps to manifest a stronger and more active sense of helpfulness towards others, and it opens one to more easily be helped by others. It is a tree with strong ties to the realm of nature spirits as well. The oak tree provides the energies to open the doorway to the inner realms and their mysteries. It can manifest in the auric field of the individual in a manner that makes for greater strength and security in all pursuits. It is a tree aligned with primal male force, which must be controlled and expressed properly. The acorn of the oak is a symbol of fertility and fruition and the manifestation of creativity. It represents the continuity of life.

## OLIVE

The olive tree is the Tree of Peace. It is tied to the archetypal energies of harmony and peace of mind, and when aligned to, its name and essence will manifest greater inner strength and faith as true forces—not just as beliefs. It brings the energies of renewal and rejuvenation—restoring a zest for life. It is also linked to the processes of regeneration—in physical healing and in spiritual unfoldment. It enables the individual to access the levels of consciousness that manifest inner guidance and deep levels of clairaudience. It increases sensitivity, and renews the individual's hope and will to enjoy life. It is also known as the Tree of Honor, and it has ties to Athena, Poseidon and Zeus.

## ORANGE

The orange tree is powerful in its ability to affect the astral body and energies of the individual. Aligning with this name and its essence can manifest an energy that assists the development of conscious astral projection, the rising on the planes. It is a tree whose energies bring clarity to the emotions and can assist in releasing gently emotional trauma. It brings calmness to highly charged states. Its energies aid in the development of counselling abilities, and it can stimulate dreams that provide clues to deep-seated fears or fears of unknown origins. It releases tensions held within the subconscious, and it can be used to create intense thoughtforms. It activates the spleen chakra, and it can put a person in the mood for marriage.

## PALM

The palm is the Tree of Peace. It has a powerfully calming energy associated with it, so much so that it can provide protection for all members of a group tied to the one who has aligned with its energies. It manifests opportunities to celebrate or to produce something worth celebrating. The leaves alone have been rumored to prevent evil from entering into an area. It is an easy plant to grow indoors, providing a protective energy for the home environment. It can open one in meditation to a realization of the divine within, and it can ultimately help one to learn to commune with members of the angelic hierarchy. It awakens one to the Christ within.

## PEACH

The peach tree is tied to awakening hidden wisdom, as with all fruit-bearing trees. In this case though, the archetypal energies behind it can help the individual to develop a new realization about immortality and how it can be attained. It can open one to magic associated with youth and the prevention of the aging process. It is tied to a renewed activation of the individual's life force, the kundalini. It stimulates artistic energies and the innovative applications of them within the bounds of the individual's life. It activates an energy within the aura of the individual that is calming to the emotions—of oneself and of those the individual comes in contact with.

## PINE

The pine tree was the Sacred Tree of Mithra. It also has ties to the Dionysian energies and mysteries. It is balancing to the emotions, and it awakens the divine spark which resides within the heart chakra for true salvation as defined through occult and Gnostic Christianity. Pine comes from a word that translates as "pain," and it is its essence that helps the individual to alleviate such within his or her life on any level. Pine has an archetypal energy that helps one eliminate feelings of guilt and over-emotionalism so that decisions can be made from as clear a perspective as possible. It heightens the psychic sensitivity while balancing the emotions as well. It helps the individual to express his or her creative energies without feelings of guilt and without allowing others to overly influence or manipulate. The pine tree is cleansing and protective against all forms of negative magic, and it helps to repel evil. It was a tree sacred to Poseidon.

## REDWOOD

The redwood tree is one of the largest and the oldest of the living trees upon the planet. They are direct descendants from the time of evolution known as Lemuria. Alignment with their name and essence can open one to understanding the evolutionary cycle of humanity. It enables the individual to put his or her life into an entirely new perspective. Its essence awakens a clear insight into one's own personal vision of life and what must be done to follow through upon it. It stimulates great spiritual vision—especially of the etheric realms. It activates the brow and crown chakras, although if not properly balanced, it will manifest as unbalanced imagination and even superstition. It awakens within the aura a vitality that is simultaneously soothing and stimulating. It awakens extended growth periods that will touch strongly upon soul levels.

## ROWAN

The rowan activates a play of archetypal energies that manifest opportunities for the individual to develop control of the senses—physical and otherwise. It is a powerful force against intrusion by outside energies (including spells and enchantment). This also involves those energies encountered throughout the day. Because the aura is partly an electro-magnetic field, contact with others throughout the day results in an accumulation of energy "debris." One who has aligned with the energies of the rowan are less likely to be affected by these extraneous energies as it serves as a cleansing force. Its essence can also help open one to understand the significance and practical application of the Norse Runes. It manifests an energy that will assist the individual in developing discrimination, especially in balancing common sense with superstition. This is the tree of protection and vision. Its energies invoke all goddesses and assist the individual in learning to call up magic spirits, guides and elementals. Its energies enhance the individual's creativity.

## SPRUCE

Spruce comes from a Russian word meaning "fine, smart." As a link to the archetypal energies of nature, it is powerfully effective in awakening realizations as to how best to detoxify one's system and to balance one's energies on all levels. It opens the individual to a clarification of disease causes—as applied to the individual. It awakens dream activity that gives greater focus to the individual, and can be used to discern proper spheres of focus for others as well. It is an excellent tree to align with for any disorientation or lack of direction. It amplifies healing on all levels, and it is calming to the emotions. It is a gentle awakener of the dynamic feminine intuition, and it can assist the individual in developing lucid dreams that lead to conscious out-of-body experiences.

## SYCAMORE

The sycamore was the sacred tree of the Egyptians. It is a tree whose name and essence can be used to draw the energies of Hathor into one's life and individual energy field. It is a tree whose name means "fig." As such, its energies when activated help prevent any atrophy of higher abilities the individual has brought into this lifetime. It can open communication between the conscious and subconscious minds. It strengthens the life force of the individual and opens the opportunities to receive "gifts" from the universe. These gifts may come in the form of assistance, compliments, etc. It is important to receive them graciously, for if we do not receive the "little" things, the universe will not bring us the "big" things. The sycamore awakens the feminine energies of intuition, beauty and nourishment. It can open one to the energies of love and nature and all their magnificent aspects.

## WALNUT

Walnut is a tree that can activate the energies of hidden wisdom within one's own life circumstances. It awakens the ability to make transitions of all kinds. Its energies are often catalytic in the manner in which changes will manifest, but once allowed to play out, *all* of the changes will be of benefit. It activates a cleansing of the auric field so that the individual can see clearly what needs to be changed and how to institute it from the clearest perspective possible. Its name and essence awaken the energy of freedom of spirit within the individual, as if breaking free of the cocoon. It manifests opportunities to follow one's own unique path in life. Whether the individual follows through on such opportunities is a free will decision. It activates the energy for initiating and initiation. It opens knowledge of the esoteric aspects of death and rebirth and how to apply them constructively within one's own life. The key is to be true to one's self when aligning with these energies. Self-deception and delusion results in chaotic disruption instead of creative transition when this tree is aligned to. It holds the power of re-birth.

## WILLOW

Willow is a magical and healing tree. Its name literally means "convolution," and there is a convolution of energies associated with it. It stimulates an energy of healing on many levels, especially though in the areas of herbology and aromatherapy. It will manifest opportunities to learn and explore these avenues. It awakens a flexibility of thought, and its energies—when properly aligned to—will help the individual to realize the very intimate link between thoughts and external events. It is associated with an awakening of the feminine energies, of going into the darkness of the womb and activating greater expression of them. It opens "night" vision, or vision of that which has always been hidden or obscured. It aligns one with the rhythms of the Moon, and it stimulates great dream activity. Individuals who align with this name and essence must learn to work with their dreams and learn to trust in their inner visions. The willow tree is associated with the goddess Bridget of Celtic mythology, and it can help one invoke and align with her energies as well. It awakens flexibility and many avenues of exploration. It awakens powerful opportunities for communication, and it has ties to all deities of other worlds. It is also linked to Orpheus who brought to Greece the teachings of music and nature and magic. It was the source of a strong religious herb in China, and has always been said to make powerful magical wands.

To the ancient Druids and Celts trees were mystifying and magical symbols of power and force. Every grove of trees was a source of a sacred spiral of energy which could be accessed for growth and enlightenment. The Druids even developed a secret tree alphabet known as the Ogham. Each letter of this alphabet was associated with the intrinsic energies reflected by the various trees. Some of the names of the trees as we now know them are simply labels, but myths have come to be associated with them. Some were named because of their characteristics. Some were named because of myths associated with them, and some had names which had no other meaning.

When we take the name of a tree as part or all of our magical name, we are giving it significance. We link specific energies with it, and by its name and all other correspondences we can apply, we activate those energies within our own life. We plant a tree of life that enables us to bridge and link our soul potentials to our physical consciousness. We begin a process of empowering our lives. We become the Tree of Life itself!

# 18

# Magical Names
# from Flowers

Flowers have been great sources of energy and inspiration. Every aspect of the flower has been used by healers and metaphysicians. The fragrances, the herbal qualities, the color and imagery serve as powerful sources of energy.

Many flowers have been associated with gods and goddesses. Individuals looking for a magical name can easily take the name of a flower that is associated with a particular god or goddess, rather than the specific name. In this way, there is a more generic association with the archetypal energies and thoughtforms behind it, and it allows for more individual expression.

Flowers in any form are sources of strong energy vibrations. Even dried flowers continue to be a source of such. It is only decayed and decaying flowers which are not. Modern spiritualists are very familiar with the energy aspects of flowers, and they take care to set flowers in the seance room or any room in which spiritual activities are going to occur. The influence of flowers upon all within its area is very subtle and very real. They raise the vibrations of the individuals, facilitating contact with the more subtle dimensions and realms.

Most people are at least superficially familiar with herbal aspects of flowers and plants, but an even newer process of using such has unfolded within this century and is growing in popularity. Flower elixirs and essences are becoming dynamic tools for healing physical and psycho-spiritual conditions. Each flower has its own unique vibration or energy pattern, and will interact with a human in definable ways.

The flower elixir is a means of drawing out the vibration or life essence of the flower and infusing water with it. This can then be taken internally to assist with particular conditions of the body, mind and spirit. (In the bibliography are several prominent works detailing this procedure for those wishing to explore further.) Although this process of healing with flowers from various plants, herbs and trees was established by Dr. Edward Bach, other groups have expanded upon his research. If for no other reason, sources of this information help to further define the very subtle influences of flowers within our lives. They help us to define and understand the archetypal energies that work through them.

All plants that flower—just as all fruit-bearing trees—are indicative of hidden wisdom that can be brought out into the individual's life. Just as with the trees that we may align with, it is important with flowers to learn as much about them as possible, especially if we intend to use a particular flower as a source for a magical name. Flowers have in the past provided great sources for the magical names of individuals, whether it is the taking of its more common name or the use of its botanical delineation (sagebrush vs. artemisia). In either case, when you take the name, you are aligning yourself with all aspects and energies of that flower. You are opening yourself to be influenced by all archetypal forces that reflect through the actual flower itself.

It is important to learn as much about the flower you choose for your name as possible. How and where does it grow? Under what climatic conditions does it best unfold? Learn all that you can about its growing process and all of its parts: roots, bulbs, stems, leaves, flowers, etc. Each aspect has significance and can help you to define how the archetypal energies working through it will manifest within your own life.

A good example can be drawn from the lily. Its fragrance awakens the divine aspects within ourselves. Its stalk is symbolic of the uplifting of the godly mind. The hanging leaves reflect the energies of humility, and its whiteness awakens the purity of the individual's soul and helps manifest its expression.

The color of the flower can reveal much about the flower's energy. In the list that follows, the colors are generally not given. You may wish to give your flower name a color association, not usually attributed to it. A study of the forces associated with colors will assist you in your understanding.

Is it a perennial (blossoms every year) or is it an annual (living only one growing season or year)? Most perennials have a cycle that lasts more than two years and longer, and thus one who links to the name of a perennial can unfold even greater energy with each passing year. With perennials, as you change, the essence to which you are aligning will change with you, adding to your overall soul energy on the etheric level. You are adding to the garden of your soul. With an annual which has a cycle of only one season or one year, you will have to replant and re-dedicate yourself ritually each year. This must be considered and aligned with your individual goals.

Make each aspect of the flower signify something, and honor it, just as was described with the trees. Buy bouquets of them on a regular basis. Paint and draw pictures of them. Plant them in your house, apartment or garden. Make an amulet upon which is a picture of it. Make a drawing on it in which the number of petals of the flower corresponds to the number of your birthdate. If numerologically, as described earlier, your birthdate comes to a 5, give your flower five petals, or five parts, or whatever. Use your imagination and find creative ways of applying it. Instead of using your birthdate, use the number for the date that you assume the magical name. There are no hard and fast rules.

By aligning yourself with the name of a flower, you are aligning with Mother Nature herself. You are opening yourself to creation, growth and sustenance.

In the following list of flowers and their energies, some of the names have specific meanings. Others do not. The ones that do, the translation of the name of the flower is given next to the name of the flower itself, enclosed in quotation marks. When possible use the name of the flower, its meaning, all the correspondences, colors, etc., to understand the energies associated with it so as to be able to more accurately discern how the energies will play within your life.

**AMARANTHUS** ("unfading flower")

This is a flower which has ties to those energies that facilitate an activation of visionary dreams. It assists in controlling radical dreams and helps maintain an alignment of all the subtle energies and bodies. It assists in overcoming fears.

**ANEMONE** ("breath, daughter of the wind")

To the Greeks, this flower was a gift from the god of wind,

Anemos. It has ties to all magic associated with the element of air. Its energies help to align the individual with sylphs and to overcome feelings of being forsaken. It also has ties to Aphrodite and Adonis. In Greek mythology it grew from the blood of Adonis, and thus it is associated with overcoming sorrow and feelings of abandonment. To the Chinese it was the "flower of death" and thus of re-birth as well. It helps the individual hear the higher voice of truth.

## ANGELICA ("angel, messenger")

This flower activates those archetypal energies which awaken clearer insight into the cause and nature of problems. Its name and essence help one to align with the angelic hierarchy and provide protection against negativity. It has ties to Atlantis where it was used to assist in achieving powerful forms of meditation. It draws good energy and fortune, and it balances the aura, so that the individual can radiate more joy. It helps in awakening the inner light, insight and inspiration. It is also associated with the archangel Michael and the Christian Feast of the Assumption.

## BABY'S-BREATH ("Gypsophila")

This wonderful flower has ties to energies which help the individual bring out greater modesty and their own unique sweet beauty. It helps the individual to unfold their abilities and potentials—to blossom without undo attention. Its biological name has a sound that is both exotic and enticing.

## BASIL ("royal")

Basil is a flower that activates those energies which help the individual to integrate sexual energies in a more dynamic and creative manner. It helps the individual to integrate sexuality and spirituality constructively. It has ties to the invoking of dragons of protection into one's environment. Its use as an incense was employed for such purposes by ancient magicians. It was also sacred to the deities of the Hindu religion and evoked within the aura an energy of romance. It awakens a higher sense of discipline and devotion.

## BEGONIA

This flower has a name and essence tied to the energies of balance on all levels. It awakens a balance of the internal with the external, the masculine and feminine. It awakens strong psychic energies, but it helps the individual learn to express them in a spiritual manner. The archetypal energies behind this flower are those of integrated balance on all levels and all planes.

## BLACK-EYED SUSAN

This flower has an energy which will awaken insight into emotional aspects of the individual. It brings light into the dark areas of the soul. It assists the individual in overcoming resistance. It is dynamically catalytic in opening the intuitive faculties and in increasing the insight. It stimulates an energy of change.

## BUTTERCUP

This flower has an energy behind its name and essence which awakens a new sense of self-worth. The individual will come to know his or her special gifts and how to apply them within this incarnation. It manifests energy for healing and understanding. It opens the individual to the power of words, especially when applied to healing. It opens opportunities for new life directions and the sharing of light with others.

## CACTUS ("thistle")

The cactus is tied to those energies which help in the manifestation of riches and beauty under all conditions. It helps the individual to rediscover the elixir of life within themselves, in spite of outer conditions. It manifests the life waters wherever one is parched.

## CARNATION ("of the flesh")

Carnation is tied to the archetypal forces of pure and deep love. It activates a dynamic healing energy that stimulates the entire body. It helps to remove blockages within the meridians of the body. It provides protection and strength to the aura. In Elizabethan times, it was a flower whose essence and energy would help "prevent untimely death upon the scaffold." It restores a love of self and of life.

## CHERRY BLOSSOM

Although this is a flower of a tree, it has some dynamic qualities associated with it, which will become active within an individual's life. It awakens the energies of faith and trust on high levels. It enables the individual to let go of the aspects of the ego which are preventing growth.

## CHRYSANTHEMUM ("gold flower")

This is a flower which has the capability of stimulating the heart chakra into greater activity. It ties the archetypal energies of vitality and suppleness to the individual, and it serves to strengthen the overall life force so that it can be expressed more lovingly and more beneficially as a healing force. It can open one to alchemical processes.

## CLOVER

Clover is a flower whose essence draws positive energies. It awakens a vibration of "luck" within the auric field. As an herb, it has magical ties to love and fidelity. It aids in psychic development and intuition, and it balances the hemispheres of the brain. The white clover is tied to the energies and goddesses associated with the Full Moon. It opens the individual to the kindness of nature.

## COLEUS ("sheath, scabbard")

This is a flower that has strong ties to the primal feminine energies of the universe. While the sword was always a symbol of the masculine, the scabbard reflected the feminine. Excalibur needed its special scabbard to protect Arthur from being killed. This is a flower that awakens the innate healing energies of the individual. It will often manifest a spiritual awakening and reveal a new path—one which will allow the individual to draw upon his or her own strength, beauty and power.

## CORNFLOWER

Cornflower is a powerful plant whose name and essence embody the energies of Mother Nature and all goddesses associated with her. It has ties to Demeter, Ceres, Artemis and Cybele, and it is a sacred flower of the Mysteries of Eleusis. It is a flower with ties to those archetypal energies which enable individuals to awaken their lives as if entering the spring of their lives. Its energies help the individual to discover a balance between things of heaven and of earth. It grounds psychic energies, while at the same time stimulates new visionary capabilities and clairvoyance. It stabilizes the auric field of the individual so that centeredness is maintained in spite of the environment. It has the capability of opening the individual to the creative forces of the universe as they play through the flora of nature. It is helpful in turning daydreams into applicable visions.

## COSMOS

This small flower has a very dynamic potential when aligned to by the individual. Its name and essence are tied to those universal energies which facilitate a linking of the heart and mind. It also has a dynamic affect upon the throat chakra, stimulating into activity any creative expression which has been lying dormant. It awakens the imagination, and it brings inspiration through the dream state. It can help the individual in the development of clairaudience.

## DAFFODIL

Daffodil is a flower whose essence draws the archetypal energies that will help the individual to link the subconscious and the superconscious mind (higher self). It stimulates an increasing realization that the true power of the innate beauty of the individual manifests most strongly through surrender to the divine. It opens deeper forms of meditation, brings clarity of thought and vitality of the body. It facilitates true contact with the higher aspects of the soul.

## DAHLIA

Dahlia is a flower whose name and essence will help manifest the archetypal energies of higher development in a unique manner. It awakens a true sense of self-worth and dignity (regardless of one's profession or position in life). An innate sense of inner nobility begins to grow within the individual. It awakens a strong realization of psychic ability, but with no sense of psychic "pettiness." It is a flower which helps the individual to overcome pride and false ego, so that the true potential can manifest undistorted.

## DAISY ("the day's eye")

This is a flower which draws to the individual an energy which increases awareness on all levels. There will occur a greater synthesis of ideas, and there will also occur a greater understanding of the archetypal forces in nature and how they manifest. This is a flower that attracts fairies and nature spirits, so those who align themselves with this name and its essence can open themselves up to commune and work with them more fully. It stimulates a spiritualizing of the intellect. In mythology it has been associated with the goddess Freyja of Teutonic lore and also the Dryads of Greek lore. It is associated with the energies of love and divination, and it helps to awaken creativity and inner strength.

## EDELWEISS ("noble white")

This is a flower tied to the archetypal energies of spiritual purity. Alignment with it will help manifest situations that will enable the individual to develop such within the confines of his or her life. It awakens the spiritual beauty that lies within all. It stimulates a sweetness of personality and an almost otherworldly purity that is necessary for entrance into some of the higher planes of life.

## FAIRY LANTERN

This is a flower tied to the fairy realm and can help open it to those who align with its name and essence. It is important to keep oneself grounded and not to become "fairy charmed" for it is within the physical that we must work and grow. It stirs the imagination, and helps to restore a child-like innocence and approach to the world. It awakens the feminine energies that are so strong in all pre-puberty children, so that the individual can learn to express it in a manner more creative and beneficial. It can awaken the sexual energies and provide opportunities for expressing them in a new and creative manner.

## FORGET-ME-NOT

This is a flower which can open the memory of the past—including past lives. It helps the individual synthesize all the experiences of the past and enables them to see them from a new perspective. It opens the individual to an understanding of karmic conditions. In meditation, it increases the spiritual experiences and brings greater contact with one's spiritual guides, be they one's ancestors or not. This flower and its energies make it easier to tap the higher realms and can lead to connecting with universal mind.

## FRANGIPANI

Powerful as both a flower and as a fragrance, this plant has a strong ability to stimulate the energies of the individual so that deeper meditational experiences occur. It is the flower of the microcosm of the universe in which all energies are reflected. It is a flower that has five petals, which in numerology is the number of man and the universal life forces expressed through humanity. It awakens a greater faith in oneself and in higher forces of the universe. It unfolds a greater sincerity within one's life, along with a greater sense of devotion and aspiration. It works upon the aura of the individual, manifesting an energy that awakens confidence and truth, so much so that others may confide secrets or place greater trust in you.

## GARDENIA ("of the garden")

This flower activates an energy which will help the individual align with almost any plant that can be found within a garden, along with any of the nature spirits that can be found there as well. Alignment with it creates a radiation of purity of action and purpose. It is a very protective flower in regard to one's emotional well-being. Its essence and name help prevent others from creating strife within your life. It repels negativity. It is especially beneficial for those who do a lot of counseling or for those who work with emotionally disturbed people, as it helps prevent becoming tied into their problems. It affects the auric field in a manner that helps one to remain objective. It awakens and increases telepathic abilities—especially with nature spirits. It draws vibrations of peace, love and healing to the individual, and it draws good spirits during ritual work. It has a very high spiritual vibration.

## GERANIUM ("crane's bill")

The crane, the animal to which this flower is also associated, is a symbol of the solar deities and the bridging of the spiritual and physical realms. This flower and its energies awaken a greater sense of happiness and stir the heart chakra into greater healing and a renewed sense of joy in life. It vitalizes the aura of the individual which has strong repercussions on all those within one's life. It helps one to pinpoint and grab life's happiness.

## GLADIOLA ("sword lily")

The gladiola is a flower whose name and essence help to make the individual receptive to divine will. It helps strengthen the individual so that he or she can follow the inner spiritual impulse. This name activates an energy which makes one receptive to more light within his or her life. It raises the lower emotions to higher aspirations. It helps move the individual from psychic energies to spiritual energies.

## GOLDENROD

Goldenrod has an energy and essence which help the individual discover his or her own "Quest for the Holy Grail"—a quest which reveals one's true essence and how best to manifest it within this incarnation. It strengthens the aura so that the individual can remain true to his or her essence, once uncovered. It facilitates the overcoming of false persona, while awakening creativity, intuition and great healing abilities. The individual learns to find the "gold" within all people and all situations.

## HEATHER ("forest")

Although also described within the section "Magical Names of Trees," it is also important to discuss it as a flower. The bloom of the heather has an energy attached to it that helps the individual link to the inner self more strongly. It is a universal healing energy which will act in the individual's life in the manner appropriate to him or her. It stimulates self-expression in those who align to its name and essence, and it facilitates the manifestation of inner forces and potentials in the outer world.

## HIBISCUS ("mallow")

Hibiscus is a flower whose name and essence activate the feminine energies in those who align with it. It stimulates positive feelings of sexuality and warmth . It is the flower of new creation. It has ties to Agni yoga and the process of spiritual purification. It assists the individual in integrating the feminine energies within the individual's life circumstances. It is the flower of the blossoming of new youth, and it assists the individual in attaining control of the inner power and enlightenment.

## HOLLY

Holly was also discussed to some extent within the section on trees. It is also covered here in that it is one of those plants that borders between being a tree and a flower. Aside from what has already been revealed about its energies, alignment with its name and essence will stimulate an opening of the heart so that true love can be expressed and experienced. It awakens compassion, and it assists the individual in understanding "misunderstood emotions."

## HONEYSUCKLE

Honeysuckle is also a tree, but its blossoms are powerful. It assists the individual in overcoming the past, and it awakens a power in one's dreams. It balances the hemispheres of the brain, enabling the individual to draw upon greater power and potential. When aligned to, it creates within the aura an air of confidence that affects others within your life. It helps awaken psychic energy and the ability to become magnetic in avenues desired.

**HYACINTH** ("blue larkspur, gem of blue color")
Ties to the myth of Apollo and Hyacinthus, this very fragrant flower has some powerful energies associated with it. Hyacinthus was fought over by Apollo and the wind god, Zephrus, who killed him when Apollo won his favors. This flower has an energy that can open one to an understanding of many of the ancient burial rituals and the esoteric mysteries within them. It is effective in overcoming feelings of grief and jealousy, and it awakens a strong sense of inner beauty. For men, it is a flower whose name and essence bring lessons of gentleness and expression of feminine energies in a creative and productive manner.

**IRIS** ("crystal, rainbow promise")
Iris was the goddess of the rainbow. As a flower, its name and essence are tied strongly to the archetypal energies associated with creativity and self-expression. It is a flower which draws to the individual higher inspiration and psychic purity. Iris, as the goddess of the rainbow, lead souls to the Elysian Fields. Alignment with the flower named for her awakens within the auric field a strong sense of peace and the hope for new birth. This flower is sacred to all who worship and reverence the virgin goddess in any of her forms.

**JASMINE**
Jasmine is the sacred flower of Persia, and it held great symbology and significance to those within the Persian Mystery Schools. To those who align with its name and essence, it draws good spirits. It stimulates an energy within the auric field of self-esteem. It is also a flower which stimulates the ability to manifest prophetic dreams. It also activates the god-spark within the heart chakra. It awakens greater discrimination, manifesting opportunities to develop such, along with mental clarity. It is a powerful flower to stimulate major transformations within one's life.

**LAVENDER**
A very sacred flower, it has many magical properties. When aligned to its name and essence, it activates an energy of stability within one's life. It assists the individual in making any magical operation permanent, and it was a powerful flower, used in rituals associated with Midsummer Eve (a dynamic time to assume this

magical name). Lavender was used by Solomon to clean sacred circles, as it activated an extremely high vibration that is impenetrable to lower thoughtforms and astral entities. It draws love and protection, and it was considered a good remedy for cruel treatment by spouses. It is a powerfully healing flower, and it activates the crown chakra and the chakra above the medulla oblongata which stimulates mental clarity, keen awareness and alertness. It stimulates the aura to a degree that spiritual beings are more visible to the naked eye. It helps integrate aspects of the higher self into the personality. It stimulates visionary states, connecting people to their higher self and helps to manifest situations for the removal of karmic blockages. It establishes emotional balance and it has ties to the kingdom of nature spirits. It can be aligned with to overcome certain emotional blocks and conflicts that hinder spiritual growth.

## LILAC

Discussed under the section on trees, the flowers of this tree need to be explored as well. Very fragrant and powerful, the lilac stimulates mental clarity, and its name and essence can help the individual to link more productively with the kingdom of nature spirits. The name and essence of this flower align all of the chakras and spiritualize the intellect. It activates the kundalini in a balanced manner. It can open the individual to the ability to explore past lives, and it activates greater clairvoyance.

## LILY

The lily is the flower of birth. It has many mythical ties. Its name and essence align one with the archangel Gabriel and the power of the Winter Solstice. It is also tied to St. Leonard, the slayer of dragons. Tradition tells us that this flower sprouted from the blood of his wounds as it touched the earth. This is a flower which is a favorite to fairies and nature spirits, and those who align with it are also aligning themselves with them. It awakens the energy of new birth on all levels. The stalk of this flower is the symbol of the godly mind being awakened within the individual. The hanging leaves are the humility that comes to life, and its whiteness is the purity being activated. Its fragrance opens the individual to the divine. It is a sacred flower of great power.

## LOTUS

A sacred flower of the Orient, it has been associated with many ancient masters, gods and goddesses. These include Isis, Osiris, Hermes, Kwan Yin, Brahma, Buddha and Horus. It is the flower of the avatar, the one striving to become the master. It stimulates high visionary states, and alignment with it opens one to healing on all levels. It stimulates great spiritual openness. It activates a higher sense of grace, harmony and synthesis in all areas of life. It aligns and balances all the chakras, and it is especially activating of the brow and crown chakra, and it stimulates within the auric field of the individual an energy of calm and serenity. It spiritualizes the psychic energies, and it opens one to newer and higher forms of knowledge.

**MANGO** ("Mangifera")

Although a tree, its flower has a dynamic quality beneficial for all who are working to unfold their psychic energies. It awakens the intuition and stimulates telepathy. Anyone who works with the nature realm in any fashion can benefit by alignment with this name and essence. It has ties to the archetypal energies that awaken within the aura the hope of true spiritual realization—one that is attained by alignment with nature. Its scientific name has an exotic sound which reinforces this.

**MARIGOLD**

This is the flower of fidelity and longevity. Its name and essence are tied to the feminine master of the true Christ Mysteries—the one known as Mary. It is a flower which can open the individual to an understanding of the power and use of words in healing processes. It awakens clairaudience and any ability towards achieving visionary states. It is a flower of love and sacrifice. One tradition tells that it sprung from the blood of the natives of Mexico after they were slain by the Spaniards. It has ties to the archetypal forces of consecration and the blessing of all departures. It has the ability to open one to the mysteries and magic of thunderstorms.

**MORNING GLORY**

Alignment with this flower through its name and essence will help put the individual in touch with those archetypal energies which assist in the breaking down of old habits. It stimulates and draws fresh life forces and it heightens the overall sensitivity of the individual. It builds within the aura an energy of spontaneity. It enables the individual to draw upon inner resources with greater effortlessness and to bring out the inner beauty as an offering in the lives of others.

## MOUNTAIN PRIDE

This wildflower is powerful for anyone wishing to become a true "spiritual warrior." Its name and essence draw strength and assertiveness out of the inner self and into greater expression. It manifests an energy which is active and positive in all confrontations. It strengthens the spiritual beliefs and attitudes, and it helps the individual remain true to that which is held most dear.

## NARCISSUS

This has ties to both the Greek and Egyptian mythologies. Its name and essence awakens an energy of self-exploration and the balance of sexual energies, a quieting of desires. Narcissus fell in love with his own reflection, and this flower can break a pattern of self-absorption. Its name and essence awaken inspiration and creativity. It is a flower tied to Isis in her maiden aspect and can invoke the energies associated with her into one's life and aura. It may manifest as an aphrodisiac within the energy of the individual which must be balanced and controlled—re-channeled into productive creativity.

## ORCHID

Orchid is a name and flower with ties to the satyrs of mythology, some of whom were teachers to humanity of the healing arts. Alignment with this essence affects the sexuality. In mythology, Orchis was born of a nymph who had been seduced by a satyr. For those interested in the spiritualizing of sexuality and in various forms of sex-magic, this is a name and flower that will assist. Its energies are strong, and they must be controlled or they will become unbalanced, so much so that sexuality can get out of control or the quelling may create abstention. This is a name and flower for those wishing to manifest the energies that will force a development of control and positive expression of the sexual energies.

### PANSY ("to weigh or consider")

Pansy is a flower with strong connections to various orders of devas and nature spirits. For those wishing to work with them, it is an excellent name and essence to align with. One source associates this flower with Lemuria and the birth of the black race upon the planet who would sow the seeds for great civilizations upon the planet in the ages to come. It is tied to those archetypal energies which help one to create and magnify thoughts into stronger more productive bands of energy. It helps in the creation of thoughtforms, and its energies touch the core of the mind to assist the individual in turning his or her thoughts to the divine.

## PEONY ("healing")

The peony is a flower that some traditions tell us was created by the goddess of the Moon to reflect her light at night. Just as the Moon reflects the light of the Sun, alignment with this flower's name and essence assists in your own inner sun in being reflected out into your life more distinctly. It helps to cleanse the aura of negative energies and it promotes the manifestation of any healing and artistic abilities within the individual. Its roots were used to carve amulets because of its protective energy.

## PERIWINKLE

Periwinkle is a small blue/purple flower that has been used by many people as both an herb and as a symbol of one's beliefs. Its name and essence are linked to thoughtforms associated with Wicca and all of those known for healing and magic in many villages and towns of older times. Its essence awakens a renewed sense of coming into a new life. It is protective to the aura, and it has ties to the energies of love and immortality.

## PETUNIA

The name and essence of this flower will activate the archetypal forces within a person's life that will manifest opportunity to develop proper behavior. It awakens a change in mental attitude, one more appropriate to one's individual life environs. It stimulates a greater, more solid fusion between the higher self and the outer personality. It awakens within the aura an energy of enthusiasm. There will begin to manifest an integration of joy and vitality in all areas of life.

## PHLOX ("flame")

Phlox is a name whose essence activates the universal forces for the unfoldment and development of skill and craftsmanship in some area of the individual's life. It awakens any latent artistic abilities, and it stimulates within the energy field a greater conscious control of all work environments, enabling the individual to become more productive in any avenue of endeavor.

## PUSSY WILLOW

A powerful plant, pussy willow is a name and essence to align with if you are wishing to open to divination in any form. It is tied to the archetypal energies of the future. It holds within its energies the promises yet to be fulfilled. It renews and revitalizes, awakening the inner fires of hope and inspiration for that which is yet to come.

## QUINCE

Often associated with the goddess Venus, it is tied to the universal energies of love. It awakens the feminine, and it stimulates within the auric field an energy which promotes greater expressions of love and mothering. Its name and essence help the individual to balance love and nurturing with power and strength. It draws to the individual opportunities for self-actualization.

## ROSE

One of the most sacred plants, its name and essence are linked with dynamic archetypal energies of love. In mythology it has been associated with Cupid, Venus and Adonis. It has also come to be associated with the blood of Christ within the Christian tradition, but even more so with the feminine expression of the Christian mysteries—Mary. Alignment with its energies activates the heart chakra for healing and increases telepathy. It awakens a greater love for divination and healing. It can help open one to exploration of the mystery of time, life and death and all that is unknown. It is tied to the energies of "strength through silence." The red rose is a symbol of the Sun, of earthly passion, love and fertility, of the divine manifesting in the physical. The white rose is a symbol of the Moon and of purity of the inner divine aspects of the soul. The pink rose is a symbol of the blending of the male and female within to give new birth and creation to one's life. The blue rose opens one to the energy that makes the impossible possible and the unobtainable obtainable.

## ROSEMARY

This herbal flower is one of the most powerful against any form of black magic, hatred and evil. It aligns the individual with those archetypal energies that protect and strengthen the individual auric fields. It is linked to the kingdom of nature spirits and elves. It promotes the awakening of healing potentials, and it draws opportunities to explore various avenues of healing within one's own life. It stimulates creativity and it brings clarity to the mind. It increases the individual's sensitivity, and alignment with it assists in integrating spiritual and soul warmth with the outer personality. It reduces the ego, and it assists in the development of out-of-body experiences.

**ROSE OF SHARON**
This flower and its essence stimulate a play of energy into the individual's life that facilitates bringing the personal will into alignment with divine will. It strengthens the individual's energies at all levels to help triumph over all obstacles. It awakens the soul power to be at the divine's service. This name and essence are tied to those energies that give one the power to live a higher form of life.

**SAGE** ("Salvia")
One of those flowers whose botanical name can be adapted and assumed for greater mystery, sage is a dynamic flower and herb. Alignment with its name and essence stimulates an energy which facilitates achieving higher states of consciousness. It aligns the subtle bodies so that a greater flow of spiritual energy can occur within the physical. It helps integrate spiritual inspiration with outer personality. It awakens psychic faculties and mediumistic abilities. It releases tension that is accumulating within the auric field of the individual. It slows the aging process, and it awakens a newfound sense of immortality and wisdom within the confines of one's own life. Alignment with it creates an increased interest in spiritual matters.

**SHOOTING STAR**
The name and essence of this flower are tied to those archetypal energies which will help the individual to feel more at home on earth. This is especially effective for those who have feelings of alienation—from home, family, study groups, etc. It manifests an energy that helps the individual's energy field connect more fully with the magnetic fields of the earth. There occurs more of a grounding and a sense of security. It awakens a sensitivity to the stars and opens one to greater knowledge and insight into astrology. It helps develop a sensitivity to the process of dowsing and the ley lines of the earth. This is a good flower to have around with any group that is beginning to form, as it helps the individuals feel less isolated and

more integral to the group process.

## SNAPDRAGON

Snapdragon is a flower whose name and essence make a powerful inner amulet and talisman for the individual who assumes it. It has ties to the energies of all dragons—those which are meant to be controlled and not slain. Ancient magicians used to invoke etheric dragons into their environments for protection, guidance and strength. The snapdragon has ties to those same energies and more. It awakens the throat chakra, stimulating the will force into greater creative expression. It can help open one to clairaudience, and it assists the individual in discovering the true power of expression and the ability to manifest. Its energies protect the individual against all unwanted influences.

## SPIDER LILY

Legends of the spider woman permeate societies around the world. The spider woman was one who spun the web of life. One either had to learn to walk the threads or be caught within them. Such is much of the energy of this plant when aligned to by an individual. Its name and essence manifest an energy of opportunity to spin new patterns within individual lives. It brings an energy that teaches versatility and suppleness. This is a name and essence of alchemy and transformation and of learning to move more freely—in new realms or within the old.

## STAR TULIP

This flower has ties to archetypal energies that can make the individual more receptive to the spiritual realms. Its name and essence can awaken opportunities to develop clairaudience. It is vitalizing to the auric field when aligned to—so much so that it can manifest direct contact with one's spiritual guides. There occurs a growing dream awareness, and a clarity of the inner voice.

## SUNFLOWER ("Helianthus")

Sunflower is a plant with dynamic energies, associated with the archetypal masculine forces of the universe. Its botanical name makes for a wonderful magical name. It manifests opportunities which help the individual find his or her inner sun. It has a name and essence that assist the individual in finding his or her own power and means of self-actualization. This flower was sacred to the

Aztecs, and thus can align the individual with their gods and goddesses. It opens one to the influence of energies associated with all of the Sun gods. It increases a sense of happiness and well-being within the auric field. Alignment with it can draw protective lions and fire dragons into one's environment. Its energies often awaken opportunities to increase one's learning of how to heal with stones and gems.

## SWEET WILLIAM
Sweet William is a flower whose name and essence awaken within the individual greater obedience to divine will. The name William means "brave and protecting." When we align to the divine will we are protected and can walk without fear. This is a flower which activates an energy within the individual's life providing opportunities to reveal the gold of the soul. It awakens higher forms of intuition and psychic sensitivity, along with creative fires.

## TIGER LILY
Tiger lily is a flower of great strength. It awakens the energy of the soul so that opportunity arises to overcome the lower self and the baser emotions. It balances the auric field when aligned to by the individual. It brings into harmony the male and the female aspects of the personality and the soul so that new expression can be given birth to. This is a flower which helps the individual to understand the power—equal but distinct—that resides within both aspects of themselves, the male and the female. It helps awaken a realization of when to draw upon which aspect for the greatest success. The individual should also explore all the energies associated with the tiger, as these will also be experienced when aligned to. This name can be invoking to etheric tigers.

## TRILLIUM ("triplet")
This is a flower\plant that is endangered, and yet it has ties to very dynamic archetypal energies. The aspect of three within it has great symbology. The trinity—in some form or another—has been a major symbol of most of the ancient mystery schools. It is the symbol of the male and the female coming together creatively to produce the "holy child" within. Alignment with this flower activates this force within your life. It brings the energies of sacrifice for higher causes and goals. It is purifying to the auric field, and it activates the seat of the kundalini so that it can be given new movement

and expression within your life. It opens opportunity for greater service. It awakens any healing abilities latent within the soul and brings a sense of peace to one's life, regardless of the circumstances. It is one of linking the physical and the spiritual into new forms of expression.

**TUBEROSE** ("swelled or raised area")

This is the flower and name of new creation—of being pregnant with new life. It has strong ties to the archetypal energies of love and attraction and the new creations that come from it. As a fragrance, it was once known as the "mistress of the night" as the most virtuous were supposed to succumb to its influence. It brings into the auric field an energy that promotes serenity and peace of mind. It is stimulating to the crown chakra when aligned to and it energizes all of the bodies, physical and subtle. It increases one's sensitivity and psychic capabilities. It manifests opportunities to turn one's vital energies toward the light.

**TULIP** ("turban")

Alignment with this flower and its name draws to one an energy of trust and success. It is clearing to the mental faculties, and it opens one to a greater sense of discernment and discrimination. Tulips come in various colors, each with its own distinct energy which must be explored. Many vary in the number of petals as well, which is quite significant. This flower has an energy that assists the individual in staying grounded and works on any "air-headed" tendencies. It stimulates greater vision in meditation, and it facilitates the individual in seeing the hidden significance of events, people and things.

**VIOLET**

Violet is a name and flower of simplicity and modesty. One myth tells how it came from the nymph IO. It is the occult symbol of twilight, the power point in time when the Sun has set and the light still remains, although diffused. It is the occult time of peace. Many legends speak of the violet being sacred to the Fairy Queen, and gathering the first wild violet in the spring brings an energy of luck and the assistance of the fairy realm into your life for the fulfillment of one's dearest wish in the year ahead. It is good to re-dedicate oneself to this name at such time. This flower and its essence assist the individual in discerning his or her relationship within groups. It awakens a psychic sensitivity—one that reveals itself strongly through dreams. This flower can open dreams as sources of information, making them more clear and understandable.

## WATER LILY

This flower and its name are tied to great psychic energies. It is associated with the water element which is the psychic sensitivity within ourselves. It awakens such sensitivity within the auric field of the individual. It can help link the individual to all the energies associated with the water nymphs of myth and lore. It is powerfully—though subtly—healing. It makes the energy of the individual more magnetic—activating receptivity toward that which is most strongly focused upon. It opens opportunities for wealth in various forms. It is tied to the feminine forces of the universe, bringing them into greater activity within the life of the individual.

## WISTERIA

This exotic flower and name are very powerful, with dynamic ties to archetypal energies. It is an excellent name to align with for those who are students and scholars as it stimulates the manifestation for greater opportunities to learn, especially that which is not normally accessible. It stimulates an awakening of inspiration in the life of the individual and, in fact, it has been known as the "poet's ecstasy." Occultists and healers have used its fragrance to draw good vibrations. This flower and its name activate the heart and throat chakras. It awakens a realization of the good that is already present within one's life; it clears the fog within the aura. It stimulates creative expression and the "power of the word." It is of a rare spiritual influence that can be a passport to higher consciousness. It opens the doors between the realm of humanity and the realm of the divine. It assists the individual in contacting other planes of life and higher forms of illumination.

## YLANG YLANG

This exotic flower is probably best known for its effects in aromatherapy, but as a magical name, it activates those qualities and more. It facilitates greater productivity in meditational experiences. It widens one's perceptions, and it is strengthening to the will of the individual. It becomes easier for the individual to hold to his or her truths without distortion. It is cleansing to the energy of the individual, cleansing the fog of doubt from it. It stimulates greater clarity of thought and perception, and the intuitive senses become more specific and more easily recognized.

## ZINNIA

This wonderful flower has a name and essence that are beautiful in the manner which activates the play of archetypal energies within the individual's life. It touches that aspect of the soul where child-like humor and innocence still reside. It helps to re-awaken the energy of the inner child, the child that can see all things new, bright and beautiful. It restores our sense of humor, and it awakens within the energy field of the individual the opportunity and ability to touch and heal others with that soft humor. It strengthens and instills a strong sense of encouragement and hope. It releases the energy of endurance and courage in all things. The beauty of the world is re-discovered.

# PART V

# CREATING NAME TALISMANS

# 19

# The Functions of
# Name Talismans

According to the Golden Dawn, a talisman is a "magical figure charged with a Force which it is intended to represent... it should be in exact harmony with those you wish to attract, and the more exact the symbolism, the more easy it is to attract the Force..." Talismans and amulets have been associated with every society, especially those involved in the teaching and working of mysticism and magic. Technically, the talisman is considered that which attracts beneficial energies and effects, while the amulet is that which wards off dangers and misfortunes. For our purposes here, we will be using the two terms interchangeably and adapting their meaning somewhat.

The name talisman is that which becomes charged with the universal forces associated with the symbols of the name, but it is also a physical reminder to the conscious mind of the inner aspects, qualities and energies associated with the name. The more conscious we become of these aspects, the easier it is for them to manifest within our lives.

Almost anything can serve as an amulet or talisman. It depends tremendously upon the significance we attribute to it. A color, a stone, a feather, etc., anything can become such if we imbue it with special significance. There are those who will say that nothing can be an amulet or talisman without being properly "charged," blessed and dedicated. Often such purists forget that it is the above processes which are used to imprint upon the conscious mind the unconscious significance of the talisman, thereby enabling the individual to first become more aware of the archetypal forces and second to manifest them more consciously.

This is not to say that amulets and talismans are not empowered through such processes, as they are dynamically affected. To understand this, we must understand basic energy patterns. Anything that has an atomic structure has an electro-magnetic energy field. It gives off (electric aspect) and it draws (magnetic aspect). This is due to the activity of the electrons and protons that comprise each atom. When we consciously focus upon and create a talisman or amulet, we are linking its electro-magnetic energies with our own electro-magnetic energy field and all of its capabilities.

When we inscribe symbols, images, etc. upon something we intend to use as a talisman or amulet, we are bringing its basic electro-magnetic energy field into a new vibrational pattern, one in accord with the symbol or image upon the talisman. We are taking the energy field of the talisman, and by what we inscribe upon it, we align its energies with various archetypal energies. The talisman then becomes a more physical bridge to those energies. Thus when we wear it or use it, it can assist in bringing our own individual energy field into greater resonance with those universal energies. The talisman becomes a tool to help align us with the archetypal forces.

This presupposes that the energy invoked by the talisman is strong enough to create a kind of "forced" resonance of the human energy field. And this is not necessarily so. It is why many groups and individuals use rituals and specific, intricate procedures in "charging" or increasing the energy of the talisman. With all this, we must remember that it is only a tool, and it can do no more than what we allow. It is an amplifier and adapter of energy patterns. Remember that every geometric shape, image, color, sound, etc. has a capability of altering energy patterns and fields to any degree that we allow them. We do not want to become superstitious with this process. We are simply employing it in a manner to assist in amplifying what we have already aligned ourselves with—the archetypal energies behind our names.

As microcosms of the universe, we have access to an infinite amount of energy. In the creating of talisman and amulet, we are drawing (magnetic) more energy form the universe and charging (electrical) the amulet or talisman with it. Since it has a capability of receiving such because of its own magnetism, it can then become a conductor or a reservoir of energy that we can use to more easily link ourselves with the archetypal forces of the universe. Those that are the most accessible to us are those associated and hidden within the name(s) we take upon ourselves.

Talismans and amulets have been used in every society, although few understand how they really work. The St. Christopher medal and the rosary are two of the more common in Western Christian societies. One who wears a cross around his or her neck is using a talismanic image. This image is a reminder and a symbol of a profession of one's beliefs and faith. It helps to keep those beliefs fresh within the conscious mind. It also interacts with the energy field of the individual altering it so that it is easier to be conscious of that which it symbolizes. Talismans are both reminders and simulators of creative forces.

Many of the oldest charms and amulets are derived from nature—stones, herbs, feathers, etc. Each takes on its own unique significance to the individual. Anything which helps us to develop a strong, conscious connection to a force or energy within us or outside of us can be considered a talismanic tool.

The images and symbols used on or with talismans and amulets serve a number of purposes:

1. Images—especially mythic images and those of nature—awaken a sense of relationship to those "mysterious" dimensions of the universe. They help us to recognize that we are connected to all things and all times.
2. They bring the basic energy pattern of the talisman into a new and specific vibrational pattern, one in accord with the individual's purpose, thereby serving as a conductor and bridging those archetypal energies reflected by the symbol and image.
3. They are reminders to the conscious mind of the archetypal energies operating within one's life.
4. They open astral doorways, enabling a greater flow of universal energy into one's life, which can help orient us to a more subtle and spiritual train of thought.
5. They link the past with the present and the present with the future, helping us to see that all things are connected.
6. They link the physical world to those spiritual dimensions and energies which influence it. They assist us in learning to recognize the interplay of the archetypal forces as they are translated into physical expression so that we can develop greater control and consciousness over all aspects of our life and energy.

Those talismans which are the most effective are those which are personally made and those which are aligned with one's name. They are the easiest to "charge" and the easiest to establish as conductors for an enhancement and new expression of personal potentials. The process is neither entirely esoteric nor complicated. *The more significance that you can attribute to your talisman, the more of an imprint it will make upon your own energies!*

For name talismans, you must know what everything upon the talisman will represent. In order to know that, you must know as much about your name as possible: meaning, sounds, rhythms, glyphs of the individual letters, the hidden potentials reflected within the vowels... You must decide which of those energies of your name you wish to activate more strongly within your life.

A good name talisman can include aspects of just the birth name, just the magical name or combinations of both. We will explore variations of all three, but before you begin the construction of your talisman, make sure you know which name and which energies you most want to activate and emphasize within your life. Once the process of focus upon the specific energies of a name or an aspect of your name begins, the increased activation of the archetypal energies behind it also will begin.

Most esoteric systems teach access to "magical states of consciousness" and archetypal energies through basic visualization and forms of meditations. This alone will initiate a new play of energy within the individual's life, in accordance with the point of focus. This applies to the making of talismans as well. As you begin to focus, the visualization and thought processes involved in its design affect a more dynamic play of the corresponding energies within your life. Know what you want!

# 20

# Considerations in Constructing Name Talismans

Decide which name you desire to use as the basis for your talisman. It may be the birth name, the magical name or both. All are powerful sources for linking to the archetypal energies most active within your life. For those just starting their studies and self-explorations, I recommend the birth name be used. There are so many energies and hidden potentials to which we have access through our name. Most individuals are unaware of that process. As we learned earlier within this work, we can easily turn the birth name into a magical name.

Learn as much about your name as possible. Study the significance of the letters, their sounds, the rhythms, the meaning, the energies and potentials—everything that you can. Meditate upon your name. Meditate upon each element. It is often said that for every one hour of study the individual should use three hours of meditation. Much insight into the specifics of the name characteristics—as they apply uniquely to your life—may only come to you through meditation.

Decide on some near and long range goals in your life, and then decide which energies associated with your name would be the best to amplify in order to assist you in the achievement of these goals. This can help you to determine which vowel you most want to stress and activate within your name—birth or magical. This vowel can become the basis for a wonderful talisman. Remember that a talisman can be an inner talisman, built into the aura through meditation. It can also take the outer, more traditional form which can enhance the creation and manifestation of these same energies within the aura.

There are some basic, preliminary considerations in the actual construction of any talisman or amulet:

1. The outer, more traditional, talisman and amulet can be made of various materials: parchment, wood, metal, stone, paper, cloth, etc. There is no hard and fast rule. Metal is more effective since it is an excellent conductor of electrical energy, but it is not practical or accessible to the average individual. It demands a degree of training and skill. Parchment and paper are easy to work with, although if worn or carried upon the person, they are not always durable. Cotton cloth is effective, as it is both durable and it is easy to charge. It has a strong magnetic aspect, allowing it to form and hold a particular energy pattern rather easily. Wood is also durable and it can be easily worked with, whether drawn upon, painted, carved or burned. Many craft stores carry small (two to three inches) circular pieces of wood that can easily be turned into a talisman or amulet. Although wood is not a great conductor of electrical energy, its other qualities make up for it.

2. The geometric shape of the talisman or used within the talisman itself will strongly affect the energy of it. Geometric shapes interact with electro-magnetic fields, creating variations. Most people are familiar with the fact that pyramidal shapes will amplify or intensify the energy field of whatever is within it. Other geometric shapes alter fields in just as a unique manner.
   a. The *square* is a form which stabilizes the energy field. It helps to establish equilibrium. It is calming and settling to an individual's energy. It also amplifies the balancing of the base chakra of the individual, the seat of the life force. It is grounding.
   b. The *triangle* (pyramid) is amplifying to all energies. If pointed upward, it raises the physical energies toward the spiritual; it lights the individual's fires. If pointed downward, it is drawing of the spiritual energies into the physical (water). It is thus a form which can be used in talismanic work to heat up or cool down any archetypal forces playing within the individual's life. It is cleansing to one's energy and

aura, and it balances the spleen chakra center, the center of our emotional creativity.

c. The *Star of David* or two interlaced triangles is a powerful geometric shape to use in the construction of talismans. It is the linking of the male and the female, the physical and the spiritual—the outer name and its inner force. It is a symbol which activates a bridging of the inner potentials and the outer personality, the heart and mind which control the archetypal energies at play within our lives. It helps bring the inner divine into play upon the physical. It affects both the heart and brow chakras, and it activates an energy that allows the archetypal forces affecting us to do so in a protective and strengthening manner without overwhelming us in the process. It helps activate the inner solar fires that resonate within our lives through the vowels within our names.

d. The *cross* is a geometric form that helps to balance the play of four elements within our lives more fully. It affects the heart chakra, and it links and balances the four expressions of archetypal energy within our lives—physical, emotional, mental and spiritual. It will also balance the male and female aspects, the electrical and magnetic energies of the individual, so that a more balanced expression of the archetypal energies of one's name can be experienced.

e. The *crescent* or Moon shape is one that enables the feminine aspects of the individual to manifest more fully. It affects the magnetic energies of the individual. It also activates the throat chakra, the center of higher creative expression, with a greater intuitive understanding of one's inner potentials. It has ties to Nada Yoga and the activation of the power of the sounds within our names.

f. The *pentagram* or five-pointed star is the symbol of the microcosm. It helps in talismanic work to activate all of the universal energies being expressed through you and your name. It helps provide a concentrated force of energy surrounding anything enclosed within it. It is also drawing to those of the nature kingdom and the angelic hierarchies who work to manifest the play of archetypal energies within our lives. The single point should always be upward, or it will turn all of the chakras backward and create a distortion and interruption of the normal flow of electro-magnetic energy within the auric field.

g. The *seven-rayed star* when used in talismanic work activates a healing energy. In the creation of name talismans it will stimulate not only a healing of the name enclosed within it, but it will also stimulate into greater activity any healing abilities or potentials of the individual. It balances all of the chakra centers of the individual so that there is a much more distinct play of archetypal forces into his or her life. It is a particularly protective geometric form for children or for the child within us. This particular shape has ties to the Celtic tradition and more specifically to the one known as Bridget (St. Bridget).

h. A study of geometry and shapes will provide even more significance of these shapes and others. These can then form the entire shape of the talisman itself, or it can be used to enclose the name, or aspect of the name, within the talisman itself.

3. The most common and the most effective shape for a name talisman is the *circle*. The circle is the most perfect and the most natural shape in nature. It builds an energy of totality and wholeness when used as a talismanic form. It sets up a vortex of electromagnetic energy which amplifies the energies within it. It links the divine with the human, the inner with the outer, the birth name with the magical, the personality expression with the archetypal force behind it.

The circle is a powerful symbol for name talismans. It is the perfect symbol. It has no beginning and no end. We can start anywhere within it in our search to understand our essence, and it will be correct. The circle is the cycle of our life energies. It separates the inner essence from the outer expression. The circle has the sacred space within its center, the point of focus. In name talismans, the name (our essence) is that point of focus. By placing something within the circle, it could be protected and its energies could be activated.

Some of the talismans demonstrated will have an inner circle along with the outer circle of the talisman itself. The outer can be the place of the outer name and its significance, and the inner can be the magical name or the aspect of the outer name to be enhanced and brought to life. Keep in mind that the circle is the womb, and with name talismans we are working to bring to life the inner soul potentials.

## SYMBOLS OF THE ZODIAC

| Sign | Symbol |
|------|--------|
| ARIES | ♈ |
| TAURUS | ♉ |
| GEMINI | ♊ |
| CANCER | ♋ |
| LEO | ♌ |
| VIRGO | ♍ |
| LIBRA | ♎ |
| SCORPIO | ♏ |
| SAGITTARIUS | ♐ |
| CAPRICORN | ♑ |
| AQUARIUS | ♒ |
| PISCES | ♓ |

| Planet | Symbol | Planet | Symbol |
|--------|--------|--------|--------|
| EARTH | ♁ | JUPITER | ♃ |
| SUN | ☉ | SATURN | ♄ |
| MOON | ☽ | URANUS | ♅ |
| MERCURY | ☿ | NEPTUNE | ♆ |
| VENUS | ♀ | PLUTO | ♇ |
| MARS | ♂ | VULCAN | ⚲ |

4. Before the actual and final construction of your talisman, make rough drafts. Draw out various versions, until you are sure of what exactly you wish and how best to express it in talismanic images and symbols.

5. Personalize it as much as possible. Nothing, of course, is more personal than one's name, but we can even personalize it further. Using the glyphs and symbols associated with one's astrological chart, we can more directly call forth the energies. Take the symbol for your Sun sign and put it on the talisman. If you are aware of it, also use the symbol for your Moon sign and your rising sign.

   If you wish to get even more particular, if there are planets in your astrological chart that are positioned in powerful points, you may include their symbols as well. You may wish to use just your Sun sign, but then along with it the symbols for its ruling planet, the planet that is exalted in its sign and the esoteric planet that rules that sign. (This information is listed on pages 153 and 154.) The chart on the previous page provides symbols for the signs of the zodiac and the major planets.

6. Another way to empower and personalize your talisman is through the use of crystals and stones. There are specific stones and metals associated with each sign and element. Many individuals are drawn to various stones which can be added to a talisman. Be fully aware of the energies and correspondences of the stones you choose. There are many books currently out on this subject. One simple way of applying the talismanic use of stones and gems is through their color associations. Earlier we discussed the various colors associated with each letter of the alphabet. Using stones of those same colors upon your talisman will amplify its effects. Keep in mind though that crystals and stones elicit more than just a color energy influence. Each crystal and stone has its own peculiar electro-magnetic energy pattern as well. It is also possible to use a cut stone as the talisman itself. At many rock and mineral shows can be found crystal and stone "tabs." These are oval shaped and slightly rounded on one side. They can be painted upon and even etched upon. They are thus effective for personal engraving of your name symbols. Learn to follow your own creative instincts in the formation of the name talisman. Once you initiate the process of creating them, it will open a flow of inspiration unique to yourself. Use your own ver-

satility and ingenuity in their construction.

7. To enhance the "magical" aspects of the talisman, you may wish to convert your name into other "magical languages" or symbols. On pages 254 to 257 I have included a chart of 8 ancient or magical alphabets. Keep in mind that the ancient alphabets were often used as a means of passing on esoteric knowledge by the shape of the letter, the sound, their numerical correspondence and any other correspondences. These eight are Egyptian, Phoenician, Hebrew, Greek, Theban, Runic, Ogham and Malachim.

*Egyptian*—primarily a pictographic alphabet, its images and symbols though had three possible correspondences. Each picture could represent a specific letter, a sound or an idea.

*Phoenician*—one of the earliest true alphabets, it formed the basis of many alphabets throughout the world. The Phoenicians were skilled in esoteric and worldly knowledge and many esoteric teachings have come down to us through them.

*Hebrew*—the 22 letters of this alphabet were considered the 22 steps to wisdom by the ancient Hebrew mystics and seers. When translating one's name to Hebrew do so from left to right. The first letter of your name will appear on the left; the second will be just to the right of it and so on.

*Greek*—Greece was a place of great magic and many ancient mystery systems. Its alphabet evolved from the Hebrew. Those who are drawn to the Greek myths for sources of magical names, may find it beneficial and more empowering to use the Greek alphabet.

*Theban*—an alphabet designed and used by those followers of the Old Religion, Wicca or forms of paganism. Its letters are flowing and artistic—a reflection of the worshipped feminine aspects.

*Runic*—of Teutonic origin, the runes were earned by Odin after sacrificing himself upon the Tree of Life. They hold the keys to all of life's mysteries and magic.(Written/read left to right.)

*Ogham*—a tree alphabet of the ancient Druids and Celts, it was a means of passing on esoteric information through various correspondences and associations.

*Malachim*—originally an alphabet designed specifically by and for those interested in high forms of ritual magic. Appropriate in name talismans, as the Malachim are angelic teachers and guides for those who touch the heart of their souls through their name.

## TALISMANIC ALPHABETS

| English | Egyptian | Phoenician | Hebrew | Greek |
|---------|----------|------------|--------|-------|
| A | | | | A |
| B | | | | B |
| C | | | | Γ |
| D | | | | Δ |
| E | | | | E |
| F | | | | Φ |
| G | | | | Γ |
| H | | | | H |
| I | | | | I |
| J | | | | I |
| K | | | | K or X |
| L | | | | Λ |

| English | Egyptian | Phoenician | Hebrew | Greek |
|---------|----------|------------|--------|-------|
| M | | 𐤛 | ם | M |
| N | 〰〰〰 | 𐤉 | נ | N |
| O | | O | ע | O or Ω |
| P | | 𐤉 | פ | Π |
| Q | | φ | ק | ϙ |
| R | | 𐤓 | ר | Ρ |
| S | or | ‡ | ם | Σ |
| T | | ⊗ | מ | T |
| U | | Y | ן | Y |
| V | | Y | ן | Y |
| W | | Y | ן | Y |
| X | | ≢ | | Ξ |
| Y | | ⅂ | י | Y |
| Z | | I | ן | Z |

## TALISMANIC ALPHABETS

| English | Theban | Runic | Ogham | Malachim |
|---------|--------|-------|-------|----------|
| A | | | | |
| B | | | | |
| C | | | | |
| D | | | | |
| E | | | | |
| F | | | | |
| G | | | | |
| H | | | | |
| I | | | | |
| J | | | | |
| K | | | | |
| L | | | | |

| English | Theban | Runic | Ogham | Malachim |
|---------|--------|-------|-------|----------|
| M | | | | |
| N | | | | |
| O | | | | |
| P | | | | |
| Q | | | | |
| R | | | | |
| S | | | | |
| T | | | | |
| U | | | | |
| V | | | | |
| W | | | | |
| X | | | | |
| Y | | | | |
| Z | | | | |

# 21

# Magical Squares
# and Name Sigils

Another means of personalizing your name talisman in a magical manner is through the use of MAGICAL SQUARES to create a "name sigil." The use of magical squares in the making of talismans comes to us through various sources. Pre-eminent is *The Sacred Magic of Abramelin the Mage* by S. L. MacGregor Mathers. It is based upon numerological correspondences drawn from planetary associations within the Hebrew Qabala. The magical squares consist of numbers that are arranged so that no matter which direction they are added—horizontally, vertically or diagonally—the sum will always be the same. Each of the seven major planets has its own magical square (refer to pages 260-262). We can align the numerical correspondences for the letters within our name, and by marking off a sigil within the square, we align our name and the energies of the planet more productively.

In name talismans this is very practical as a means of manifesting more abundantly the archetypal energies that so strongly affect our lives. The two predominant energy signatures that influence us within our lives are those of our name and those reflected within the astrological chart. If we can bring them into greater harmony, we link their corresponding archetypal energies, intensifying opportunities to manifest our inner potentials.

Most people are aware of the sign of the zodiac under which they were born. As has been mentioned, each sign has a planetary ruler. We can use the planetary ruler of our individual sign as a means of creating a sigil for our name talisman. For example, an individual born in the sign of Capricorn might want to use the magical square for Saturn to create a name sigil, as Saturn is the ruling planet of Capricorn.

The creation of a name sigil, using the magical squares is simple. It begins with translating one's name into numbers, much like we did earlier, only we will not add them together this time. Some of the magical squares have numbers that go beyond the nine digits normally used in numerology. In those cases, we can use a second method of converting the letters to numbers. Both are shown below:

| 1 | 2 | 3 | 4 | 5 | 6 | 7 | 8 | 9 |
|---|---|---|---|---|---|---|---|---|
| a | b | c | d | e | f | g | h | i |
| j | k | l | m | n | o | p | q | r |
| s | t | u | v | w | x | y | z | |

EXAMPLE: J O H N
            1 6 8 5

(SECONDARY METHOD)

| A | B | C | D | E | F | G | H | I | J | K | L | M |
|---|---|---|---|---|---|---|---|---|---|---|---|---|
| 1 | 2 | 3 | 4 | 5 | 6 | 7 | 8 | 9 | 10 | 11 | 12 | 13 |
| N | O | P | Q | R | S | T | U | V | W | X | Y | Z |
| 14 | 15 | 16 | 17 | 18 | 19 | 20 | 21 | 22 | 23 | 24 | 25 | 26 |

EXAMPLE:    J   O  H   N
                10 15 8 14

One way is no better nor worse than the other. They are simply different means of conversion to create a name sigil that aligns with the archetypal forces symbolized by the planets.

| 6 | 32 | 3 | 34 | 35 | 1 |
|---|----|---|----|----|---|
| 7 | 11 | 27 | 28 | 8 | 30 |
| 19 | 14 | 16 | 15 | 23 | 24 |
| 18 | 20 | 22 | 21 | 17 | 13 |
| 25 | 29 | 10 | 9 | 26 | 12 |
| 36 | 5 | 33 | 4 | 2 | 31 |

**Magical Square of the Sun**

Activates such qualities as love, healing, devotion, success and harmony. Vision of beauty and the energies of the rainbow.

| 37 | 78 | 29 | 70 | 21 | 62 | 13 | 54 | 5 |
|----|----|----|----|----|----|----|----|----|
| 6 | 38 | 79 | 30 | 71 | 22 | 63 | 14 | 46 |
| 47 | 7 | 39 | 80 | 31 | 72 | 23 | 55 | 15 |
| 16 | 48 | 8 | 40 | 81 | 32 | 64 | 24 | 56 |
| 57 | 17 | 49 | 9 | 41 | 73 | 33 | 65 | 25 |
| 26 | 58 | 18 | 50 | 1 | 42 | 74 | 34 | 66 |
| 67 | 27 | 59 | 10 | 51 | 2 | 43 | 75 | 35 |
| 36 | 68 | 19 | 60 | 11 | 52 | 3 | 44 | 76 |
| 77 | 28 | 69 | 20 | 61 | 12 | 53 | 4 | 45 |

**Magical Square of the Moon**

Activates psychic energies and sensitivities, greater independence, confidence. Can open one to greater dream activity and awareness. Opens to true work with omens and rhythmic cycles.

| 4 | 9 | 2 |
|---|---|---|
| 3 | 5 | 7 |
| 8 | 1 | 6 |

**Magical Square of Saturn**

Activates energies for understanding and the primal feminine. Strength through silence and concentration. Opens to understanding of mysteries of birth and death and karma.

**Magical Square of Jupiter**

Abundance and justice. Hearing the inner call, financial opportunities and obedience to higher.

| 4 | 14 | 15 | 1 |
|---|----|----|---|
| 9 | 7 | 6 | 12 |
| 5 | 11 | 10 | 8 |
| 16 | 2 | 3 | 13 |

| 11 | 24 | 7 | 20 | 3 |
|----|----|---|----|---|
| 4 | 12 | 25 | 8 | 16 |
| 17 | 5 | 13 | 21 | 9 |
| 10 | 18 | 1 | 14 | 22 |
| 23 | 6 | 19 | 2 | 15 |

**Magical Square of Mars**

Strength and endurance. Vitality, courage, initiating change, and critical judgment.

| 8 | 58 | 59 | 5 | 4 | 62 | 63 | 1 |
|---|----|----|---|---|----|----|---|
| 49 | 15 | 14 | 52 | 53 | 11 | 10 | 56 |
| 41 | 23 | 22 | 44 | 48 | 19 | 18 | 45 |
| 32 | 34 | 38 | 29 | 25 | 35 | 39 | 28 |
| 40 | 26 | 27 | 37 | 36 | 30 | 31 | 33 |
| 17 | 47 | 43 | 20 | 21 | 46 | 42 | 24 |
| 9 | 55 | 54 | 12 | 13 | 51 | 50 | 16 |
| 64 | 2 | 3 | 61 | 60 | 6 | 7 | 57 |

**Magical Square of Mercury**

Activates energies for greater truthfulness and communication. Opens one to knowledge of healing techniques and knowledge of magic. Aligns one with any scientific or educational endeavor.

**Magical Square of Venus**

Awakens sense of unselfishness and the energy for greater understanding of relationships. Aligns one with energies of love and sexuality and can open one to greater contact with elements of nature. Greater love and idealism.

| 22 | 47 | 16 | 41 | 10 | 35 | 4 |
|----|----|----|----|----|----|---|
| 5 | 23 | 48 | 17 | 42 | 11 | 29 |
| 30 | 6 | 24 | 49 | 18 | 36 | 12 |
| 13 | 31 | 7 | 25 | 43 | 19 | 37 |
| 38 | 14 | 32 | 1 | 26 | 44 | 20 |
| 21 | 39 | 8 | 33 | 2 | 27 | 45 |
| 46 | 15 | 40 | 9 | 34 | 3 | 28 |

Having converted the name into numbers, the steps to then translate it into a planetary name sigil are simple:

A. Choose the planetary square whose influence you wish to align your name with.

B. You may wish to create a sigil for your birth name along with your magical name, and you may wish to choose a planet whose energies you wish to activate more than those of your birth sign. There are no hard rules.

C. Locate within the square, the box which has the number for the first letter within your name. Draw a small circle within it to indicate it is the beginning of your name. Refer to the example on the following page.

D. Locate the number in the magical square that corresponds to the second letter in your name. Draw a straight line from the small circle to this number.

E. Continue connecting each square until your name is converted. When you reach the number for your last letter in your name, draw a small vertical line to indicate this is the end.

F. For letters that are doubled, next to each other in a name (*i.e.* Billy), make a loop at the number for the double letter and then continue the line to the next letter/number of your name.

G. You can convert any name to a sigil in this manner: birth, first, last, magical, names of gods and goddesses. The only limits are your own.

## Magical Square for the Moon

| 37 | 78 | 29 | 70 | 21 | 62 | 13 | 54 | 5 |
|----|----|----|----|----|----|----|----|----|
| 6 | 38 | 79 | 30 | 71 | 22 | 63 | 14 | 46 |
| 47 | 7 | 39 | 80 | 31 | 72 | 23 | 55 | 15 |
| 16 | 48 | 8 | 40 | 81 | 32 | 64 | 24 | 56 |
| 57 | 17 | 49 | 9 | 41 | 73 | 33 | 65 | 25 |
| 26 | 58 | 18 | 50 | 10 | 42 | 74 | 34 | 66 |
| 67 | 27 | 59 | 10 | 51 | 2 | 43 | 75 | 35 |
| 36 | 68 | 19 | 60 | 11 | 52 | 3 | 44 | 76 |
| 77 | 28 | 69 | 20 | 61 | 12 | 53 | 4 | 45 |

**SIGIL FOR "JOHN"**

The name JOHN has four numbers (1, 6, 8, 5). Starting with #1, lines are drawn connecting each number in sequence. At the beginning is a circle; at the end a vertical line.

The sigil for John is now drawn upon the talisman, along with any other appropriate symbols.

Having converted our name to numbers, it is drawn upon the magic square, eliciting the sigil or symbol for your name. A smaller duplication of it is then drawn upon your talisman, along with any other personal symbols, *i.e.* astrological correspondences, as in the illustration.

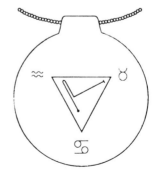

# 22

# Name Talisman Designs

As mentioned, a talisman can be made of any material. Metals and stones can be rather expensive, and they do require some skill and training to craft them properly. Cotton cloth works quite effectively and is not nearly as expensive. It can also be fashioned into an effective pendant. Before drawing and cutting upon the cloth, make rough drafts of the design you wish to use as the basis for your name talisman. Experiment, as there are many possible variations. Keep in mind also that the front and the back of the talisman can be used if you desire, or just one side. In the front and back designs, there are variations that can be employed according to one's own purpose:

—The front can be the birth name and the back the magical name.

—The front can be the birth name and the back the design for the inner vowel and its energies you wish to stress.

—The front can emphasize the activation of the primary vowel within the birth name and the back the magical name.

—The front can be the magical name, and the back the birth name. *Whatever the design pattern is, make sure that you choose it consciously with good reason. Everything you do in the construction of the talisman should be imbued with significance.*

Some sources will tell you that in the construction of the talisman, your shadow should never touch it. Some will tell you that it should be done at certain times of the day and certain days of the week. If you believe it is of importance then it will be. What is most important is the symbology and the reverence you give it personally while constructing it. Remember that the name talisman is a way of honoring and reverencing the divine within yourself. It is a means of realizing and manifesting the innate power of the soul.

1. Having decided upon the design for your name talisman, it is important to choose the color of the cloth upon which you will be drawing it. This can be a color associated with the primary vowel within your name. You may wish to use a color of cloth to which you are drawn. Remember that colors also activate certain energies, and it is good to familiarize yourself with the associations and energies of colors. If undecided, simply go with white cotton.

2. Draw upon the cloth a double circle (approximately two inches in diameter), connected by a half-inch square section. Refer to the diagram on the following page.

3. Draw upon the cloth, on one or both of the two circles, your name design or sigils. Use other symbols that also help identify you personally. Use colored pens, or many craft stores have coloring devices that are permanent upon cloth. On the upper circle, you must draw the design upside down, for when the material is cut and this section is folded over then it will appear upright.

4. As you draw upon the cloth focus upon all aspects and significances of the design. The more you keep it in mind, the more the talisman becomes infused with the appropriate energy.

5. Cut out the talisman, along the edges of the two circles and the adjoining half inch square. Cut it all in one piece, then fold it over at the square section, so that the two circular parts are back to back.

6. Before sewing these together, you may wish to place between the two parts a crystal, stone, a flower, herb, etc. that may be appropriate either to your birth name or to your magical name. For example, if your magical name is "VIOLET," you may wish to place within the talisman a wild violet that you have found and picked yourself. This kind of fetish intensifies the energy.

7. Sew around the edges of the circle, tying the front and back of the talisman together. You are also tying the birth name and the magical name together, or you may be symbolically tying the birth name and the inner vowel's activation together. Everything in the construction of the talisman has significance. The half inch square that connects the two circles is not sewn. By sewing only the circles, a loop is formed through which you can now slip a ribbon, a chain or any form of necklace so that you can wear the talisman.

## Cloth Design Talismans

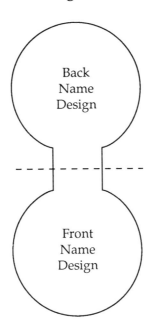

Sketch out the design for your talisman upon the cloth prior to cutting. Use name sigils or names that you converted to other more magical alphabets.

Back Name Design

Front Name Design

Make sure you understand the significance of everything that goes on the front or back of your talisman. The design on the back is drawn upside down, so when it is cut out and folded over, it will be right side up.

Once the design is drawn upon the cloth, cut it out and fold it over, sewing along the edges to enclose the circular talisman. Sew only upon the circular part of the talisman so that there remains a loop for you to run a necklace through.

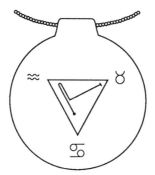

Before sewing, you may wish to enclose in the middle any stone, crystal, flower, herb, etc. that may be appropriate to your birth name or to the magical name that you are taking.

8. It is always beneficial to construct this and any other talisman when you know that you will be undisturbed. This is a very powerful form of meditation and activation of the archetypal energies within your life. Interruptions can distort the flow of energy within your life. Visualize and concentrate on each part of the construction of the name talisman. Focus upon those aspects you want to bring to greater life. Visualize the potentials within the name manifesting in as many ways as possible. The more you invest your own time, energy and significance in this process, the more the symbols will be able to trigger a greater release of the archetypal energies operating within your life. The more conscious we are in formulating and constructing them, the more the symbols and designs will stimulate the subconscious mind which directs the play of the archetypal forces within your individual life circumstances.

9. It is also good at the conclusion of the construction to perform a blessing and meditation with your talisman. This does not have to be complicated, and it can be a part of the dedication ceremony of your magical name, as discussed earlier. Smudging it with incense and offering a prayer to whatever divine source you worship and reverence is beneficial. Meditate upon its significance and what it represents to you. Visualize it as a physical reminder of the inner potentials of your soul that you will from that point on express more fully and productively. Dedicate it with thought and prayer for your growth and enlightenment.

10. This process should be basic to creating any of the talismans described through the rest of the chapter, and they can easily be adapted to their construction.

## BIRTH NAME FOUNDATION TALISMAN

This is one of the simplest of the name talismans to create, its steps are quite easy to follow:

1. As discussed, the foundation of archetypal energies playing within our lives and reflected through our name is found in three primary elements—the cornerstone consonant (the first consonant of the name, especially if it is the initial letter of the name), the primary vowel and the capstone consonant (the final consonant of the name). Review the significance of each of these elements.

2. On the talisman itself, they are arranged in a manner that the individual finds suitable. The individual may wish to enclose them

within a geometric shape appropriate to their energies or may wish to translate them into an alphabet to which the individual is drawn.

3. It is good for this type of talisman to have these letters in both English, as well as any other alphabetic translation. This adds emphasis to the fact that we are translating the energies of our name and life into a new form of expression—one which will add magic to one's life.

4. This design, as reflected below, is simple and basic and extremely functional. It is one which can easily be enhanced with one's own creative expression. It simply emphasizes the elements of energy that we should be most aware of in our life.

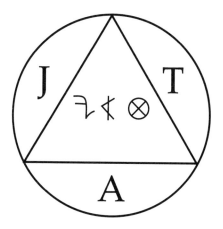

*Talisman for the birth name "Janet"*

## Birth Name Foundation Talisman

*This is an example of a basic talisman that activates predominant energies of one's name. The cornerstone, the primary vowel and the capstone consonant are the three key elements within the birth name. They are tied to the strongest archetypal forces playing within the individual's life. This is a simple talisman for one who has the birth name of "JANET." In this name, "J" is the cornerstone consonant, the letter most indicative of the energies brought over to help the individual in this incarnation. The "A" is the primary vowel, the hidden potential to be developed in this incarnation. The "T" is the capstone. On this talisman, they have been translated into the Phoenician alphabet. It is a simple design, but powerfully effective.*

## THE INNER VOWEL TALISMAN

This particular talisman is one of the most effective for assisting in the manifestation of the inner potentials and energies reflected within the primary vowel of one's birth name. An appropriate design for this would involve a front and back talisman design. The front would signify the outer name and forces in which the inner potentials are enclosed and must be expressed through. The back would be an amplification of the energies of the inner vowel.

1. On the outer front surface of the talisman, draw a smaller circle. Within this circle you will place the primary vowel within your name. This may be the birth name or the magical name, although this is most effective when applied to the birth name itself. This stresses to the mind that we want to manifest the inner potentials represented by this vowel.

2. Around the outer edge of the front side of the talisman, outside of the inner circle, inscribe your birth name (or magical name). I recommend doing this three times. Three is the creative, birth giving rhythm, and thus it has great significance for giving birth to new expressions of the potentials of the vowel. You may wish to inscribe your name in three different languages as depicted on page 271.

3. On the back side of this talisman, the emphasis of the design will be upon the activation of the energies of the vowel itself, and not just its expression through the name. It is important to inscribe a large form of the primary vowel of your name. Keep in mind that you want to begin looking at the letter not as an element of the alphabet, but rather look at it as a glyph, a symbol reflecting forces both mystical and magical that are operative within your life.

4. To further emphasize and activate its manifestation into your life, you may wish to enclose it in a particular geometric shape or color it appropriately.

5. A dynamic way of activating it even more intensely is translating it into the corresponding symbols as were used in other parts of the world. In our example on page 271 we have encircled it with the corresponding letters from other alphabets. This emphasizes the universality of the energies behind the symbol of the vowel, no matter how it is expressed or written.

## The Inner Vowel Talisman

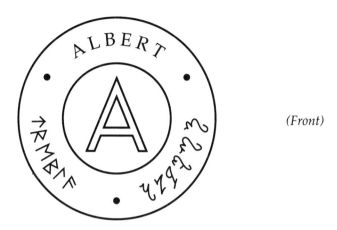

*(Front)*

This talisman is designed to stimulate into greater expression the archetypal forces inherent within the primary vowel of one's birth name. On the front is the birth name, in several languages, surrounding the primary vowel.

*(Back)*

On the back of this talisman is the primary vowel again, but written in a variety of languages, reflecting the universality of the energies inherent within it and thus within the individual's life.

## The Mirrored Name Talisman

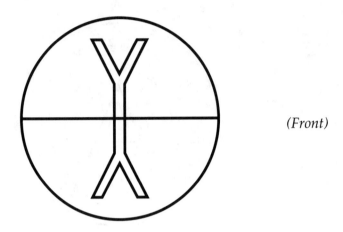

*(Front)*

*This is a variation of the talisman which activates and stresses the play of energies associated with the primary vowel. This can be used with the birth name or the magical name. The talisman is divided into two halves, as if the bottom were a reflecting pool. The vowel is drawn upright and reversed— the mirror effect. This symbolizes the outer always reflecting the inner, the physical reflecting the spiritual. On the back are drawn any other personal symbols, images, etc. that have correspondence and significance. It is also powerfully effective to place some mirrored glass upon the talisman itself. All it takes is some glue and ingenuity.*

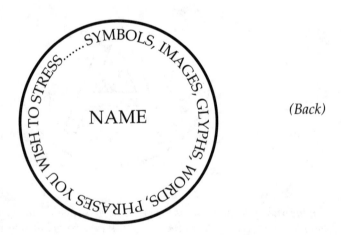

*(Back)*

## THE MIRRORED NAME TALISMAN

This is a talismanic design to emphasize the mirroring effect of our names and the archetypal energies behind them. More importantly, it amplifies the inner potentials of the name and its primary vowel so that its energies are more strongly "reflected" into outer world manifestation and expression.

1. Use a two-sided design for this talisman. On the front, we will draw or inscribe a mirror image of the primary vowel within your name. This is accomplished simply by dividing the front side in half horizontally. On the upper half draw or inscribe the primary vowel. On the bottom half, draw or inscribe its reverse image, as if it is being reflected in a mirror or a still pool of water. Refer to the diagram on page 272. This is a dynamic reminder that the inner forces and potentials of the vowels are going to be reflected into greater expression.

2. On the reverse side of the talisman you may place your full name and any other images, symbols, glyphs, words, phrases—anything you are wishing to further stress.

3. A dynamic way of amplifying the mirroring effects of the inner to the outer, the spiritual to the physical is by employing mirrored glass in the talisman construction. Small pieces can be cut, and with some glue and ingenuity this talisman can be a tremendous amplifier of inner potentials, reflected into outer expression.

## THE NAME AFFIRMATION TALISMAN

This is a wonderfully empowering talisman, based upon the meaning of one's name and the affirmation that can be created from it. In the index is a listing of names, their meanings and suggested affirmations. You are not limited to those variations, as you may be able to create an even more effective one for yourself, based upon your name's meaning. For this talisman, we will employ both sides again.

1. First determine your name's meaning and then construct an affirmation based upon such.

2. In the center of the front side of the talisman, inscribe your name. You may wish to do so in one of the alphabets listed earlier.

3. There are several ways of inscribing the affirmation itself

upon the talisman. You can convert it into another language, using the alphabets given within the previous chapter. You may wish to translate it into Latin, if you remember your high school courses or find a good book on it. You may wish to keep it in English. It is all a matter of choice, but be sure to be conscious of what you are choosing and why. Inscribe around the outside of the front face of the talisman the affirmation for your name. The affirmation is then circling, creating a spiral of energy around the name that you have placed within the center. This amplifies the activation of the energy.

4. You may also wish to use just the initials for the major words within the affirmation, rather than writing out the entire affirmation itself. In the example on page 275, we are using an affirmation for the name "IRIS"—"I AM THE PROMISED RAINBOW." Instead of writing out the entire affirmation, we used the first letter of the main words within it, establishing a code of a sort that only you can truly define. This is significant in that only you can define how those archetypal forces behind you will manifest. The I, A, P, and R of the affirmation are then spaced about the name on the front of the talisman.

5. On the reverse side, you may place the primary vowel, as is shown within the sample on page 275, along with any other symbols and images that are significant and can be used to personalize the talisman for you. An effective way of empowering it, is to use the astrological symbol for your birthdate if you are using your birthname, or you can use the sign for the month in which you take your magical name. Include with this the symbols for the ruling planet of that sign, the planet that is exalted and the esoteric ruler of the sign. It is extremely energizing and it helps to bring out the hidden forces of the name more emphatically and more recognizably.

### THE NAME COLOR TALISMAN

This is an excellent form of talisman to use to link the birth name with the magical name. It helps one to become more sensitive to the color energies associated with one's name and can be used for healing and balancing on all levels. Chromotherapy is a growing science with legitimate recognition of the effects of color upon the human energy system.

This is one which can also be adapted into a "NAME MANDALA." The mandala is a visual doorway between two worlds. It is a tool that has been used to focus the mind and concentrate its ener-

## The Affirmation Talisman

In the center is the name "Iris," written in Theban alphabet. Outside are the initials from the affirmation: "I Am the Promised Rainbow!"

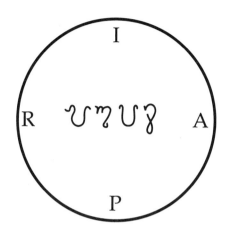

*Affirmation Talisman for "Iris"*

*The name "Iris" means "promise; rainbow." An affirmation based upon this could be: "I am the Promised Rainbow!"*

*This variation of the name talisman is based upon the affirmation that can be constructed from the basic meaning of one's name. (Refer to the Index at the end of this book for more information regarding this process.)*

*On the back of the talisman is the primary vowel of the individual's name and any other personal symbols.*

*If one desires, it is also possible to write out the affirmation around the edges of the talisman on either side.*

gies. In Eastern philosophy, they are known as yantras, and they can be a melange of pictures, images, geometric patterns, etc. designed to elicit a specific effect. They can be viewed somewhat as a larger version of the talisman.

The image or picture of the mandala holds the essence of a specific thought, concept and its corresponding energies—much like a talisman. It is designed to draw our consciousness more fully into that concept and energy. Mandalas stimulate the creative forces in a manner peculiar to their design and, like talismans, they can be psychic transformers, helping us to connect with our missing or unrecognized energies and potentials. They help us to draw into the inner realities of the essence of our name.

When constructed, just like talismans, they are imbued with significance. Once completed, they should be hung at a point where you can focus on them at regular intervals. Your meditation area is an effective place, as it will activate the energies of your inner essence, facilitating the meditational process. You may also hang them in the bedroom across the room from you. This serves to remind you of the inner essence and potential of your name each day when you awaken, and it activates an energy at night that imparts a growing sense of new reality as you sleep. Just as talismans affect the electro-magnetic energy of the aura, mandalas will affect larger areas, bringing the energy of a room into a particular vibrational frequency.

The following procedure for a "Name Color Talisman" is adaptable to creating a "Name Color Mandala"—as are all of the talismanic variations discussed.

1. For this talisman we will again use both sides. We will also be focusing upon the colors associated with the letters within our names.

2. On both the front and back of the talisman, inscribe an inner circle. On the front, within that inner circle, write your birth name in any alphabet desired. On the back, within the inner circle, write your magical name in any alphabet desired.

3. Determine the colors associated with each letter of each name—birth and magical. Use the chart on page 103 to assist you with this.

4. On the front side, the side with your birth name, divide the outer circle into sections that equal the number of letters within

**The Name Color Talisman**

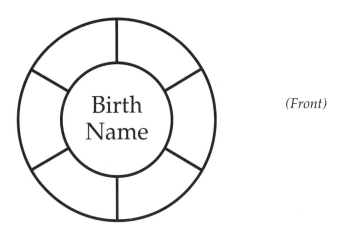

*(Front)*

On the front of this talisman one writes the birth name (in any language desired). As we learned earlier, every letter has a color correspondence. The outer circle is then divided into a number of sections equal to the number of letters within the name. Each section is then painted or colored accordingly.

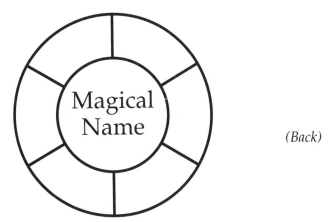

*(Back)*

On the back, one writes the magical name (in any alphabet desired). The outer circle is then divided into sections equal to the number of letters within the magical name and colored accordingly. With the magical name and birth name both placed within an inner circle, we initiate a process of linking their energies.

your birth name. If the birth name has six letters, divide the area out-side the inner circle into six sections. Refer to the sample on page 277.

5. Color each section in accordance with the appropriate color for each letter. If you desire, you may wish to inscribe within each section the letter that goes with each color. This is most effective if done in an alphabet other than English.

6. On the back side, the side with the magical name, divide the outer circle into sections equal to the number of letters within the name. If the magical name has six letters, divide the area outside of the inner circle into six sections.

7. Color each section appropriate to the letter/color relation-ships as have already been determined. You may wish also to in-scribe the letter of the magical name within the section of its appro-priate color. As with the birth name, this is more enhanced when one uses one of the "magical" alphabets.

8. This is just a basic and simple design, and you can get as crea-tive with the process as you desire. You can color each letter within the name appropriately, and you may apply color to all of the other forms of talismans. We are treating it separately to simplify the ex-planation, but you should feel free to adapt and combine the various talismanic techniques.

### THE NAME TALISMAN OF SACRED GEOMETRY

We have discussed the manner in which geometric shapes and forms will alter energy fields. This concept can easily be applied in the talisman-making process. We can choose various geometric shapes that are harmonious to the inner energies we are working to manifest more strongly. We can do this in a variety of ways:

1. We can enclose elements of our name within geometric shapes within the talisman itself. Refer to the example on page 279.

2. We can enclose the whole name within a geometric shape. For example, enclosing the name within a square will help to bal-ance the inner forces of the name as they are expressed and experi-enced within the outer world and life.

3. We can construct the talisman in specific geometric shapes other than in the basic circular form we have elaborated upon within this chapter. We can construct triangular talismans, square talismans, oval talismans, etc. Each shape will influence the manner

in which the inner potentials and forces reflected within the name will manifest and be experienced.

4. We can alter and amplify any aspect of our name's energy through the use of geometry and enclosure of the symbols and images of our name within the geometric forms.

5. There are no limits other than those which are self-imposed.

## Name Talisman of Sacred Geometry

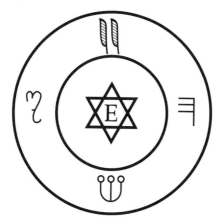

*In this first example, the primary vowel is placed within two interlaced triangles, linking the inner with the outer—amplifying the opportunity for the outer expression of the inner potentials reflected by the vowel. This is placed within an inner circle, surrounded by other alphabetic variations of the same vowel, symbolizing the many ways in which the inner potentials can be outwardly expressed.*

*In the second example the magical name is placed within a square. The square is a geometric shape which activates the energies to establish new foundations and grounding within one's life. In this case the magical name is being activated so as to become a new foundation of energy for the individual.*

PART VI

# NAME ENCHANTMENT

# 23

# Awakening the Inner Life Through the Magical Name

All names are tied to archetypal energies, even the ancient names of the various deities. Those archetypal energies play within our life, translated by the subconscious mind into various manifestations. The magical name then can become a means by which we stimulate the deeper recesses of the subconscious in order to awaken our inner energies. The inner life is the energy of our essence and how it operates on realms other than the physical. The magical name provides a matrix of energy which can become a more substantial vehicle for consciously exploring those inner realms.

We discussed earlier the imagickal body that we need to develop. Having a magical name facilitates the formulation of this energy so that it can be a source for drawing greater archetypal forces out into our physical life consciousness. Awakening this energy and inner life activation more consciously begins with the assuming of a magical name. There are a number of things though to keep in mind when using it to initiate greater inner life activity:

1. You must infuse the name with energy and create a thoughtform around it. This means study all of the significance of it. Have a conscious reason for employing and formulating it.

2. If you choose to use a name of a deity, read the entire mythol-

ogy of the tradition from which the name comes. Read and study especially all the tales and myths in which the name of your deity appears. Become familiar with this person and his / her qualities and characteristics. Don't stop with the obvious. Remember that most myths and tales have deeper significance than what is often attributed to them.

3. Meditate upon the name, its significance, its energy correspondences. Visualize yourself in the image of the name—an image that you choose. This is more easily accomplished when the specific name of a deity is used, but in those cases where you create your own magical name, create an image of yourself within your mind that suits all the energies and forces associated with all of its elements. Try to come up with a magical symbol(s) that most seems to reflect the energy of the name you are associating with and assuming.

4. In the case of names taken from nature learn as much about that plant, tree or animal as you are capable of learning. Study its behaviors, its growing patterns—all aspects of it. Find books on symbology and learn what it has represented to others in the past. In your meditations upon this name and its energies, see yourself as the plant, the flower, the tree, or the animal. In all of your meditations—not just those centered around the name—visualize it always with you. Learn to see the image at any moment. Remember you are taking upon this energy, and the more we focus upon it, the quicker it is to align with it.

5. Meditate upon all aspects of its energy. Use creative visualization and affirmation. Affirm that you are this new name and all that it represents. Use altered states of consciousness to enhance the effects of the visualization and affirmation. Perform them when relaxed, quiet and undisturbed. Experiencing an altered state of consciousness is not the same as a spiritual experience, but we can use the altered state to create an energy thoughtform around the magical name to enable us ultimately to build to the spiritual energies inherent within it.

6. Do not allow others to know your magical name, unless they are part of your private meditation and study group, coven, etc. Many do not understand the impact and force of the magical name. Informing others of it—especially those who do not have a foundation in the metaphysical sciences—can open you to ridicule, gossip, raised eyebrows, etc. All of these things can create blocks to access-

ing the archetypal energies of the name or can dissipate the energy thoughtform you have been building, thus weakening its effectiveness within your own life.

7. Practice calling upon its energy throughout the day. To do so, all one needs to do is close the eyes briefly. Mentally say the name three times, visualizing the image and energy you are building into this name awakening and overshadowing your "normal" presence. Doing this periodically over the first couple months that you have a new name, develops the ability to call forth the energies at will, and serves to add energy to its thoughtform so as to more easily establish a matrix of energy for awakening the inner life. After several months, you do not have to be calling it up, as there will establish an ability for it to come forth as it is needed.

8. Pay attention to how individuals begin to respond to you over the next few months. As you develop, strengthen and attune to the new energy of this magical name and its manifestation, people will respond. You may only hear vague comments, such as "you seem to be changing" or "Gee, you look different today," etc. All of these confirm that the energy is beginning to work itself out into the outer auric field. You are bridging the inner and the outer. Pay attention to how you handle people and situations.

9. Pay attention to the changes in your meditation and/or ritual experiences. They will begin to take on a different tone, clarity and vibrancy. Keep a record of the meditational experiences. Record them in a journal. Unless you are part of a development or esoteric group of some kind, keep your experiences to yourself. By sharing all the "visions" and "new experiences" you dissipate the energy you had accumulated and you counteract your own efforts. By recording them in a journal of some kind, you are physically acknowledging a recognition of a shift in energy around you. If you must discuss the experiences, it is often enough for others to know that there are changes occurring and that you are experiencing some new results—without getting explicit in the description. Often other people can unconsciously set up blocks as there is the very human tendency to compare personal experiences with those of others. Comparisons must be avoided. We each have our own unique energy system. One experience is no better or worse than another— simply different.

10. Do not change your magical name too frequently. This will require that you set some far range goals. They do not have to be ex-

tensive, but knowing what you wish to accomplish within the next three to seven years, how you wish to develop, etc. is important. This must be kept in mind in the formulating of the magical name. You must either choose or create a name that has inherent within it energies that will assist you in the achievement of these goals. Keep in mind goals that are physical, emotional, mental and spiritual. The name must help you with all aspects, if it is going to do the most for you. Changing the name too frequently scatters one's energy and can create imbalance and disruption. Except in extreme situations, I recommend it not be changed for a minimum of three years. It takes time to fully attune to the energy of a name. Yes, there may be immediate results, but that does not indicate complete attunement to all the subtleties within it. And if it must be changed, use specific techniques to either dissipate the energy of the old magical name or to integrate its energy with the new. (This will be discussed within the next two chapters.) Be patient and persistent. It takes time for the full magic of a name to be experienced. Remember that you are creating a vehicle that will open the inner realms more productively and empower the outer more creatively. Allow yourself time to enjoy the experience.

## EMPOWERING THE MAGICAL NAME

Part of the process of empowering the magical name, strengthening it so that it can become a beneficial tool occurs simply through setting the process in motion in a powerful manner. The attention given it, as explained within the previous pages, helps to initiate the building of that energy. What needs to be done in order to set up a catalytic motion for the formulation of energy around the name is a Ritual of Self-Dedication. (This can be adapted for group situations.)

A ritual can be anything done with strong intention and emphasis. It provides a rewarding means of self-expression, self-discovery and self-empowerment. Aquarian forms of ritual are more mental. It is in the mind that most of the work is done, but it is extremely beneficial to have a physical ritual in order to trigger the process in motion.

1. There are always preliminary considerations in any ritual. What is the purpose? What is needed to make it work? When is the best time? What sort of results do you expect? How do you wish it to be performed?

2. The first step is to decide upon the magical name. Having

done this, you may wish to make a list of all the energies and correspondences associated with the name and have them accessible to read during your dedication ceremony.

3. You may also wish to make an amulet or talisman for your name. This is described in part five. If you decide to do this, this should be finished before you perform the dedication ceremony so that it can be blessed and energized as well.

4. Decide on the best time. Remember that the taking of a new name is like a new birth. The Full Moon is the time of birth, and thus during the period of the waxing Moon, as close to the Full Moon as possible, is best. Choose a date that resonates with the numerological correspondence of your new name. Use the earlier section in this chapter to determine the number. This date is going to be a new birth date for you.

5. Make preparations ahead of time. All materials—candles, incense, prayers, etc.—should be ready on the day you choose to perform the ritual. Rehearse the procedure within your mind periodically the week before. You do not have to be rigid in following this, as you may well be inspired within the ceremony itself, but you also do not want to be floundering, wondering what you should do next.

6. Have a definite beginning and end. This may be a gesture or prayer or invocation of some kind. You may wish to write a prayer that is designed to reflect the energies of the new name or you may wish to use a childhood prayer that has always held significance for you.

7. Prepare the room ahead of time on the day of the ceremony. You may wish to smudge in order to cleanse it and to raise the vibration of the energy. Have candles ready (if you choose to use them) of colors appropriate to the colors associated with your name. Have at least one white candle. This will enhance the energies of all the others, it raises the vibrations and it is purifying and protective. You may wish to create a small altar upon which you have set everything you need. Incense and symbols appropriate to the name you have chosen (even in the form of pictures) are beneficial.

8. Bathe yourself before the ritual. Use visualization during this ritual bath to see yourself being cleansed of the old energy to be born into a new.

9. Make sure you will not be disturbed. All phones off the hook and if there are others within the home, make sure they have orders to not disturb you.

10. Performing this ritual completely naked is recommended. When we are born, we come into the world naked with only a name which we grow into. It is this process we are consciously re-manifesting. Clothing and jewelry associated with the name you are going to be taking can be in the room and donned as part of the ritual itself.

11. Light the candles and incense. Begin your opening prayer or invocation.

12. Affirm your birth name and your magical name, as in: "I am Patricia. I am Freyja!" Repeating it three times activates the creative energies of the name and of ourselves.

13. Read the list of energies and correspondences associated with the name. A powerful way of doing so is by using the "I Am..." phrase before each correspondence. If the name you have taken is one of a god or goddess, and helps promote the awakening of prophecy, use the words "I am a prophet" or anything similar. You are affirming your relationships and your alignment with this energy. Pause after each characteristic, and visualize yourself with that aspect. See yourself using it daily. See that aspect adding to all avenues of your life. See your entire existence being assisted by it. Do so in as many ways as you can.

14. After reading the list, affirm who you are again as you did in #12. Use your birth name and your magical name and repeat the affirmation three times again.

15. If you have created a talisman or amulet, hold it now with both hands, and dedicate it to helping you unfold your highest inner potential. You may wish to pass it through the flames of the candles as a symbol of infusing it with force. You may wish to dedicate it according to the four elements and four directions. If you have made a robe for this occasion, put it on now, along with the amulet.

16. Assume a suitable meditation pose and meditate upon the image of the magical you that you are initiating. Visualize yourself and meditate upon your new name and all of its qualities. See yourself as the new ideal you. See yourself in the image of the new name.

17. When you finish meditating, if you feel like celebrating such as with cakes and wine or singing, feel free to do so. Remember that part of the magical name process is to free our energies, so do not worry about being embarrassed or silly. This is the secret and magical you that is being born.

18. Give thanks to whatever divine source you worship for the

blessing of the ritual and the blessing of your life through the taking of this new name.

19. Do your closing prayer. Extinguish candles, ending the ceremony.

20. Do not limit yourself to just these guidelines. Adapt and create within the course of the ceremony as is suitable to the energies of your magical name. The important thing to remember is to imbue everything within the ritual with significance and to dedicate the taking of this name to manifesting physical, emotional, mental and spiritual goals for this time in your life. You are limited only by your own imagination. As the old saying goes, "change your imaginings and you change the world." Make sure that you see yourself as the new, ideal you!

### BLENDING THE MAGICAL NAME WITH THE OUTER LIFE

The first step—and most important—in this process is being able to visualize yourself in the ideal image that you have created in association with your magical name. By the time we take a magical name, we have strong intentions of applying its energies in specific areas of our life. We need to be able to call upon those energies during those times.

The mental calling of the name in some form serves as the trigger. The mental calling can be like a magical "incantation." You may wish to construct a little poem or chant to serve as the transitional device. Simple quatrains—four line poems—serve as wonderful devices and they are fun to create. You can create one for each aspect of the magical name's energy that you wish to call upon.

A very simple exercise for bridging the magical name and the birth name involves breathing and toning:

1. Breath, esoterically, is the quick intake of energy. It is that which carries an image or thought to the subconscious. It is life itself, and breath with the sound of our name activates our most intimate life forces.

2. Find a time in which you will not be disturbed. Take a few moments just to relax and to draw your attention away from the outer world. Use rhythmic breathing—inhale for a count of four, hold for a count of four and then exhale for a count of four.

3. When you are relaxed, inhale silently and sound the magical name. Try to see and feel its energies come alive. As you exhale,

sound the magical name audibly. In, silently. Out, audibly. We begin a process of bridging the inner magical into the outer aura.

4. Next, repeat the same process, only using the birth name. As you inhale, sound it silently. As you exhale, sound it audibly. Repeat for as many times as you did the magical name.

5. The last step of this exercise involves the birth name and the magical. As you inhale, sound the magical name silently. (Remember to perform the appropriate visualization along with it.) As you exhale, sound the birth name audibly. Inhale, silent magical name. Exhale, audible birth name. We are infusing the outer persona—reflected by the birth name with the inner forces activated by the magical name. I recommend this be done every day for a week after assuming the birth name, and then periodically thereafter as needed.

It is important to begin to see the inner magical form, activated by your magical name, merging and forming within you and extending into your outer life. It is like looking in a mirror and seeing your reflection, but also an ideal image faintly visible within it. We bring the inner magical energy into an outer expression.

# 24

# Effective Name Changes

Our myths and fables are filled with individuals seeking out special magical words that will solve their life problems, instill wealth and prosperity and manifest love and all its joys. Even today people are still fascinated with the possibility of discovering a magical word or phrase. In every man, woman and child's heart there comes a time when he or she wishes there existed a magic word that could "make the world right." What few realize though is that there does abide within us all a deep-seated, ancient memory of the reality of the WORD! At some level is that child-like faith and hope that there really is something to it all. Unfortunately, what have been lost are the understanding and the techniques for activating those deeper levels of consciousness that would allow us to re-discover and use magical words and sounds.

All of the ancient mystery schools taught their students the power of the word. They taught the sacredness of names and the means to employ them for various functions. They taught the use of the name to touch the soul and awaken its potentials. Ancient forms of mysticism and magic were centered around words and names. They recognized that every word was tied to some force within the universe, and special effort was given to identify such forces and thus attach great significance and meaning to the figures and sounds that comprise our words and names.

Word and name magic was pre-eminent among the magical arts. Students of the ancient mysteries learned to attach meanings to the figures of names. They learned to draw them in a manner that invoked the forces they symbolized. They learned to tone the sounds that corresponded to them in a manner that would elicit great power, healing and enlightenment. The master of the Word was a worker of miracles.

The process was simple, but it did require great practice to perfect it. It began by attaching definite meanings to the sounds and the infinite combinations, so that with their use there would occur an invocation of energy. The script of those sounds—that which we call our various alphabets—had specific meanings attached to them, aligned with specific forces operative within the universe. When the script was combined with the sounds, an amplified and very specific manifestation of energy would occur within the individual's life circumstances. It grounded, invoked, the energy into a crystallized expression within the physical realm.

This art of "name enchantment" and "word magic" has not been lost. It may be somewhat obscured, but it still exists. The art of empowering and activating the forces inherent within and reflected by our names is still accessible for those willing to put forth the effort.

The magical word which we all have and which can restore the enchantment of life is our name It is the outer reflection of the inner matrix of energy operating within your life. As we learn to activate it more consciously and dynamically, it imbues our lives with greater control and greater power. It helps us to recognize the significance of everyone and everything within our lives.

All names are magical or non-magical, according to how much spiritual significance we attach to them. They activate the energies behind us whether we are aware of them or not. By becoming aware, we can learn to direct them more fully, creating a more "magical" existence. This is not to say that we are controlled by them, as we have free will and can learn to assert our will over the subtle play of archetypal energies within our physical lives.

Uncovering the mystery of our name and its effects is a high form of esoteric initiation. Learning to use our name and the forces inherent within it can open one to the true "cosmic language"—the language of the divine, wherein rests all knowledge. For one who learns to bridge to the cosmic language—through his or her own name—nothing is kept secret. All knowledge begins to unfold. The mysteries are revealed, the universal rhythms and patterns are more understood and the individual creative life force is expressed more fully in all things and to all people. It is the epitome of the spiritual path. It reveals our true spiritual essence and how best to manifest it within this incarnation.

### CONSIDERATIONS IN NAME CHANGES

The name is a direct link to the soul and its potentials, and the manner in which those potentials can most productively be developed. Unfortunately, the assigning of names is not given the consideration it once was. Names are now viewed as mere labels. We must return to understanding the influence of names in all aspects of life.

The ancients recognized that the time of pregnancy was a time for the parents to attune to the child that would be entering into physical life. It was a time to discern the energies and purposes of the incoming soul and thus a name could be chosen that would assist this soul in manifesting its highest potentials.

Names label us and represent us. They take on stereotypes. People associate names with physical, emotional, mental and personality characteristics. The individual may not actually reflect such characteristics, and thus there must be effort to overcome the stereotypes. This may be part of the learning process that the soul has chosen to take upon itself, or it may be the result of a name that a parent assigned without thinking of the effects or attuning to the soul entering into new life.

We can choose a name whose meaning, sounds and rhythms make life tasks and learning of the new soul much easier. We have each come into the physical world to express our energies in a highly individualistic and creative manner. In order to do that most effectively, we must break the limitations that we have imposed upon ourselves and those that others have imposed upon us. Sometimes, this may require an actual name change or adaptation; but we should first consider other important factors.

1. Find out the hidden significance of your name as it is. Name education is sorely lacking within society, and there may be greater significance to your name than what you may realize. Changing the name should be a last resort, and should occur only when the name is completely out of harmony with who you are and where you are going in life, and this does happen.

2. Know what your future goals are—short and long range. Do the energies of your name reflect qualities and forces that can assist

you in achieving your goals?

3. Keep in mind that the name and its elements are links to specific spiritual and archetypal forces. Learn what those forces are, how to access them and if they are in harmony with your goals and desires for the future. Remember that as we grow and change so do our goals and desires. Does the name you have presently contain elements and ties to energies that will assist you and benefit you, even if your goals and desires change?

4. The name you were given at birth has set in motion an energy matrix around you that you have had time to resonate with in varying degrees. The longer you hold to that matrix, the more difficult it is to break free from its influence entirely. This is not to say that the energy pattern cannot be altered or changed, but rather that the longer it has been allowed to establish itself around you, the more effort will be required to adjust or change it. This is why the first year of marriage for most women is the most difficult. Women who change their name upon marriage are thrown into an entirely new matrix. I most often recommend that the woman either keep her maiden name within the marriage or at least in a hyphenated form, so that the shift is not so catalytic.

5. The taking of a nickname is a means of compromising the disharmony with the actual birth name. Nicknames limit and alter the energies of the individual, and the energies may be more easily "lived up to" and expressed more productively. Many times, the assumption of a nickname—especially when it is a shortened form of the birth name, as in the case of Tom vs. Thomas—allows for the individual to evolve into the full birth name. It enables the individual to bridge to the full force of the energies behind the full birth name. This is often reflected biologically. As the child with the nickname grows up and moves out on his or her own, they will often return to the full name.

6. It was often considered taboo in many societies to take the name of a living relative—the belief being that it would draw the life force away from the relative, splitting it so that neither person could feel the full benefit of the energies behind the name. Along these same lines, it is common to find many juniors within families. Daughters are often named after mothers and grandmothers, and sons, more commonly, are named after their fathers. These are names which should be changed or adjusted so as not to be identical to the parents in many cases. When a son shares a name with the fa-

ther, there will occur a sharing of karma as well. The child becomes more bound to the karma of the parent than may have ever been necessary. It can make it difficult for the child to develop individual creativity and expression.

7. In cases of divorce, it is important for the woman to change her name. This helps to remove one's own individual energy from the energy of the partner. Any time there has been sexual intimacy of an extended nature—such as in marriage—the energies of the two become entwined and linked on an atomic level. Keeping the last name of the spouse keeps you tied to that energy, and it delays the separation of the energy between the two. No divorce is easy, but the more we can do to disentangle the energy the easier it will be to re-establish one's own individual creative expression again. (Children of divorce should keep their names. Their names tie them to both parents as they should. When they are independent adults, then they can choose to change their names as they see fit.)

8. Rather than change the entire name, you may simply want to try changing a letter or two within the name. Each letter, as we have seen will activate certain energies. It is also not unusual to find many people who discover that the name they have been going by is different than what actually appears upon the legal birth certificate. Any difference in spelling or essence will cause a different play of energy within your life. This alone can sometimes explain the negative attitude that many hold toward their names.

9. Often there may exist at the time of birth confusion and difference of opinion as to what name the child should be given. If at all uncomfortable with your name, even after studying its esoteric significance, question your parents about it. This may reveal much. It would do to analyze any name that either one or both of the parents had felt strongly about but did not give—for whatever reason. This name can reveal energies and essences that you have come to unfold and evolve by first overcoming and learning to manifest the energies of the given name. Remember that nothing is insignificant—especially when it concerns something as intimate as one's name.

10. If you discover another name that you could have been named or that you have always been drawn to, it does not mean that you must legally change to that name. You can assume it as a nickname or as a magical name. In either case its energies will then come more into play within your life.

11. Changing one's name will not necessarily solve all prob-

lems. Any name change that does occur, especially if legally inaugu-
rated, can take as long as seven years before harmony with its energies and rhythms can be established. With some names, it may occur
almost simultaneously, with others, there will have to be a resonance established. This cannot be determined truly until the change
is instituted which is why any name change should always be seri-
ously considered.

12. People need to learn to rejoice in the energies of their name.
No name is inherently good or bad. What we must understand are
the energies operating through that name within your life. Changing the name legally should be as a last resort because names are living and changing anyway. As you grow and unfold, so do the perceptions of others concerning this label. So too will the manifestation of its archetypal forces. If you are uncomfortable with your
given name, alter its spelling, or give yourself a nickname and enforce its use. You may also want to take on a magical name whose
essence you can use to overcome the negative associations of the
birth name, along with enhancing its positive aspects and energies.
It is always much easier to unfold the "magic" within a name we already use and are aligned to than it is to take on a new one and unfold its energies. Changing names is not like changing tires that are
worn out or don't seem to fit. Names are intimate links to spiritual
forces operating within the universe and within our lives.

No name change should occur without understanding the esoteric influence of it. It begins with an objective and accurate assess-
ment of your own attitude toward your name. How do you feel
about it? How do you react when others call you by your name? Are
you proud of it? Do you enjoy it? Do you hurry to tell others your
nickname? Do you even know what your name means? Do you
know the significance of its elements? Do you know what affect the
sounds of your name have upon you and others? If you have not
fully explored the energies associated with your name, then you
should not yet consider changing it. It is foolish to make judgments
about something you do not understand.

Learn to use your full name. Enforce its use. If you don't wish to
be called by a nickname, correct others that refer to you in such a
manner. Take pride in your name and the essence and forces behind
it. If you must change your name, avoid fad names, and be aware
that any dislike for a name may indicate low self-esteem or a lack of
realization of the innate divinity inherent within each of us—*and reflected by our names!*

# 25

# Changing the Magical Name

Just as in any name change, the changing of one's magical name should be given great consideration and thought. No name change should be forced, nor should a name be taken simply because you feel you should have one or to hold you over until you can think of one that is better or more appropriate. If you cannot decide upon a magical name, relax and be patient. The time to take it upon yourself may not be quite appropriate. Maybe your goals are not clarified at the moment, and thus the most beneficial magical name will be obscure as well. Remember the Law of Synchronicity: "Things will happen in the time and manner that is best for us—if we allow them to!" In the meantime, consider the following points in regards to taking or changing the magical name.

1. Never force a change. When the time is appropriate, you will know. The idea of "you will know" sounds like one of those vague metaphysical axioms that is passed around from time to time, but it is true. You do not want to take a magical name just so you can say that you have one. We use them as a means of empowerment and accessing of the soul energy more effectively, to bridge the intuitive aspects into greater expression and harmony with the outer life. Trust that you will know.

2. If you choose to take a name and then hear of another who is using the same name, don't get upset. Many of the more popular magical names are used by a wide variety of people. If you are truly drawn to the name, use it, unless the person is part of the same meta-

physical group as yourself. Keep in mind that many people have taken "magical names" that they thought had a power that could bolster their own individual egos. It is amazing how many people have used the name "Merlin" as the magical name, so that they could try and pass themselves off as part of the line of true magicians descendent from him. Remember that there is much more reflected within a name than the thoughtform and history behind it. Calling oneself Isis or Merlin does not make one so. What you will be doing is learning to access and express the archetypal energies inherent with the name in a manner unique to yourself.

3. When you have chosen your magical name, keep it a secret, unless it is a name you will be using as part of a group. Most people outside of occult, metaphysical or spiritual groups will not understand the significance and essence of the magical name. Their doubts and their remarks and even their "scoffing disbelief" can set up blockages and hindrances to you manifesting the energy of the name. If they notice changes in you, acknowledge that you have been working on personal development, but there is no need to go any further. More harm can be done by revealing it than if you had just kept silent. One of the precepts that all who are working toward their unfoldment must learn is that "there is strength in silence."

The magical name is used to bridge to and awaken energies that can help make our lives more creative and productive. One of the ways in which this occurs is through its impact upon the auric field—which in turn impacts upon the physical body. The magical name can be part of what is often called the "alchemical marriage." We are marrying the energies of the soul more intimately to those of the physical expressions of life. For this to occur, the physical body must be able to handle the more intense energy of the soul. The assumption of a magical name helps to create an energy within the auric field of the individual that as it builds, it will impact upon the entire energy structure of the body.

It begins a cleansing of the karma held within the cellular memory of the body and begins a process of transmuting the cells of the body so that higher, more spiritual energy can be handled and expressed through the physical life. It institutes energy changes on the cellular level, helping to bring the body into a new vibrational pattern, one that is more in tune with the soul. Discussing the magical name, revealing what one experiences through it, especially in circles where there may be resistance to such beliefs, or negative attitudes, that will dissipate much of that new energy before it can accumulate and institute the permanent changes in your energy that you desire.

4. Attunement with the energies of the magical name varies in the length of time required. Those magical names that are based upon one's birth name are often the easiest to attune to and activate—but not in all cases. When you assume a new name, you are opening yourself to a new expression of energy that will affect you on physical, emotional, mental and spiritual levels. To a great degree, the amount of time and energy you put into understanding and working with the energy of the new name will accelerate the harmonizing and activating of it. Some names—often those associated with gods and goddesses—are aligned with abstract energies which may not always be clearly discernible in how they are manifesting within your own life. It can take up to seven years to be able to touch the core of energy associated with some names and to be able to manifest it and direct it into your life in a controlled and balanced manner.

The taking of a magical name is a form of initiation. The individual is initiating a change of energy that will provide opportunity for growth and evolvement. Many hold the concept that an initiation is a period of three days or so in which occurs a great testing, followed by great enlightenment. Initiation is a day to day process of growth. With the assumption of the magical name we are setting an energy in motion that will help provide for growth along certain avenues. How long it takes the individual to extract the essence of the learning and the heart of the energy associated with the name will vary from individual to individual.

5. How often to change one's magical name is another concern that often arises. My usual recommendation is that the change not occur more often than every three years, but it is not a hard and fast rule. It depends greatly upon the individual's efforts to touch the core of the name and the long and short range goals.

Three is recommended, as it is a creative rhythm, and anything done in "threes" helps to give new birth. Keep in mind though that even when the energy is born, it still must be developed and controlled and expressed fully. The birth process is only the beginning of the development process.

Some individuals find it beneficial to change their magical names every year, as they only focus upon the immediate and the short range goals of life. If changed every year, over a period of time the individual can become scattered and there can occur a splintering of the personality in varying degrees. We must remember that we are trying to bridge the energies of the magical name with the energies of the birth name for greater empowerment in life. Changing the name too frequently will not allow harmony and resonance to be established between the archetypal forces of the magical name with those of the birth name. It can create discordant energy within the auric field, and imbalance will show itself at some point on either physical, emotional, mental or spiritual levels.

Seven years is often considered an ideal minimum length of time to use a specific magical name. The number seven has a long history of mysticism about it. Astrologically, Saturn is the teacher of the solar system. It makes a revolution around the Sun in approximately 28 years. Every seven years, it moves into a new quadrant within the astrological chart, triggering a whole new set of energies and lessons within the individual's life. One can change the magical name so that the energies of Saturn are harmonized and the learning process is accelerated.

Most often the frequency of change should be determined by the amount of effort and the degree of success that the individual has had in touching the core of the essence of a name. Names have an outer expression of energy and an inner esoteric aspect as well. If we are changing our names frequently and according to whatever whim hits at the moment, then we are doing no more than dabbling in things that would be best left alone. The choosing of a name is a mystical process that needs to be reverenced. As we approach it from such an angle, we begin to see that all aspects of our life take on greater reverence and light as well.

6. There are times when it may be necessary to change the magical name somewhat prematurely. Sometimes an individual will choose a name, wishing to initiate change and transition in all areas of life. The assumption of that name can become a catalytic triggering of those desired changes. Unfortunately, the changes may come at a rate and intensity that is unexpected, unprepared for and difficult to handle in a balanced manner. It is quite easy to try and bite off more than one can chew, and within the psychic and metaphysical realms, it happens more frequently than many are aware. In such cases it may be necessary to adjust the name that has been chosen. This could mean changing it entirely, or altering

the spelling so that the energies associated with the name are softened or altered to a degree that they can be more easily balanced. When situations such as this occur, it is usually an indication that the person has not fully explored all the significance of the name and the manner in which it could manifest within the physical life. This is learning, and all learning is beneficial. It just is not always easy.

7. Sometimes it is necessary to change one's magical name when the individual leaves a group to whom the name was known and used. Many covens, metaphysical study groups, etc. use magical names as a means of creating a group harmony. All individuals are called during group meetings by their magical names, rather than their birth names.

When you leave such a group, to embark on individual studies, to work as a solo practitioner or to join another group, it is beneficial to change the magical name. The old name is one that has an energy tied to the past and to the energy of the group from which you are departing. When you move away, you are establishing a new, more independent expression of energy, and it should have a name that is suitable to it. The old name ties you to the old group.

One often hears tales about individuals who leave esoteric groups, and because they don't change their magical names, the group continues to draw on the individual's energy and manipulate the individual. Most of these occurrences are little more than tales, and although they may occur in extreme circumstances and in groups in which there was no true balance to begin with, most groups send the individual on with blessings and light. We must remember though that the name ties us to whatever we have awakened and associated with it.

There are some who—even though they leave a group—do not want to leave the magical name. The energies of the name may still be unfolding for the individual. There may be strong resonance and harmony with this name. In such cases, one does not need to necessarily change the entire name. Altering the spelling somewhat may be all that is necessary to break the connection with the group and still retain the essence of the name and the rhythm of its energies within your life. The individual should keep in mind also that as he or she moves from the group, the name will begin to manifest a more independent expression of energy.

Usually though when an individual leaves a group, the goals

and desires have changed and evolved. New goals are being formulated by the individual. New goals are often best achieved by new
energies and new expressions of energy that can be instituted more
effectively with a new magical name. (This does not mean that every
time one's goals change, so should the name. As the archetypal energy behind a name is unfolded within the individual's life, it will
institute changes in attitudes and goals. One should make sure that
the goals are met or are no longer suitable for where you are at the
present and for where you want to be in the future before the name
is changed.)

8. As we decide to change the magical name, we must re-assess
and assimilate all of the energy of the old. When we use a name, we
create a thoughtform around it which as it builds assists us in expressing the energy of the name we have assumed. As we move to
the process of taking the new name, we must integrate the old.

Old names are like old friends, each unique unto themselves—
each special in the way they touched our lives. We do not just dis-
card them and jump into the new. Before we take a new name, it is
good to take at least a month to re-assess, honor and integrate it
fully. A month is a miniature reflection of the cycle of change. It is
then a time in which we can meditate upon and contemplate the cycle of change that the old name instituted within our life. We must
focus upon the fact that as we aligned ourselves with its energies,
they became a permanent part of our soul expression, a resource
that we can build upon and tap whenever needed.

Meditations during this month should be upon the relationship between the old name and how having taken it has opened us
now to the even newer expression of soul energy within our lives,
reflected by the new name whatever it is or may be. The focus
should be on how the old magical name has helped you to draw
even closer to manifesting all of your soul potentials within the
physical. Thus we do not just release the old, but we see it as a bridge
that has strengthened you and shaped your life to help you move to
an even more unique expression and experience of the soul.

The old name should be viewed as a permanent part of you, for
anything that touches us and affects us on any level becomes a
manifest part of our soul memory. It is an awakened resource for
our continuing life experience and evolvement. It becomes as much
a part of the energy matrix of our life as that of the birth name. It will
forever help to define and express the soul's greater potentials and

energies.

9. When we decide to change the magical name, we must use a transitional period. Remember that we have been aligning with and harmonizing with the energies of another name. These may or may not be in complete resonance with the new name you wish to take. Make sure your future goals are well defined. Make sure that you know the essences of the energy matrix of the new name. Make sure that it is aligned and compatible with your goals. Meditate upon it. Don't just immediately drop the old and move into the new. As mentioned above, allow for a transitional period to honor and reverence what you have already achieved and how it has laid a foundation for that which you will achieve in the future.

There may come a point where you know the old magical name is no longer suitable for you, but you do not have a magical name that is. Do not force it. Honor the old name and allow it to become a part of your energy matrix. Assimilate it and absorb its influence through meditation upon all that it accomplished for you. When it is no longer suitable, then no longer use it.

How long the transition may be between the old name and the realization of the new one will vary from individual to individual and from one time in your life to the next. Simply realize that during the period in which you do not have a magical name is a time in which your energy system is assimilating and absorbing all of the essence of the old name. It is a transition period that allows the old name and its energies to become part of the foundation matrix of energy of you. As this occurs, and becomes fully ensconced within the soul memory, there will occur a crystallizing of one's future goals, along with a growing idea of a possible new magical name. This may be something entirely new, or it may lead you to awakening more fully and dynamically the magic of the birth name.

10. The names we use or choose reveal only what we allow them to beyond the basic energy foundation they manifest. They reflect energies from our soul essence that we can learn to manifest and express in all avenues of life. They define the expressions of our energies for this incarnation or for specific parts of it. We are not bound by them, but unless we become aware of their very real influences, we will never unfold the potentials of which we are capable. Our names—magical or birth—are special creations. Inherent within them is the creative principle that operates throughout nature and the universe. It is this same creative aspect that we can

awaken through our names and through a greater reverence for the sacred energies inherent within them.

# Afterword

# The Blessing Way
# of Name Enchantment

The ancient mystery schools had but one precept: "KNOW THYSELF!" If we truly wish to become more than what we are now, if we truly wish to manifest the creativity that resides deep within each of us, if we wish to become active within our lives rather than allowing events to play upon us, we must discover the new patterns of energy to which we have access. We must come to understand that we are capable of manifestation. We must expand our perceptions beyond the tangible and the visible.

Part of our responsibility in the evolvement process is to learn to build upon what we have. We must learn to re-synthesize teachings and abilities in the manner that works best for us as individuals and within the unique environs of our lives.

What should be the first step in this process is a re-awakening of the "BLESSING WAY" of naming ceremonies. We must become aware of the intricate play of energies that occur so that a soul can take physical form to unfold even more of its potential. We must become aware of the forces active within the birthing process so that they can be used to bless our lives and assist the incoming soul in manifesting greater potentials.

We must learn to proclaim the holiness of birth—not from a mere biological point of "wonder"—but as a time of recognition of the holiness of the incoming child. We must learn to attune to that incoming soul, and we must learn to create and offer a blessing of love—a prayer of blessing and faith that will live on through the name of the child.

In the infinity of life, everything is possible. We all have limitations that we must learn to transcend, but by focusing upon the infinite possibilities, rewards and blessings to which we have access within this life we become living prayers and blessings in the lives of those we touch. Our name and essence become soft touches of comfort and healing.

In this universe of infinite possibilities and energies, that which expands our awareness and unfolds our creativity can only benefit us. By opening ourselves to the blessing way of name enchantment, we open ourselves to the realization of those possibilities. We open ourselves to the worlds and wonders of which we have dreamt of exploring. We open ourselves to the true mysteries of life. When we assumed our names, the doors to these mysteries and wonders were opened to us. That is the blessing way. When we learn to use our names and touch the heart of the divine that touches us through them, then we may walk through those open doors!

# Appendix

# The Name Analysis Process

1. Determine your real name at birth—the way it appears upon your birth certificate.

2. Note any key meanings or associations with the name.

3. Develop an affirmation based upon the name's meaning.

4. Determine its primary vowel, and all of its energies.

5. Determine the cornerstone consonant and the capstone and the energies and meanings associated with them.

6. Make a list of all other letters and their meanings and energies. Although secondary they will also strongly influence.

7. Determine astrological correspondences and compare to your own astrological natal chart.

8. Note the rhythms of your name and its significance.

9. Use as many ways of exploring your name's significance as possible: numerology, astrology, meditation, musical and any other means to confirm your highest potential.

"WE ARE NOW READY TO DANCE TO THE RHYTHMS OF CREATION!"

# Dictionary of Names
# and Affirmations

One of the most powerful techniques of working with your name is that of creating an affirmation from its meaning. Every name has its origin, and even though the meanings may have been obscured over the years, whatever meaning can be uncovered provides a wonderful starting point for self-exploration. The meanings we attribute to many names may now be more symbolic than literal, but they will still provide a means of opening ourselves to the soul energies reflected within it. The name is a symbol. It suggests a quality and thereby links us to the archetypal energy that lies behind that quality.

We can take the meaning of our name—be it symbolic or literal—and we can create a powerful affirmation that will energize and balance not only the metabolic system but the entire energy system, physical and subtle. We can use it to strengthen the auric field and open to higher consciousness and realization of our true essence.

In this index is a listing of several hundred names and their basic meanings. With each name are two examples of affirmations which can be used by anyone who has the particular name. The first affirmation is one which has more of a Judeo-Christian slant for those who are more orthodox in their approach to the spiritual realms. The second is an affirmation more likely to be favored by those of the Old Religion or Wiccan persuasions. Neither is better or worse than the other. Neither is more effective than the other. They are simply two different variations on a technique that can be employed effectively, regardless of belief system or religious persuasion.

If you are not comfortable with either, construct your own. These are given as examples, but often the best affirmations are those constructed by the individual. Use the meaning of your name, and before affirming the essence of the meaning, affirm who you are: "I am     (name)     ! I am (name's meaning)  !"

Always phrase your affirmation in the present. There is no past, and the future is always future. We live in an ever-present moment. Including references to spiritual or divine sources adds greater power to your affirmation. (Refer to the examples in the index if unsure.)

With this process, you are expressing and affirming your divine essence—reminding yourself of your origins. It ignites the aura and it lights the inner fires of the soul. It affirms and reminds of the central presence of the divine operating in and through you at all times.

1. *AARON* (the light bringer)
   "I am Aaron. I am God's bringer of light."
   "I am Aaron. I bring the light of the Goddess."

2. *ABNER* (trustworthy; of the light)
   "I am Abner. I am the trustworthy light of God."
   "I am Abner. I am the trustworthy light of the Goddess."

3. *ABRAHAM* (protector and father of many)
   "I am Abraham. I am God's righteous protector."
   "I am Abraham. I am the divine protector."

4. *ADA* (one of happy, cheerful spirit)
   "I am Ada. I am the happy child of God."
   "I am Ada. I bring the cheerful spirit of the Mother Goddess."

5. *ADAM* (a man of the earth; God's creation)
   "I am Adam. I am God's creation for the earth."
   "I am Adam. I am the child and blessing of Mother Earth."

6. *ADELL* (woman of noble esteem)
   "I am Adell. I am God's woman of noble esteem."
   "I am Adell. I am the divine woman of noble esteem."

7. *ADRIAN* (creative soil and heart; of the black earth)
   "I am Adrian. I am the creative heart of God."
   "I am Adrian. I am the fertile soil of Mother Earth."

8. *AGNES* (purity; the pure one)
   "I am Agnes. I am the pure child of God."
   "I am Agnes. I am the pure child of the Divine Feminine."

9. *AL* (cheerful; of good cheer)
   "I am Al. I am the cheerful child of God."
   "I am Al. I am the Goddess' child of good cheer."

10. *ALAN* (of good cheer; harmonious and handsome)
    "I am Alan. I live the harmony of God."
    "I am Alan. I embody the harmony of the Goddess."

11. *ALBERT* (noble; industrious and full of honor)
    "I am Albert. I am filled with the nobility of Christ."
    "I am Albert. I honor the noble Feminine."

12. *ALEXA* (brave, protecting and secure soul)
    "I am Alexa. I am God's brave and secure protector."
    "I am Alexa. I protect bravely the Divine Feminine in all."

13. *ALEXANDER* (brave, protecting and secure soul)
    "I am Alexander. I am the brave protector of God."
    "I am Alexander. I am secure in the protection of the Goddess."

14. *ALICE* (truthful one)
    "I am Alice. I am the truthful child of God."
    "I am Alice. I am the truthful child of the Goddess."

15. *ALICIA* (the truthful one)
    "I am Alicia. I am the truthful child of God."
    "I am Alicia. I am the truthful child of the Goddess."

16. *ALLEN* (of good cheer; harmonious and handsome)
    "I am Allen. I live the harmony of God."
    "I am Allen. I embody the harmony of the Goddess."

17. *ALVIN* ( the noble friend)
    "I am Alvin. I am the noble friend of all God's people."
    "I am Alvin. I am the noble friend of the Goddess."

18. *AMANDA* (beloved; worthy of being loved)
    "I am Amanda. I am the beloved of God."
    "I am Amanda. I am the beloved child of the Goddess."

19. *AMOS* (the bearer of burdens; compassion)
    "I am Amos. I bear God's spirit of compassion."
    "I am Amos. I am the divine spirit of compassion."

20. *AMY* (beloved)
    "I am Amy. I am the beloved of God."
    "I am Amy. I am the beloved child of the Mother Goddess."

21. *ANDREA* (womanly; woman who is like a god)
    "I am Andrea. I am the godly woman."
    "I am Andrea. I am like a goddess."

22. *ANDREW* (strong, manly one)
    "I am Andrew. I am the strong child of God."
    "I am Andrew. I am the gentle strength of the Divine Feminine."

23. *ANGELA* (messenger of truth; angel)
    "I am Angela. I am God's messenger of truth."
    "I am Angela. I am the angel of truth."

24. *ANITA* (graceful and gracious child)
    "I am Anita. I am the gracious child of God."
    "I am Anita. I embody the graciousness of the Goddess."

25. *ANN* ( graceful and gracious child)
    "I am Ann. I am the gracious child of God."
    "I am Ann. I embody the graciousness of the Goddess."

26. *ANNA* (graceful and gracious child)
    "I am Anna. I am the gracious child of God."
    "I am Anna. I embody the graciousness of the Goddess."

27. *ANNE* (graceful and gracious child)
    "I am Anne. I am the gracious child of God."
    "I am Anne. I embody the graciousness of the Goddess."

28. *ANNETTE* (graceful and gracious child)
    "I am Annette. I am the gracious child of God."
    "I am Annette. I embody the graciousness of the Goddess."

29. *ANTHONY* ( priceless; of inestimable value)
    "I am Anthony. I am priceless in the eyes of God."
    "I am Anthony. I am the Goddess' priceless child."

30. *APRIL* (new opening; new birth; new in faith)
"I am April. I live in God's renewed faith."
"I am April. I am born anew to the Mother Goddess."

31. *ARLENE* (the promise; the pledge; the faithful one)
"I am Arlene. I fulfill the promise of God."
"I am Arlene. I am the promise of the Goddess."

32. *ARNOLD* ( brave and strong; like an eagle)
"I am Arnold. I am God's strong eagle of life."
"I am Arnold. I am the Divine Eagle of strength."

33. *ART* (the bear; noble one of integrity)
"I am Art. I am God's noble bear of integrity."
"I am Art. I am the noble bear of Mother Nature."

34. *ARTHUR* (the bear; noble one of integrity)
"I am Arthur. I am God's noble bear of integrity."
"I am Arthur. I am the noble bear of Mother Nature."

35. *AUDREY* (strong nobility)
"I am Audrey. I am God's noble strength."
"I am Audrey. I am the noble strength of the Divine Feminine."

36. *BARBARA* (bringer of joy)
"I am Barbara. I am God's bringer of joy."
"I am Barbara. I am the Divine bringer of joy."

37. *BARRY* ( pointed spear; courageous weapon)
"I am Barry. I am God's spear of light."
"I am Barry. I am the Divine spear of light."

38. *BEATRICE* (she who makes others joyful and blessed)
"I am Beatrice. I am God's blessed bringer of joy."
"I am Beatrice. I am the blessed bringer of joy."

39. *BENJAMIN* (the favored son)
"I am Benjamin. I am the favored son of God."
"I am Benjamin. I stand at the right hand of the Goddess."

40. *BERNARD* (brave as a bear; powerful and victorious)
"I am Bernard. I am the powerful bear of God."
"I am Bernard. I am the divine bear of might and victory."

41. *BETH* (house of God; consecrated to God)
"I am Beth. I am consecrated to God."
"I am Beth. I am consecrated to the Goddess."

42. *BETSY* (house of God; consecrated to God)
    "I am Betsy. I am consecrated to God."
    "I am Betsy. I am consecrated to the Goddess."

43. *BETTY* (house of God; consecrated to God)
    "I am Betty. I am consecrated to God."
    "I am Betty. I am consecrated to the Goddess."

44. *BEVERLY* (diligent; at the meadow of the beaver)
    "I am Beverly. I am the diligent worker of God."
    "I am Beverly. I am the beaver of the Earth Mother."

45. *BONNIE* (sweet; of good heart)
    "I am Bonnie. I live the good heart of God."
    "I am Bonnie. My heart is filled with the sweet."

46. *BRADLEY* (from the broad meadow; good provider)
    "I am Bradley. I provide abundance."
    "I am Bradley. I am from the broad meadow of Earth Mother."

47. *BRENDA* (the beacon; strong and enthusiastic)
    "I am Brenda. I am God's beacon unto others."
    "I am Brenda. I am the beacon of the Divine Feminine."

48. *BRENT* (the beacon; strong and enthusiastic)
    "I am Brent. I am God's strong beacon."
    "I am Brent. I am a beacon of the Divine Feminine."

49. *BRIAN* (strength, virtue and honor)
    "I am Brian. I am strong in virtue and honor."
    "I am Brian. I live the virtuous strength of the Blessed
       Feminine."

50. *BRUCE* (dweller in thicket; secure)
    "I am Bruce. I am secure in thicket of God's light."
    "I am Bruce. I am secure in thicket of the Divine."

51. *BURT* ( bright, abundant provider)
    "I am Burt. I am God's abundant provider."
    "I am Burt. I am the abundant provider of brightness."

52. *BYRON* (bear; full of strength)
    "I am Byron. I am the strong bear of God."
    "I am Byron. I am the great bear of the Earth Mother."

53. *CANDICE* (glittering white; woman of honor)
    "I am Candice. I am God's glittering white light."
    "I am Candice. I am the divine woman of honor and light."

54. *CARL* (farmer; strong and manly)
    "I am Carl. I am the farmer of all life."
    "I am Carl. I am the Earth Mother's farmer of life."

55. *CARLA* (little womanly one; strong)
    "I am Carla. I am the strong woman of God."
    "I am Carla. I am the strong woman of the Divine."

56. *CAROL* (womanly; song of joy)
    "I am Carol. I am God's song of joy."
    "I am Carol. I am the woman's song of joy."

57. *CAROLINE* ( womanly; song of joy)
    "I am Caroline. I am God's song of joy."
    "I am Caroline. I am the woman's song of joy."

58. *CARRIE* (womanly; song of joy)
    "I am Carrie. I am God's song of joy."
    "I am Carrie. I am the woman's song of joy."

59. *CATHERINE* (one of purity)
    "I am Catherine. I am the pure child of God."
    "I am Catherine. I am the pure child of the Divine."

60. *CHARLENE* (strong and womanly)
    "I am Charlene. I am strong in God's life."
    "I am am Charlene. I am strong in the Women's Mysteries."

61. *CHARLES* (strong and manly)
    "I am Charles. I am strong in God's life."
    "I am Charles. I am strong in the life of the Goddess."

62. *CHARLOTTE* (strong and womanly)
    "I am Charlotte. I am strong in God's life."
    "I am Charlotte. I am strong in the Feminine Mysteries."

63. *CHERYL* (beloved and cherished)
    "I am Cheryl. I am the cherished child of God."
    "I am Cheryl. I am the beloved of the Goddess."

64. *CHRISTINE* ( the follower and bearer of Christ)
    "I am Christine. I am at one with the Christ."
    "I am Christine. I am at one with the Archangelic Christ."

65. *CHRISTOPHER* (follower and bearer of Christ)
   "I am Christopher. I am at one with the Christ."
   "I am Christopher. I am at one with the Archangelic Christ."

66. *CINDY* (goddess of the Moon; reflector of light)
   "I am Cindy. I reflect the light of God."
   "I am Cindy. I am the Goddess reflecting light for all."

67. *CLAUDE* (of humble heart; humility)
   "I am Claude. I am filled with humility of God."
   "I am Claude. I am humble before the Divine Feminine."

68. *CLAUDIA* (of humble heart; humility)
   "I am Claudia. I am filled with the humility of God."
   "I am Claudia. I live the Divine Feminine with humility."

69. *CLIFFORD* (from the cliff; vigilant)
   "I am Clifford. I am the vigilant child of God."
   "I am Clifford. I am vigilant to the expression of the Divine."

70. *CLYDE* (heard from far away; of good heart)
   "I am Clyde. My heart hears the words of God."
   "I am Clyde. My heart is felt near and far."

71. *CONSTANCE* (firmness; constancy; devotion)
   "I am Constance. I am devoted to all God's endeavors."
   "I am Constance. I am firm in devotion to the Divine."

72. *CRAIG* (strong; enduring; dwells at the crag)
   "I am Craig. I am strong with God in all things."
   "I am Craig. I am strong in the Feminine Mysteries."

73. *CYNTHIA* (goddess of the Moon; reflector of light)
   "I am Cynthia. I reflect the light of God."
   "I am Cynthia. I am the Moon Goddess, reflecting light for all."

74. *DALE* (one who dwells in the valley; courageous)
   "I am Dale. I am courageous in life."
   "I am Dale. I live forever in the valley of the Earth Mother."

75. *DANIEL* (God is my judge)
   "I am Daniel and God is my judge."
   "I am Daniel. I am fulfilled through judgement of the Goddess."

76. *DARLENE* (dear little one; tender love)
"I am Darlene. I am the dear one of God."
"I am Darlene. I am filled with the tender love of Divine Mother."

77. *DARREN* (bountiful; great one who is beloved)
"I am Darren. I am bountiful in all things."
"I am Darren. I share in the bounty of the Blessed Mother."

78. *DARRYL* (bountiful; one who is beloved)
"I am Darryl. I am bountiful in all things."
"I am Darryl. I am filled with bounty of the Earth Mother."

79. *DAVID* (beloved one)
"I am David. I am the beloved child of God."
"I am David. I am the beloved child of the Goddess."

80. *DAWN* (new day; joy and praise)
"I am Dawn. I sing for God's new day."
"I am Dawn. I am joyful for the new day of the Goddess."

81. *DEBORAH* (the bee; the seeker)
"I am Deborah. I am the seeker of God's life."
"I am Deborah. I am the bee seeking the honey of life."

82. *DENISE* (follower of Dionysus; discerner)
"I am Denise. I am the wise discerner."
"I am Denise. I am the blessed child of Dionysus."

83. *DENNIS* (follower of Dionysus; discerner)
"I am Dennis. I am blessed with God's gift of discernment."
"I am Dennis. I am the blessed child of Dionysus."

84. *DIANA* (goddess; divine one; living in God's glory)
"I am Diana. I am the divine child of God's glory."
"I am Diana. I am the Goddess of divine glory."

85. *DIANE* (goddess; divine one; living in God's glory)
"I am Diane. I am the divine child of God's glory."
"I am Diane. I am the Goddess of divine glory."

86. *DONALD* (mighty world ruler; one who overcomes)
"I am Donald. I am the mighty child of God."
"I am Donald. I overcome all through the blessing of the Goddess."

87. *DONNA* (lady; dignity of character)
"I am Donna. I am dignified through God's blessing."
"I am Donna. I am the lady of the Goddess."

88. *DORIS* (gift of God)
"I am Doris. I am the gift of God."
"I am Doris. I am the gifted child of the Goddess."

89. *DOROTHY* (gift of God)
"I am Dorothy. I am the gift of God."
"I am Dorothy. I am the gifted child of the Goddess."

90. *DOUGLAS* (from the dark water; seeker of light)
"I am Douglas. I seek and find God's light in all things."
"I am Douglas. I seek and find the light of the Earth Mother."

91. *DUANE* (song; of cheerful heart)
"I am Duane. I am God's song of the cheerful heart."
"I am Duane. I am the song of cheerful heart of the Divine."

92. *EDGAR* (prosperous; cheerful and friendly guardian)
"I am Edgar. I am the prosperous guardian of all."
"I am Edgar. I share in the guardianship of the Goddess."

93. *EDITH* (prosperous; cheerful and friendly guardian)
"I am Edith. I am the propserous and cheerful child of God."
"I am Edith. I share the cheer and prosperity of the Goddess."

94. *EDWARD* (prosperous; cheerful and friendly guardian)
"I am Edward. I am the prosperous guardian of all."
" I am Edward. I am the cheerful guardian of the Feminine."

95. *EILEEN* (light)
"I am Eileen. I am the light of God."
"I am Eileen. I walk in the light of the Goddess."

96. *ELAINE* (the lily maid; the bright one)
"I am Elaine. I am the bright lily of God."
"I am Elaine. I am the bright lily of the Earth Mother."

97. *ELIZABETH* (house of God; consecrated to God)
"I am Elizabeth. I am consecrated to God."
"I am Elizabeth. I am a consecrated child of the Divine."

98. *ELLEN* (bright one)
"I am Ellen. I am the bright child of God."
"I am Ellen. I am the bright child of the Divine Goddess."

99. *EMILY* (industrious; diligent and caring)
   "I am Emily. I am the caring child of God."
   "I am Emily. I am the diligent and caring child of the Divine Feminine."

100. *ERIC* (ever powerful; godly power; ever the ruler)
   "I am Eric. I am ever powerful in life."
   "I am Eric. I am blessed with the power of the Goddess."

101. *ERICA* (ever powerful; godly power; ever the ruler)
   "I am Erica. I am ever powerful in life."
   "I am Erica. I am blessed with the power of the Goddess."

102. *EVELYN* (light; full of life)
   "I am Evelyn. I am filled with the light of God."
   "I am Evelyn. I am full of the light of Life."

103. *FERN* (abundant life and growth)
   "I am Fern. I grow abundantly day by day."
   "I am Fern. I have abundant life through the Mother Earth."

104. *FLORENCE* (blooming; flower; fragrant spirit)
   "I am Florence. I am the flower of God."
   "I am Florence. I embody the fragrant spirit of the Divine."

105. *FRANCES* (living in freedom)
   "I am Frances. I am free to live to my fullest."
   "I am Frances. I live freely through the Goddess."

106. *FRANK* (honest; living in freedom)
   "I am Frank. I live honestly and freely through God."
   "I am Frank. I live honestly and freely through the Divine."

107. *FREDERICK* (one who is at peace)
   "I am Frederick. I am at peace through God."
   "I am Frederick. I am the peaceful ruler of my life."

108. *GABRIEL* (man of God)
   "I am Gabriel. I am the man of God."
   "I am Gabriel. I hold the blessings of the archangels."

109. *GAIL* (gay; lively; source of joy and cheer)
   "I am Gail. I am a source of joy for others."
   "I am Gail. I bring joy and cheer from the Goddess."

110. *GARY* (the spear; loyalty)
     "I am Gary. I carry God's spear of loyalty to all."
     "I am Gary. I am the Divine's spear of loyalty."

111. *GENE* (well-born; noble and pure)
     "I am Gene. I am the noble and pure child of God."
     "I am Gene. I live the divine nobility and purity."

112. *GEORGE* (industrious; worker or farmer)
     "I am George. I am the worker of God."
     "I am George. I am the industrious farmer of the Earth
     Mother."

113. *GEORGIA* (industrious; worker or farmer)
     "I am Georgia. I am the worker of God."
     "I am Georgia. I am the worker for the Earth Mother."

114. *GERALD* (the mighty warrior; spear)
     "I am Gerald. I am God's courageous warrior."
     "I am Gerald. I am the mighty warrior of the Divine."

115. *GERALDINE* (the mighty warrior; the spear)
     "I am Geraldine. I am God's courageous warrior."
     "I am Geraldine. I am the mighty spear of the Divine."

116. *GLEN* (dweller in the valley; prosperous one)
     "I am Glen. I share in God's prosperous valley."
     "I am Glen. I share the prosperity of the Earth Mother."

117. *GLORIA* (glory)
     "I am Gloria. I am the glorious child of God."
     "I am Gloria. I am the glorious child of the Goddess."

118. *GRACE* (thanks; graciousness)
     "I am Grace. I am the gracious and thankful spirit of God."
     "I am Grace. I embody the Divine spirit of thankfulness."

119. *GREGORY* (watchman; ever watchful)
     "I am Gregory. I am the observant child of God."
     "I am Gregory. I am the Divine watchman."

120. *HAROLD* (ruler in the army; strong leader)
     "I am Harold. I am a strong leader in life."
     "I am Harold. I am a strong leader for the Divine Life."

121. *HEATHER* (heather flower or shrub; joyful spirit)
"I am Heather. I am God's flower of joy."
"I am Heather. I am the Earth Mother's flower of joy."

122. *HELEN* (light, torch; the bright one)
"I am Helen. I am the bright torch of God."
"I am Helen. I am the bright light of the Divine."

123. *HENRY* (ruler of home or estate; industrious)
"I am Henry. I am the keeper of God's estate."
"I am Henry. I am the ruler of my life."

124. *HOWARD* (chief; guardian; reasonable one)
"I am Howard. I am the guardian of life."
"I am Howard. I am the chief guardian of the Divine."

125. *HUGH* (one of mind and reason)
"I am Hugh. I live the reason of God."
"I am Hugh. I see the reason of the Divine in all things."

126. *IAN* (God's gracious gift)
"I am Ian. I am God's gracious gift."
"I am Ian. I am the gracious gift of the Divine Mother."

127. *IRENE* (peace; peaceful spirit)
"I am Irene. I am the peaceful spirit of God."
"I am Irene. I embody the peace of the Divine."

128. *IRIS* (the rainbow; God's promise)
"I am Iris. I am the rainbow of God."
"I am Iris. I am the divine Goddess of the promised rainbow."

129. *ISAAC* (laughter; cheerful and strong faith)
"I am Isaac. I am filled with God's cheer and faith."
"I am Isaac. I embrace all life with cheer and faith."

130. *JACK* (the supplanter; noble in truth)
"I am Jack. I am noble in truth."
"I am Jack. I embrace the noble truth of all mysteries."

131. *JACOB* (the supplanter; noble in truth)
"I am Jacob. I am noble in truth."
"I am Jacob. I embrace the noble truth of all mysteries."

132. *JACQUELINE* (the supplanter; noble in truth)
"I am Jacqueline. I am noble in truth."
"I am Jacqueline. I embrace the noble truth of all mysteries."

133. *JAMES* (the supplanter; noble in truth)
"I am James. I am noble in truth."
"I am James. I embrace the truth of all divine mysteries."

134. *JANET* (God is gracious; God's gracious gift)
"I am Janet. I am God's gracious gift."
"I am Janet. I am the gracious gift of the Goddess."

135. *JANICE* (God is gracious; God's gracious gift)
"I am Janice. I am God's gracious gift."
"I am Janice. I am the gracious gift of the Goddess."

136. *JASON* (the healer; one who heals)
"I am Jason. I am the healer of God."
"I am Jason. I am the healer of all life."

137. *JEAN* (God is gracious; God's gracious gift)
"I am Jean. I am God's gracious gift."
"I am Jean. I am the gracious gift of the Goddess."

138. *JEFFREY* (divinely peaceful; one at peace)
"I am Jeffrey. I hold the peace of God within my heart."
"I am Jeffrey. I bring the gift of peace from the Divine."

139. *JENNIFER* (white wave or phantom; the fair lady)
"I am Jennifer. I am the fair lady of life."
"I am Jennifer. I am the fair lady of the Blessed Goddess."

140. *JEREMY* (appointed by God; devout and consecrated heart)
"I am Jeremy. I am the appointed of God."
"I am Jeremy. I manifest the consecrated heart of the Divine Feminine."

141. *JEROME* (appointed by God; devout and consecrated heart)
"I am Jerome. I am the appointed of God."
"I am Jerome. I hold the devout heart of the Goddess."

142. *JESSICA* (wealthy and blessed one; God exists)
"I am Jessica. The blessedness of God lives in me."
"I am Jessica. The blessedness of the Goddess lives in me."

143. *JILL* (the youthful one; the youthful heart)
"I am Jill. I am the youthful child of God."
"I am Jill. I am of youthful heart."

144. *JOAN* (God is gracious; God's gracious gift)
   "I am Joan. I am God's gracious gift."
   "I am Joan. I am the gracious gift of the Goddess."

145. *JOANNE* (God is gracious; God's gracious gift)
   "I am Joanne. I am God's gracious gift."
   "I am Joanne. I am the gracious gift of the Goddess."

146. *JODI* (praised of God)
   "I am Jodi. I am the praised child of God."
   "I am Jodi. I am the praised child of Divine Blessing."

147. *JOEL* (the Lord is God; declarer of God)
   "I am Joel. I proclaim God in all life."
   "I am Joel. I proclaim the Divine in all expressions."

148. *JOHN* (God's gracious gift)
   "I am John. I am God's gracious gift."
   "I am John. I am the gracious gift of the Divine."

149. *JOSEPH* (one who adds; increasing faithfulness)
   "I am Joseph. I add faithfulness in God to the world."
   "I am Joseph. I increase the faith of all in the Divine."

150. *JOSHUA* (God of salvation; the salvation)
   "I am Joshua. I am God's gift of salvation."
   "I am Joshua. I embrace the divine salvation of all life."

151. *JOY* (the joyful one)
   "I am Joy. I am the joyful child of God."
   "I am Joy. I awaken the joy of the Divine Feminine."

152. *JOYCE* (joyful)
   "I am Joyce. I am the joyful child of God."
   "I am Joyce. I awaken the joy of all Divine Expressions."

153. *JUANITA* (God's gracious gift)
   "I am Juanita. I am the gracious gift of God."
   "I am Juanita. I am the gracious gift of the Goddess."

154. *JUDITH* (praised of God)
   "I am Judith. I am praised of God."
   "I am Judith. I live the praises of the Divine."

155. *JULIA* (youthful; young at heart)
    "I am Julia. I am young in heart and spirit."
    "I am Julia. Divine youth lives within my heart and spirit."

156. *JUNE* ( benevolent heart; born in June)
    "I am June. I express the benevolent heart of God."
    "I am June. Divine benevolence lives through me."

157. *KAREN* (dear beloved one; purity)
    "I am Karen. I am the beloved child of God."
    "I am Karen. I am the beloved child of the Divine Universe."

158. *KATHLEEN* (one of purity)
    "I am Kathleen. I am the pure child of God."
    "I am Kathleen. I am the Divine child of purity."

159. *KATHRYN* (one of purity)
    "I am Kathryn. I am the pure child of God."
    "I am Kathryn. I am the Divine child of purity."

160. *KEITH* (from the battle place; secure and safe)
    "I am Keith. I am secure and safe in all things."
    "I am Keith. I live and manifest Divine security."

161. *KELLY* (warrior; excellent virtue)
    "I am Kelly. I live the virtues of God."
    "I am Kelly. I am the spiritual warrior."

162. *KENNETH* (handsome; manly and gracious)
    "I am Kenneth. I am the gracious one of God."
    "I am Kenneth. I am blessed with the graciousness of the
    Divine Feminine."

163. *KEVIN* (gentle; loveable and kind)
    "I am Kevin. I am the gentle and kind child of God."
    "I am Kevin. I embody the gentle strength of the Earth
    Mother."

164. *KIM* (from the royal fortress; strong and noble warrior)
    "I am Kim. I am the noble warrior of God."
    "I am Kim. I live within the fortress of the Divine Goddess."

165. *KURT* (bold counselor; strong in counsel)
    "I am Kurt. I am strong in counsel."
    "I am Kurt. I counsel through the Divine Sophia."

166. *LAURA* (crowned with victory)
"I am Laura. My victorious spirit is crowned by God."
"I am Laura. I am the Divine spirit of victory."

167. *LAWRENCE* ( crowned with victory)
"I am Lawrence. My victorious spirit is crowned by God."
"I am Lawrence. I am the Divine spirit of victory."

168. *LEO* (the courageous lion)
"I am Leo. I am the lion of God."
"I am Leo. I am the courageous lion of the Earth Mother."

169. *LEONA* (the courageous lion)
"I am Leona. I am the Lion of God."
"I am Leona. I am the courageous lion of the Earth Mother."

170. *LESLEY* (dweller at the gray fortress; calm spirit)
"I am Lesley. I am the calm spirit."
"I am Lesley. I embody the calm spirit of Sophia."

171. *LINDA* (pretty one; beauty; refreshing)
"I am Linda. I am the beautiful child of God."
"I am Linda. I embody the beauty of the Divine Feminine."

172. *LISA* (consecrated one)
"I am Lisa. I am the consecrated child of God."
"I am Lisa. I am consecrated to the Divine spirituality."

173. *LOIS* (warrior-maid; victorious)
"I am Lois. I am the warrior-maid of God."
"I am Lois. I am the victorious warrior of the Divine."

174. *LOUIS* (warrior; victorious)
"I am Louis. I am the warrior of God."
"I am Louis. I am the victorious warrior of the Divine."

175. *LOUISE* (warrior-maid; victorious)
"I am Louise. I am the warrior-maiden of God."
"I am Louise. I am the victorious warrior of the Divine."

176. *LUKE* (enlightened; bringer of light and knowledge)
"I am Luke. I am the enlightened child of God."
"I am Luke. I am the bringer of Divine light and knowledge."

177. *MARDELL* (the bittersweet delight; myrrh)
"I am Mardell. I am the delightful myrrh of God."
"I am Mardell. I embody the bittersweet delight of the Divine upon the earth."

178. *MARGARET* (the pearl)
"I am Margaret. I am the pearl of God."
"I am Margaret. I am the pearl of spirituality."

179. *MARIE* (myrrh; from the sea; the living fragrance)
"I am Marie. I am the living fragrance of God."
"I am Marie. I am the living fragrance from the sea of life."

180. *MARILYN* (myrrh; from the sea; the living fragrance)
"I am Marilyn. I am the living fragrance of God."
"I am Marilyn. I am the living fragrance from the sea of life."

181. *MARK* (warlike; brave heart)
"I am Mark. I am the mighty warrior of God."
"I am Mark. I live the brave heart of the Divine."

182. *MARLENE* (myrrh; the living fragrance; from the sea)
"I am Marlene. I am the living fragrance of God."
"I am Marlene. I am the fragrance from the sea of life."

183. *MARTHA* (lady of discretion)
"I am Martha. I embody the discretion of God."
"I am Martha. I am the Divine Goddess of discretion."

184. *MARY* (the living fragrance; myrrh; from the sea)
"I am Mary. I am the delightful myrrh of God."
"I am Mary. I draw forth life from the Divine seas."

185. *MATTHEW* (gift of Jehovah; gift of the Lord)
"I am Matthew. I am the gift of the Lord."
"I am Matthew. I am the Divine gift to all."

186. *MICHAEL* (one who is like God; godliness)
"I am Michael. I am like God."
"I am Michael. I embody the Goddess."

187. *MICHELLE* (one who is like God; godliness)
"I am Michelle. I live a life of godliness."
"I am Michelle. I embody the Goddess."

188. *NANCY* (grace; gracious one)
"I am Nancy. I am the gracious child of God."
"I am Nancy. I embody the grace of the Divine Goddess."

189. *NATHAN* (given of God)
"I am Nathan. I am the gift of God."
"I am Nathan. I am the Divine gift of life."

190. *NEAL* (champion)
    "I am Neal. I am the champion of life."
    "I am Neal. I am the champion of the Divine Feminine."

191. *NICHOLAS* (victory; victorious heart)
    "I am Nicholas. I am of victorious heart."
    "I am Nicholas. I embody the victorious heart of the Divine."

192. *NORMAN* (the pattern; from the north; strong)
    "I am Norman. I live the strong example of life."
    "I am Norman. I hold the strong pattern of the Divine Life."

193. *OLIVIA* (the olive branch; peaceful spirit)
    "I am Olivia. I am the peaceful spirit of God."
    "I am Olivia. I embody the spirit of peace."

194. *OSCAR* (spirit of the divine; blessed through service)
    "I am Oscar. I am God's blessing through service."
    "I am Oscar. I am the spirit of the Divine."

195. *PAIGE* (attendant; obedient spirit)
    "I am Paige. I am the obedient attendant of God."
    "I am Paige. I am the obedient attendant of the Divine Feminine."

196. *PAMELA* (honey; sweet spirit)
    "I am Pamela. I am the sweet honey of God."
    "I am Pamela. I am the sweet honey of the Earth Mother."

197. *PATRICIA* (noble; full of honor)
    "I am Patricia. I am the noble and honorable child of God."
    "I am Patricia. I live the spirit of nobility and honor."

198. *PATRICK* (noble; full of honor)
    "I am Patrick. I am the honorable child of God."
    "I am Patrick. I live the spirit of nobility and honor."

199. *PAUL* (little; follower of God)
    "I am Paul. I am the follower of God."
    "I am Paul. I am open to follow the Divine Spirit."

200. *PETER* (rock; strong in spirit)
    "I am Peter. I am the rock of God."
    "I am Peter. I build upon the rock of spirit."

201. *PHILLIP* (lover of horses; strong in spirit)
"I am Phillip. I am strong in God."
"I am Phillip. I recognize the strength of spirit in all."

202. *PHYLLIS* (leaf; tender hearted)
"I am Phyllis. I am a leaf on the plant of God."
"I am Phyllis. I embody the tender heart of the Earth Mother."

203. *RACHEL* (little lamb)
"I am Rachel. I am the little lamb of God."
"I am Rachel. I am the Goddess' lamb of life."

204. *RAYMOND* (counsel and protection; mighty and wise)
"I am Raymond. I am the mighty and wise protector."
"I am Raymond. I am mighty in the counsel of Sophia."

205. *REBECCA* (yoke; earnestly devoted one)
"I am Rebecca. I am the devoted child of God."
"I am Rebecca. I am devoted to the Divine feminine."

206. *RHONDA* (grand strength of character)
"I am Rhonda. I express God's strength of character."
"I am Rhonda. I am the divine strength of character."

207. *RICHARD* (powerful ruler; brave one)
"I am Richard. I am God's powerful ruler."
"I am Richard. I rule with the power of the Divine."

208. *RITA* (the pearl)
"I am Rita. I am the great pearl of God."
"I am Rita. I am the pearl of Divine Spirituality."

209. *ROBERT* (shining with fame and worth)
"I am Robert. I reflect God's excellent worth."
"I am Robert. I shine with Divine worth."

210. *ROBERTA* (shining with fame and worth)
"I am Roberta. I reflect God's excellent worth."
"I am Roberta. I shine with Divine worth."

211. *ROBIN* (shining with fame and worth)
"I am Robin. I reflect God's shining worth."
"I am Robin. I shine with Divine worth."

212. *ROGER* (famous spear carrier; God's warrior)
"I am Roger. I am God's spear of light."
"I am Roger. I carry the spear of light for the Divine Feminine."

213. *RONALD* (mighty power)
     "I am Ronald. I manifest the mighty power of God."
     "I am Ronald. I draw from the mighty power of the Earth Mother."

214. *ROSE* ( the rose; the giver of love)
     "I am Rose. I am God's giver of love."
     "I am Rose. I am the Goddess of love."

215. *ROSEMARY* (giver of sweet fragrance of love)
     "I am Rosemary. I am God's sweet gift of love."
     "I am Rosemary. I draw from the Goddess' sweet gift of love."

216. *RUSSELL* (red-haired one; wise discretion)
     "I am Russell. I am wise and discrete."
     "I am Russell. I wisely manifest the Feminine Mysteries."

217. *RUTH* (compassionate and beautiful)
     "I am Ruth. I am the compassionate child of God."
     "I am Ruth. I am the Goddess of compassion and beauty."

218. *RYAN* (little king; man of distinction)
     "I am Ryan. I am God's man of distinction."
     "I am Ryan. I am a King of great distinction."

219. *SAMUEL* (his name is God; asked of God; integrity)
     "I am Samuel. I am the integrity of God."
     "I am Samuel. I embody the Divine integrity."

220. *SANDRA* (helper; defender with compassion and humility)
     "I am Sandra. I defend and strengthen others with compassion and humility."
     "I am Sandra. I embody divine compassion and humility."

221. *SARAH* (princess; God's princess)
     "I am Sarah. I am God's princess."
     "I am Sarah. I am the princess of the Divine mother."

222. *SCOTT* (loyalty)
     "I am Scott. I am loyal in all things."
     "I am Scott. I live the life of divine loyalty."

223. *SEAN* (God's gracious gift)
     "I am Sean. I am God's gracious gift."
     "I am Sean. I am the gracious gift of the Divine."

224. *SHERYL* (cherished womanly one)
   "I am Sheryl. I am the cherished child of God."
   "I am Sheryl. I am the cherished child of the Goddess."

225. *SHIRLEY* (from the bright meadow; restful spirit)
   "I am Shirley. I am from the bright meadow of God."
   "I am Shirley. I embody the restful spirit of Blessed Mother Earth."

226. *SONJA* (woman of wisdom)
   "I am Sonja. I am a woman of wisdom."
   "I am Sonja. I live the wisdom of the Divine."

227. *STACEY* (resurrected; transformed heart)
   "I am Stacey. I am the resurrected heart of life."
   "I am Stacey. I express the Divine's transformed heart."

228. *STAN* (sturdy in spirit; lives at the rocky meadow)
   "I am Stan. I am sturdy through God."
   "I am Stan. I am sturdy in spirit."

229. *STEPHANIE* (one who is crowned)
   "I am Stephanie. I am crowned with God's light."
   "I am Stephanie. I am crowned through the expression of Divine."

230. *STEVEN* (one who is crowned)
   "I am Steven. I am crowned in God's light."
   "I am Steven. I am crowned through the expression of Divine."

231. *STUART* (caretaker; the helpful spirit)
   "I am Stuart. I am the helpful spirit of God."
   "I am Stuart. I am the caretaker of the Earth Mother."

232. *SUSAN* (lily; full of grace)
   "I am Susan. I am the lily of God."
   "I am Susan. I am the lily of grace."

233. *TAMARA* (the twin; the seeker of truth)
   "I am Tamara. I am the seeker of truth."
   "I am Tamara. I seek the truth of the Divine Feminine."

234. *TANIA* (the fairy queen; noble in spirit)
   "I am Tania. I am noble in spirit."
   "I am Tania. I am the Fairy Queen."

235. *TED/THEODORE* (gift of God)
"I am Ted. I am the gift of God."
"I am Ted. I manifest the gifts of the spirit."

236. *TERRENCE* (smooth, polished one)
"I am Terrence. I am the polished gem of God."
"I am Terrence. I am polished in Divine Expressions of life."

237. *THERESA* (the reaper; industrious one)
"I am Theresa. I reap the rewards of life."
"I am Theresa. I reap the blessings of the Earth Mother."

238. *THOMAS* (the twin; the seeker of truth)
"I am Thomas. I am God's seeker of truth."
"I am Thomas. I seek the truth of Divine Life."

239. *TIMOTHY* (honoring God)
"I am Timothy. I honor God with my life."
"I am Timothy. I honor the Divine in all expressions."

240. *TODD* (the fox; the wise one)
"I am Todd. I am the wise one of life."
"I am Todd. I express the Feminine Wisdom of Sophia."

241. *VALERIE* (strong; of determination)
"I am Valerie. I am strong and determined."
"I am Valerie. I hold the divine strength and determination."

242. *VICTORIA* (conqueror; victorious one)
"I am Victoria. I live God's victorious spirit."
"I am Victoria. I am of Divine victorious spirit."

243. *VIOLET* (violet flower; humble)
"I am Violet. I am God's humble flower."
"I am Violet. I am the humble wildflower of life."

244. *VIRGINIA* (maiden; the pure maiden)
"I am Virginia. I am the pure maiden of God."
"I am Virginia. I am the maiden of the Mother Goddess."

245. *WALTER* (powerful warrior)
"I am Walter. I am the powerful warrior of God."
"I am Walter. I am the Divine warrior spirit."

246. *WANDA* (wanderer; one who walks with God)
"I am Wanda. I walk with God."
"I am Wanda. The Divine spirits travel with me."

247. *WENDY* (wanderer; one who walks with God)
"I am Wendy. I walk with God."
"I am Wendy. The Divine Mother walks with me."

248. *WILLIAM* (resolute; brave and protecting)
"I am William. I am God's brave protector."
"I am William. I am resolute with the Divine Life."

249. *YVONNE* (courageous heart and soul; the hero)
"I am Yvonne. I am of courageous heart and soul."
"I am Yvonne. I manifest the courage of the Divine soul."

250. *ZACHARY* (Jehovah remembers)
"I am Zachary. I am remembered by God."
"I am Zachary. The memory of the Divine Feminine lives in me."

# Bibliography

## Mysteries of Languages and Names

Ames, Winthrop. *What Shall We Name the Baby?* Workman Publishing: New York, 1941.

Anderson, Christopher P. *The Name Game.* New York: Simon and Schuster, 1977.

Bardon, Franz. *The Key to the True Quabballah.* Germany: Dieter Ruggeberg, 1986.

Baskin, Wade. *The Sorcerer's Handbook.* New Jersey: Citadel Press, 1974.

Bischoff, Eric. *The Kabbala.* Maine: Samuel Weiser, 1985.

Browder, Sue. *New Age Baby Book.* New York: Workman Publishing, 1974.

Busse, Thomas V. *The Professor's Book of First Names.* Pennsylvania: Green Ball press, 1984.

Claiborne, Robert. *The Birth of Writing.* New York: Time-Life Books, 1974.

Cottle, Basil. *Names.* London: Thames and Hudson, 1983.

Dunkling, Leslie Alan. *First Names First.* New York: Universe Books, 1977.

_____. *Our Secret Names.* New Jersey: Prentice-Hall,1981.

Etiemble, Rene. *The Written Word.* New York: Orion Press, 1961.

Jackson, Donald. *The Story of Writing.* New York: Taplinger Publishing, 1981.

Katan, Norma Jean. *Hieroglyphics—The Writing of Ancient Egypt.* New York: Athenum Press, 1982.

Langacker, Ronald. *Language and Its Structure.* New York: Harcourt, Brace and World, 1968.

Logan, Robert K. *The Alphabet Effect.* New York: William Morrow and Company, 1986.

Ludovici, L. J. *Origins of Language.* New York: G.P. Putnam, 1965.

Moss, Miriam. *Language and Writing.* New York, Bookwright Press, 1988.

Ober, J. Hambleton. *Writing: Man's Greatest Invention.* Baltimore: Peabody Institute, 1965.

Ogg, Oscar. *The 26 Letters.* New York: Thomas Y. Crowell Company, 1961.

Palmquist, Al. *What's in a Name?* Minneapolis: Ark Products, 1976.

Rees, Ennis. *The Little Greek Alphabet Book.* New Jersey: Prentice-Hall, 1968.

Robertson, Stuart. *The Development of Modern English.* New Jersey: Prentice-Hall, 1954.

Tracy, Martita. *Stellar Numerology.* California: Health Research.

Watkins, Calvert. *American Heritage Dictionary of Indo-European Roots.* Boston: Houghton Mifflin, 1985.

## Myth and Magic

*Sixth And Seventh Books Of Moses.* California: Egyptian Publishing, 1972.

Bailey, Alice. *Esoteric Astrology.* New York: Lucis Publishing, 1951.

Blum, Ralph. *The Book of Runes.* New York: Martin's Press, 1982.
_____. *Rune Play.* New York: St. Martin's Press, 1985.

Bonwick, James. *Irish Druids and the Old Irish Religion.* New York: Dorset Press.

Buckland, Raymond. *The Complete Book of Wirtchcraft.* St. Paul: Llewellyn Publications, 1988.

Budge, E. A. Wallis. *Egyptian Book of the Dead.* New York: Dover Press, 1967.

Budge, E. A. Wallis. *Egyptian Magic.* New York: Dover Press, 1971.
_____. *Amulets and Superstition.* New York: Dover Press, 1978.
_____. *Egyptian Language.* New York: Dover Press, 1983.

Burkert, Walter. *The Greek Religion.* Massachusettes: Harvard University Press, 1985.

Burt, Kathleen. *Archetypes of the Zodiac.* St. Paul: Llewellyn Publications, 1988.

Campbell, Joseph. *The Power of Myth.* New York: Doubleday, 1988.

Crossley-Holland, Kevin. *The Norse Myths.* New York: Pantheon Books, 1980.

D'aulaire, Ingri and Edgar. *Norse Gods and Giants.* New York: Doubleday, 1967.

Hamilton, Edith. *Mythology.* Massachusettes: Mentor Books, 1942.

Hope, Murry. *Practical Egyptian Magic.* New York: St. Martin's Press, 1984.
_____. *Practical Greek Magic.* Northamptonshire: Aquarian Press, 1985.
_____. *Practical Celtic Magic.* Northamptonshire: Aquarian Press, 1987.

Howard, Michael. *The Runes and Other Magical Alphabets.* Northamptonshire: Aquarian Press, 1978.

MacKenzie, Donald A. *German Myths and Legends.* New York: Avenal Books, 1985.

Mathers, S. L. MacGregors. *Book of Sacred Magic of Abramelin the Mage.* New York: Dover Press, 1975.

Murray, Liz and Colin. *The Celtic Tree Oracle.* New York: St. Martin's Press, 1988.

Oken, Alan. *Complete Astrology.* New York: Bantam, 1980.

Regardie, Israel. *How to Make and Use Talismans.* Northamptonshire: Aquarian Press, 1972.

Rutherford, Ward. *The Druids—Magicians of the West.* Northamptonshire: Aquarian Press, 1978.

Shorter, Alan. *The Egyptian Gods.* California: Newcastle Publications, 1985.

Steiner, Rudolph. *Egyptian Myths and Mysteries.* New York: Anthroposophical Society, 1971.

Stone, Merlin. *Ancient Mirrors of Womanhood.* Boston: Beacon Press, 1979.

Thorsson, Edred. *Futhark—A Handbook of Rune Magic.* Maine: Samuel Weiser, 1985.
_____. *Runelore.* Maine: Samuel Weiser, 1987.

## Herbs, Flowers and Trees

Adams, George and Olive Whicher. *The Plant Between Sun and Earth.* London: Steiner Press, 1980.

Beyerl, Paul. *The Master Book of Herbalism.* Washington: Phoenix Publishing, 1984.

Cunningham, Scott. *Magical Herbalism.* St. Paul: Llewellyn Publications, 1983.

Cunningham, Scott. *Cunningham's Encyclopedia of Magical Herbs.* St. Paul: Llewellyn Publications, 1985.

de Claremont, Lewis. *Legends of Incense, Herbs and Oils.* Texas: Dorene Publishing, 1966.

F.E.S. Society. *Flower Essence Repertory.* California: Flower Essence Society Publications, 1987.

Gurudas. *Flower Essences.* Boulder: Cassandra Press, 1983.

Junius, Manfred. *Practical Handbook of Plant Alchemy.* New York: Inner Traditions International, 1985.

Sturzaker, James. *Aromatics in Ritual and Therapeutics.* London: Metatron Publishing, 1979.

Thompkins, Peter and Christopher Bird. *The Secret Life of Plants.* New York: Harper and Row, 1973.

## STAY IN TOUCH

On the following pages you will find listed, with their current prices, some of the books and tapes now available on related subjects. Your book dealer stocks most of these, and will stock new titles in the Llewellyn series as they become available. We urge your patronage.

However, to obtain our full catalog, to keep informed of new titles as they are released and to benefit from informative articles and helpful news, you are invited to write for our bi-monthly news magazine/catalog. A sample copy is free, and it will continue coming to you at no cost as long as you are an active mail customer. Or you may keep it coming for a full year with a donation of just $2.00 in U.S.A. ($7.00 for Canada & Mexico, $20.00 overseas, first class mail). Many bookstores also have *The Llewellyn New Times* available to their customers. Ask for it.

Stay in touch! In *The Llewellyn New Times'* pages you will find news and reviews of new books, tapes and services, announcements of meetings and seminars, articles helpful to our readers, news of authors, advertising of products and services, special money-making opportunities, and much more.

### The Llewellyn New Times
### P.O. Box 64383-Dept. 014, St. Paul, MN 55164-0383, U.S.A.

● ● ●

## TO ORDER BOOKS AND TAPES

If your book dealer does not have the books and tapes described on the following pages readily available, you may order them directly from the publisher by sending full price in U.S. funds, plus $1.50 for postage and handling for orders *under* $10.00; $3.00 for orders *over* $10.00. There are no postage and handling charges for orders over $50. UPS Delivery: We ship UPS whenever possible. Delivery guaranteed. Provide your street address as UPS does not deliver to P.O. Boxes. UPS to Canada requires a $50 minimum order. Allow 4-6 weeks for delivery. Orders outside the U.S.A. and Canada: Airmail—add retail price of book; add $5 for each non-book item (tapes, etc.); add $1 per item for surface mail.

## FOR GROUP STUDY AND PURCHASE

Because there is a great deal of interest in group discussion and study of the subject matter of this book, we feel that we should encourage the adoption and use of this particular book by such groups by offering a special "quantity" price to group leaders or "agents."

Our Special Quantity Price for a minimum order of five copies of *The Magical Name* is $38.85 cash-with-order. This price includes postage and handling within the United States. Minnesota residents must add 6% sales tax. For additional quantities, please order in multiples of five. For Canadian and foreign orders, add postage and handling charges as above. Credit card (VISA, Master Card, American Express) orders are accepted. Charge card orders only may be phoned free ($15.00 minimum order) within the U.S.A. or Canada by dialing 1-800-THE-MOON. Customer service calls dial 1-612-291-1970. Mail Orders to:

### LLEWELLYN PUBLICATIONS
### P.O. Box 64383-Dept. 014 / St. Paul, MN 55164-0383, U.S.A.

## HOW TO SEE AND READ THE AURA
### by Ted Andrews

Everyone has an aura, the three-dimensional, shape- and color-changing energy field that surrounds all matter. And anyone can learn to see and experience the aura more effectively. There is nothing magical about the process. It simply involves a little understanding, time, practice and perseverance.

Do some people make you feel drained? Do you find some rooms more comfortable and enjoyable to be in? Have you ever been able to sense the presence of other people before you actually heard or saw them? If so, you have experienced another person's aura. In this easy-to-read and practical manual, you receive a variety of exercises to practice alone and with partners to build your skills in aura reading and interpretation. Also, you will learn to balance your aura each day to keep it vibrant and strong so others cannot drain your vital force.

Learning to see the aura not only breaks down old barriers—it also increases sensitivity. As we develop the ability to see and feel the more subtle aspects of life, our intuition unfolds and increases, and the childlike joy and wonder of life returns.
**0-87542-013-3, 160 pgs., mass market, illus.**                    **$3.95**

## THE SACRED POWER IN YOUR NAME
### by Ted Andrews

In ancient and modern forms of both high and low magick, the essential power of sounds and words is a common element. Using names as a tool for attaining higher consciousness and for divination (onomancy) was a part of most ancient esoteric societies. This art has not been lost; it has been rediscovered by Ted Andrews in *The Sacred Power in Your Name*.

Everyone is seeking some method to help them upon the spiritual path. Learning the power and energy inherent within our names is the ideal place to start. The name is a direct link to the soul. By learning how to use the name and its elements to more fully and more consciously communicate with the soul, we can begin to understand the rhythms and patterns of events within our life circumstances. We can then begin to control and direct our creative energies.

Unveil the metaphysical and esoteric potentials that lie hidden within your name! Explore ancient naming ceremonies, the divine essence and mystical vowels, names and the chakra system and the magickal music of names. Included is a Metaphysical Dictionary of Names containing 196 names and their meanings, each with an affirmation and meditation.
**0-87542-012-5, 336 pgs., 6 x 9, illustrated**                    **$12.95**

## SIMPLIFIED MAGIC
### by Ted Andrews

In every person the qualities essential for accelerating his or her growth and spiritual evolution are innate, but even those who recognize such potentials need an effective means of releasing them. The ancient and mystical Qabala is that means.

A person does not need to become a dedicated Qabalist in order to acquire benefits from the Qabala. *Simplified Magic* offers a simple understanding of what the Qabala is and how it operates. It provides practical methods and techniques so that the energies and forces within the system and within ourselves can be experienced in a manner that enhances growth and releases our greater potential. *A reader knowing absolutely nothing about the Qabala could apply the methods in this book with noticeable success!*

The Qabala is more than just some theory for ceremonial magicians. It is a system for personal attainment and magic that anyone can learn and put to use in his or her life. The secret is that the main glyph of the Qabala, the Tree of Life, is *within* you. The Tree of Life is a map to the levels of consciousness, power and magic that are within. By learning the Qabala you will be able to tap into these levels and bring peace, healing, power, love, light and magic into your life.

0-87542-015-X, 210 pgs., illus.                                            $3.95

## IMAGICK: The Magick of Images, Paths & Dance
### by Ted Andrews

The Qabala is rich in spiritual, mystical and magickal symbols. These symbols are like physical tools, and when you learn to use them correctly, you can construct a bridge to reach the energy of other planes. The secret lies in merging the outer world with inner energies, creating a flow that augments and enhances all aspects of life.

*Imagick* explains effective techniques of bridging the outer and inner worlds through visualization, gesture, and dance. It is a synthesis of yoga, sacred dance and Qabalistic magick that can enhance creativity, personal power, and mental and physical fitness. This is one of the most personal magickal books ever published, one that goes far beyond the "canned" advice other books on pathworking give you. You will learn how the energies reflected in such things as color vibration, names, letters, Tarot associations and astrological relationships radiate from the "temple" of each sephiroth.

0-87542-016-5, 312 pgs., 6 x 9, illus.                                    $12.95

## SACRED SOUNDS
### by Ted Andrews

*Sacred Sounds* is a manual of self-transformation and esoteric healing through the use of simple sound and toning techniques. On a physical level, these techniques have been used to alleviate aches and pains of all kinds, lower blood pressure and balance hyperactivity in children. On a metaphysical level, they have been used to induce altered states of consciousness, open new levels of awareness, stimulate intuition and increase creativity.

Author Ted Andrews reveals the magical and healing aspects of resonance and music, the tones and instruments that affect the chakras, the use of kinesiology and "muscle-testing" in relation to sound responses, techniques for using musical astrology, the healing aspects of vocal tones, how to use mystical words of power, the art of magical storytelling, how to create prayer-poems, how to write magical quatrains and sonnets, how to form healing groups and utilize group toning for healing and enlightenment, and much more.

0-87542-018-4, 208 pgs., 5 1/4 x 8                                    $7.95

## PRACTICAL SIGIL MAGIC
### by Frater U.D.

This powerful magical system is right for anyone who has the desire to change his/her life! Frater U.D. shows you how to create personal sigils (signs) using your unconscious. Artistic skill is not a necessity in drawing sigils, but honest, straightforward, precise intentions are, and this book gives samples of various sigils along with their purpose.

Based on Austin Osman Spare's theory of sigils and the Alphabet of Desire, *Practical Sigil Magic* explores the background of this magical practice as well as specific methods, such as the word method with its *sentence of desire*. The pictorial and mantrical spell methods are also explained with many illustrations. The last chapter is devoted solely to creating sigils from planetary cameas.

Once you've created your sigil, you'll learn how to internalize or activate it, finally banishing it from your consciousness as it works imperceptibly in the outer world. Let Frater U.D., a leading magician of Germany, take you on this magical journey to the center of your dreams.

0-87542-774-X, 166 pgs., 5 1/4 x 8, illus.                           $8.95

## THE MAGICAL DIARY
### by Donald Michael Kraig

Virtually every teacher of magic, whether it is a book or an individual, will advise you to keep a record of your magical rituals. Unfortunately, most people keep these records in a collection of different sized and different looking books, frequently forgetting to include important data. *The Magical Diary* changes this forever. Each page of this book has headings for all of the important information including date, time, astrological information, planetary hour, name of rituals performed, results, comments, and much more. Use some of them or use them all. This book was specially designed to be perfect for all magicians no matter what tradition you are involved in. Everybody who does magic needs *The Magical Diary*.

**0-87542-322-1, 160 pgs., 7 x 8 1/2**                                         **$9.95**

## MODERN MAGICK
### by Donald Michael Kraig

*Modern Magick* is the most comprehensive step-by-step introduction to the art of ceremonial magic ever offered. The eleven lessons in this book will guide you from the easiest of rituals and the construction of your magickal tools through the highest forms of magick: designing your own rituals and doing pathworking. Along the way you will learn the secrets of the Kabalah in a clear and easy-to-understand manner. You will also discover the true secrets of invocation (channeling) and evocation, and the missing information that will finally make the ancient *grimoires* such as the **Keys of Solomon**, not only comprehensible, but usable. *Modern Magick* is designed so anyone can use it, and is the perfect guidebook for students and classes. It will also help to round out the knowledge of long-time practitioners of the magickal arts.

**0-87542-324-8, 608 pages, 6 x 9, illus.**                                    **$14.95**

## Llewellyn's MAGICKAL ALMANAC
### Edited by Raymond Buckland

*The Magickal Almanac* examines some of the many forms that Magick can take, allowing the reader a peek behind a veil of secrecy into Egyptian, Shamanic, Wiccan and other traditions. The almanac pages for each month provide information important in the many aspects of working Magick: sunrise and sunset, phases of the Moon, and festival dates, as well as the Tarot card, herb, incense, mineral, color, and name of power (god/goddess/entity) associated with the particular day.

Following the almanac pages, are articles addressing one form of Magick, with rituals the reader can easily follow. An indispensable guide for all interested in the Magickal arts, *The Magickal Almanac* features writing by some of the most prominent authors in the field.

**State year**                                                                **$9.95**

## PRACTICAL COLOR MAGICK
### by Raymond Buckland

The world is a rainbow of color, a symphony of vibration. We have left the Newtonian idea of the world as being made of large mechanical units, and now know it as a strange chaos of vibrations ordered by our senses; however, our senses are limited and designed by Nature to give us access to only those vibratory emanations we need for survival.

We live far from the natural world now. The colors which filled our habitats when we were natural creatures have given way to grey and black and synthetic colors of limited wavelengths determined not by our physiological needs but by economic constraints.

• Learn the secret meanings of color.
• Use color to change the energy centers of your body.
• Heal yourself and others through light radiation.
• Discover the hidden aspects of your personality through color.

This book will teach all the powers of light and more. You'll learn new forms of expression of your innermost self, new ways of relating to others with the secret languages of light and color. Put true color back into your life with the rich spectrum of ideas and practical magical formulas from *Practical Color Magick*!
0-87542-047-6, 160 pgs., 5 1/4 x 8, illus.                                        **$5.95**

## THE NEW MAGUS
### by Donald Tyson

*The New Magus* is a practical framework on which a student can base his or her personal system of magic.

This book is filled with practical, usable magical techniques and rituals which anyone from any magical tradition can use. It includes instructions on how to design and perform rituals, create and use sigils, do invocations and evocations, do spiritual healings, learn rune magic, use god-forms, create telesmatic images, discover your personal guardian, create and use magical tools and much more. You will learn how YOU can be a *New Magus*!

The New Age is based on ancient concepts that have been put into terms, or metaphors, that are appropriate to life in our world today. That makes *The New Magus* the book on magic for today.

If you have found that magic seems illogical, overcomplicated and not appropriate to your lifestyle, *The New Magus* is the book for you. It will change your ideas of magic forever!
0-87542-825-8, 346 pgs., 6 x 9, illus.                                        **$12.95**

**WHEELS OF LIFE: A User's Guide to the Chakra System**
**by Anodea Judith**

An instruction manual for owning and operating the inner gears that run the machinery of our lives. Written in a practical, down-to-earth style, this fully-illustrated book will take the reader on a journey through aspects of consciousness, from the bodily instincts of survival to the processing of deep thoughts.

Discover this ancient metaphysical system under the new light of popular Western metaphors—quantum physics, elemental magick, Kabalah, physical exercises, poetic meditations, and visionary art. Learn how to open these centers in yourself, and see how the chakras shed light on the present world crises we face today. And learn what you can do about it!

This book is a vital resource for: Magicians, Witches, Pagans, Mystics, Yoga practitioners, Martial Arts people, psychologists, medical people, and all those who are concerned with holistic growth techniques.

The modern picture of the chakras was introduced to the West largely in the context of Hatha and Kundalini Yoga and through the theosophical writings of Leadbeater and Besant. But the chakra system is *equally* innate to Western Magick: all psychic development, spiritual growth, and practical attainment is fully dependent upon the opening of the chakras!
0-87542-320-5, 544 pgs., 6 x 9, illus.                                         $12.95

**WHEELS OF LIFE AUDIO CASSETTE**
**by Anodea Judith**

Here is the ultimate listening experience. A journey through the sounds and sensations of the chakras created by Anodea Judith especially for Llewellyn and you! With guided meditations, powerful poetry, and original music composed and performed by Bay Area keyboardist/producer Rick Hamouvis, *Wheels of Life* will entertain and enlighten in the tradition of the best Llewellyn has to offer. If you are reading this book, you must have the tape!
0-87542-321-3                                                                    $9.95